Yoga inVision 13

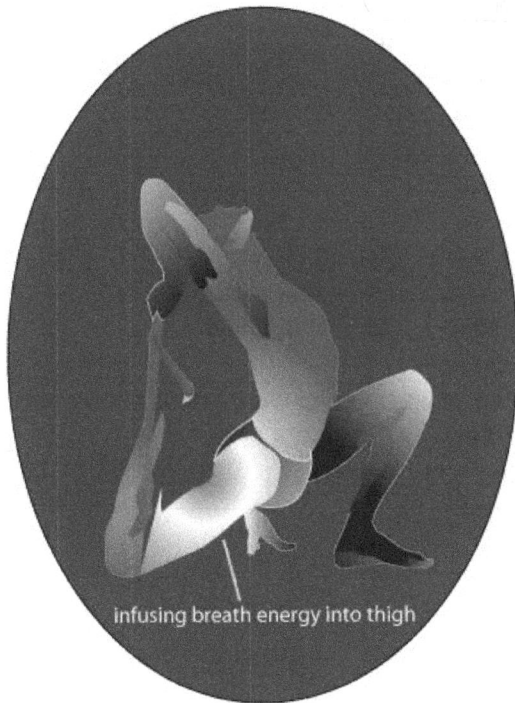

infusing breath energy into thigh

Michael Beloved

Illustrations: Author
Correspondence:
Michael Beloved
19311 SW 30th Street
Miramar FL 33029
USA
Email: axisnexus@gmail.com
                michaelbelovedbooks@gmail.com

Paperback ISBN: 9781942887324
eBook ISBN: 9781942887331
LCCN: 2020921176

Mi-Beloved

Table of Contents

INTRODUCTION

This is the thirteenth of the Yoga inVision series. It relates experiences and practices done in 2012-2013. These give beginners ideas of the physical, psychological and spiritual experiences one may have when doing asana postures, pranayama breath-infusion and *pratyahar* sensual energy withdrawal. Beyond that is higher yoga, which Patañjali named the *samyama* procedures. He defined *samyama* as a combination of *dharana* deliberate focus, *dhyana* spontaneous focus and *samadhi* continuous spontaneous focus. During practice, these progress one into the other. If one is expert at *pratyahar* sensual energy withdrawal, one may graduate to *dharana* which is deliberate focus of the attention to a higher concentration force or person. As soon as one masters *dharana* one may slip into *dhyana* which is an effortless focus on a higher concentration force or person. Once you practice *dhyana*, *samadhi* happens as the continuous effortless focus on a higher concentration force or person.

Many persons on a spiritual path feel that they can construct a process as they advance. This idea denotes failure. After all, if the supernatural and spiritual environment, is not already there, no one can create it now. It is either there or it is not. For instance, if one intends to moves to a different country, then of course one will fail if the country intended does not exist. It has to be there prior. Similarly, what you aim for as spiritual life, must be there already, or one will find that the aspiration is incorrect. This is why I speak of a concentration force or person. I could have said concentration person or divine person, or God. I did not because I do not know how anyone's spiritual path will develop.

One may leave an island in the safest boat and still the vessel may sink. One should keep one's mind open and be willing to work with fate. In spiritual development, there is providence too. What one desires to have one may not achieve. What one wishes to see may never appear.

These Yoga inVision journals show how sporadic my course of yoga was. This is after years of practice. It gives some idea of what to expect. Once you get through the lower yoga practice, you will see advancement in a more stable way but it may be incremental, accruing little by little, with bright flashes here and there.

Part 1

Yogi Bhajan: Teacher's Pride

This morning during exercises, Yogi Bhajan came. He said that I should push harder to increase the amount of infusion into the subtle body.

Before he arrived, I noticed that even though this physical body is now sixty years in surviving, still I improve postures. Of course, physically that has no value because ultimately, in fact in a few years, this body will be no more. Nature will take steps to erase its integrity. The value of this is for the subtle body which will exist for as long as the subtle backdrop of physical energy continues, which is for millions of years, and for as long as my coreSelf is on this side of existence.

Who knows how long that will be? Taking care of the physical body just for the sake of itself makes sense only if one knows the self as a physical object. As soon as one knows the self as something else, even as a psychological unit or compartment, taking care of the physical body for its own sake, makes less and less sense.

Human beings can talk about existing forever as physical forms in the future when technology and science improves, but that is like in religion where there is hope that a savior will resurrect dead bodies, raising them from coffins in graveyards. It is an empty promise.

The postures and stretches still improve even in a physical body which is sixty years of age, but the real adjustment occurs in the subtle form, which usually mimics the physical system. So long as the two bodies are fused, there is a give and take between them. One can use that to one's advantage by taking care of the physical one in so far as it affects the subtle one positively.

Yogi Bhajan said this,

"Push harder. Why play around? I taught these disciplines of breath infusion in the hope that somebody, perhaps one or two persons, would take this seriously and attain the status of siddha.

"Do not play with kundalini. Get it under your thumb. Get it harnessed. Uproot it so that its instincts are abolished by infusion of energy from higher levels. Go with the siddhas. Why stay with the human profile when something higher is available.

"It is not about religion. I was Sikh by culture but I did not insist that anyone become a Sikh. That is not it. If you take birth in a certain country,

in a certain area, the system is that you become obligated to that culture, to that lifestyle. You may change after leaving the parents. Still, some obligation is there.

"But that is not it. That is superficial. The real thing is your bare spiritual advancement. The monkey is running. The lion and cheetah are too. Which is the most proficient?

"Outstride the system! Move ahead! Do not be idle with spiritual advancement! Steal time to practice. Push harder! Push harder! Let teachers be proud of you!"

Yoga Practice Demolished

Sometimes a yogi is overcome by a negative energy which cancels the desire to do practice on a particular day. This energy is a dulling force which stops a yogi dead in his spiritual tracks. It causes him to neglect practice. It may last for a day, week, month, or year. In some cases, it lasts for a lifetime.

Last night I had an astral encounter with a lady who lives in South America. She came astrally with her teenage daughter. Subsequently because of that association, my early morning session was destroyed completely.

When the motivation and energy for practice is dissipated by someone or a group of persons, one should not be discouraged. One should wait to be rescued. A yogi must be confident that negativity will pass.

The usual time for practice is 4am, for the latest 6am. At that time there was no energy for practice, no motivation, nothing. At about 8am I felt that the negative energy was lifted. I immediately went to practice.

It appears that not only did I have a dose of bad association with that lady and her daughter, but I had a dose of bad subtle energy. When that energy disappated the energy of motivation for practice returned.

Students inquired previously about why they feel dull and why they have no motivation for practice at certain times. Actually, it is not so important to know why, as it is to be ready to resume practice as soon as the discouragement disappears.

We cannot control this universe. We cannot design reality to perfectly match our desires. We must agree to sit it out on some occasions and wait for providence to flip in the direction desired.

Association with people who do not have a breath infusion practice even if they are religious people, even if they meditate regularly, even if they are moral people of worth, will result in a down time for yoga practice. We must accept that and tolerate the obstructions. There is no excuse for not completing practice as soon as the negative energy disappears.

Thought Potency

The main disturbance while doing postures and breath infusion is random thoughts which come from the psyche of others, who just happen to be thinking of the yogi at the time of the exercises or whose thoughts arrived at the edge of the psyche while doing the exercises.

Even though a thought is a tiny psychic energy it comes with potency. It may distract the focus. This is because the initial receptor of thoughts is the psychic skin of the subtle body. This sensation in turn, transmits received thoughts with rapid speed to the analytical function of the mind. This function has direct access to the coreSelf, just as a private secretary of an executive has access to the office of that important person.

The psychic touch sensation is not under the control and command of the coreSelf. Its controller is the intellect. It does not care about the particulars of the core. The coreSelf does not have direct access to the touch sensation grid.

At any moment a private secretary may barge into the office of an important person. She may make an announcement, without considering if it is an interference. This is exactly what happens to the yogi, when the errand boy of the touch sensation invades the intellect which is like a private secretary to the self. The intellect forces its way to the coreSelf and makes the announcement about a sensual intrusion.

Imagine a scene in which an important man is tucked away with his darling in a penthouse bedroom, high above a city in the most prestigious building in that place. He makes love to his darling and is at the moment just before reaching the climax of the experience.

Suddenly the door of his bedroom opens. In comes his secretary with what she considered to be an important message. "My dear sir, she says, "I am here to alert you that there is an ant on my desk. The little creature seems to be hungry. Which restaurant should I call? What meal should I order for the poor insect?"

This is the kind of disturbance a yogi may get when doing a session of exercises or meditation. It is for this reason that the ancient yogis, way back from the time of the Upanishads, discovered and introduced the process of *pranayama*, which is breath infusement for suspending the job of the private secretary, which is the intellect. With breath infusion the yogi suspends the functions of the intellect for a time. Its interfering powers are put on hold for the duration of the practice according to the effectiveness of the breath infusion.

Patanjali alerted that this intellect is the nuisance for yogis. He suggested that it should be disabled during yoga practice. The attack of thoughts upon a yogi who does kundalini practice, or meditation or a related discipline, must be dealt with effectively if there is to be progress.

Repeated defeats suffered by a yogi, gives the yogi firsthand experience about his lack of control of the psyche. It lets him plan to increase his knowledge of the outlay of the components of consciousness. By being repeatedly defeated in the effort to directly manhandle the analytical functions, a yogi comes to the honest conclusion that he is a loser in his psyche, a mere slave to sensations and mental analytics.

Taking Command of *Sri Vidya* (kundalini)

In the astral world, Swami Rama said this.

The three aspects of Sri Vidya *are:*

- *The beneficent deity* Lalita Tripurasundari.

- *Her mantra.*

- *The* yantra *known as* Sri Chakra.

Sri Vidya *can be approached without a guru but with little success.* Sri Vidya *has three main avenues of approach which are through the murti deity, through the sound mantra and through the diagram mandala.*

Each of these in turn have an internal and external entrance.

Lalita Mahadevi *is existing as the most fabulous appealing goddess in the creation. She can be reached in the supernatural world in her form as the ultimate voluptuous goddess. That is the external approach.*

Lalita Mahadevi *can be reached on the internal plane as kundalini* shakti *in the subtle body of the yogi. In this place she has two aspects namely the individual partial expression for the yogi's personal kundalini lifeForce, and the collective power as the cosmic kundalini lifeForce. Both are tremendous. They are frightening to a yogi who is not a siddha.*

As a bee may drown in a teacup or ocean of honey so a yogi's spiritual progress may be compromised if he approaches either the individual or collective kundalini in uninformed way.

Sri Vidya can be approached by using a call prayer, which is a bija *mantra through which one may contact the deity or her energy.*

One gets a mantra either inspired into the mind or from a guru who is a master ritualist. Each of the Sri Vidya *mantras is a link to the deity.*

There is an internal route where a mantra is not used but the chakras and the other deity locations in the body of the yogi serve the purpose. The yogi goes to these locations. He either repeats the appropriate mantra which causes the location to vibrate or he enters the locale and then finds the vibration of the place and allows that to be converted into a sound energy in which he becomes absorbed.

If he is successful, he transits from that location to the supernatural world of the deity.

Arriving there, the yogi finds that the beauty of that goddess is far beyond anything he could sustain. She demolishes his ability to experience pleasure. Because it is so unbearable to be in the presence of the beauty and pleasure yielding nature of the deity, the yogi begs for release from that heaven.

Sri Vidya can be reached also by using a yantra externally. This is a diagram which is drawn as per instructions in the related tantra. After drawing this and entering it into a ritual as directed by an able knowledgeable priest, the disciple may make contact with the deity. This path usually leads to ritual worship and one becomes a pujari or purohita.

Some yogis find this yantra configuration within the sushumna nadi passage or at some other place in the subtle body. After reaching there in samadhi, the yogi focuses to become absorbed by the location. Then he is transited to the world of the Devi.

Sri Vidya should not be approached without a guru because the power involved is beyond a limited being's control. It is possible to approach her without a guru but it is not advisable. In other words, if you will concentrate and compress uranium ore, it would be foolish to do so without informing other more advanced physicists. This is because while handling it, the compressed energy may lethally affect you.

Therefore, since kundalini or cosmic lifeForce is so powerful, one should not think of controlling it to an absolute degree. That is not possible. Consider that it is already within the control of something or someone. There is no need for a controller at this stage of the cosmic development.

Limited kundalinis can be controlled by limited beings but the cosmic kundalini cannot be controlled by those persons.

In so far as Sri Vidya *is the* Mahadevi Lalita Sundari, *a limited being cannot control her. She is the ultimate mother, the cosmic vagina. It is best to get it out of one's head about controlling such a reality. Try to imaging a woman who is the sum total of all beautiful women on this earth and in the celestial and subterranean places. Put all those beautiful women into one female and consider if one can compel or control her.*

Now take that woman. Make her a million trillion times more sexually appealing. Consider if you could deal with that. Where and what would you be in the presence of Someone like that?

Lastly, I request that the students focus on getting their individual limited kundalinis in order and under control, to eradicate its animal instincts and to elevate it to the crown chakra. If a student does this, I would be pleased.

Kundalini Under Military Attack

1st Stage Kundalini Attack

In the first stage in the war with kundalini the yogi must infuse breath into the lungs. He should focus on that alone. The energy of the fresh air which comes into the lungs, should fully invade the lung cells and the chest area cavity, including its contents like the heart and other organs.

This first stage of the attack does not affect kundalini but it is vital. As in a war one cannot attack the enemy stronghold initially because the enemy has defenders which must first be subdued. The coreSelf must first shatter the power of the parts of the psyche which sides with kundalini against the core.

The kundalini lifeForce has a protective mechanism which makes it near impossible for the self to subdue it. For instance, many people feel that by subduing the ego, the iSense of the self, one can subdue everything but that is not true. The kundalini is not worried about the subjugation of the ego, because it knows that the self no matter what it does must directly attack it, for conquest. Tearing down other components of the psyche, does nothing to subdue the lifeForce which maintains its privacy while the coreSelf runs here and there in the name of self-subjugation.

Notice that I said that kundalini knows. Can the kundalini know? The answer is that it can know. It has a knowing instinct. Even though that is not an objective education, it is as effective as having one.

2nd Stage Kundalini Attack

In the second stage of the attack, the yogi infuses breath to the navel. He will find that this is like a strong fort which cannot be breached with light ammunition. Arrows, bows, riffles and the like are useless in attacking this fort. It is highly fortified.

What happens is that he must go to this place, drill a hole and force some explosive into it. This is not easy. Many yogis never get past this stage, because they have neither the determination nor engineering capacity to demolish this bunker. Until the yogi learns how to accumulate the breath energy by doing rapid breathing beyond the burning point, all efforts to crash this place, are laughed at by kundalini.

This burning point is felt when during breath of fire, there is a burning sensation above the navel. If the yogi can tolerate that and increase the burn, there will come a time when he can explode the energy and rip apart this fort. At that time kundalini will hear the explosion. It will become worried about the yogi's attack on its kingdoms.

Even though a yogi may successfully cause an explosion at this place once, that does not mean that it is subdued. This area will be repair itself if he blows it apart, such that during the next session of exercise, he finds that it is just as it was before without the damage he inflicted. He must repeatedly return to this place and blow it up repeatedly until he reaches the stage when there is one final blast which blows this place into oblivion. When that happens, he will find that the burning at the navel ceases. Unstead, the energy passes the navel with ease with no obstruction. It goes to the sex organ area and becomes dissipated.

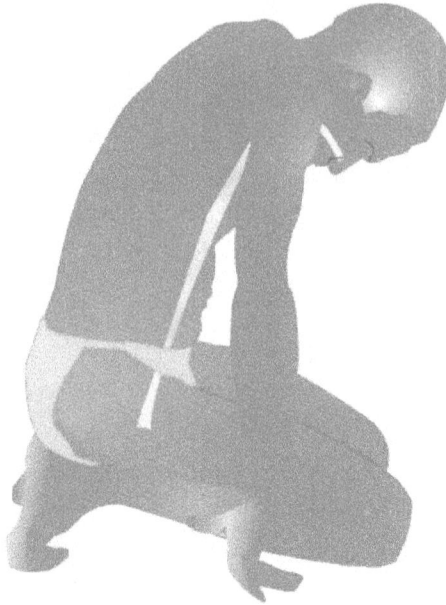

3rd Stage Kundalini Attack

The third stage kundalini attack is complicated because the sex area which is under assault is an absorbing energy. While at the navel chakra there is a repelling resistant energy, the sex area has an absorbing energy which takes the energizing force from the breath energy and leaves the yogi working on and on endlessly without having an exposure to kundalini which hides behind the sex force.

The yogi must practice celibacy and make an effort to compress the sex energy, so as to stop the dissipation. If he does this, a high charge will be at the sex organ chakra. That charge will jump to kundalini at the base chakra.

This jumping action is the first stage of a direct attack on kundalini. Some yogis get spaced out while doing the exercises. Some others are afflicted by drifting thoughts. Some are bogged by lack of focus. This is due to the influence of kundalini on the intellect in the head of the subtle body.

A yogi must keep the mind introspective and be determined to focus the attention of the self. If this is done, the yogi will find that the energy of the breath which gets down to the sexual organs, mixes with and attracts the sex hormones.

While at the navel there is an expansion which causes an explosion. At the sexual organs there is a contraction which causes the explosion. The energy contracts to the point where it can no longer tolerate compression and then it jumps to the base chakra.

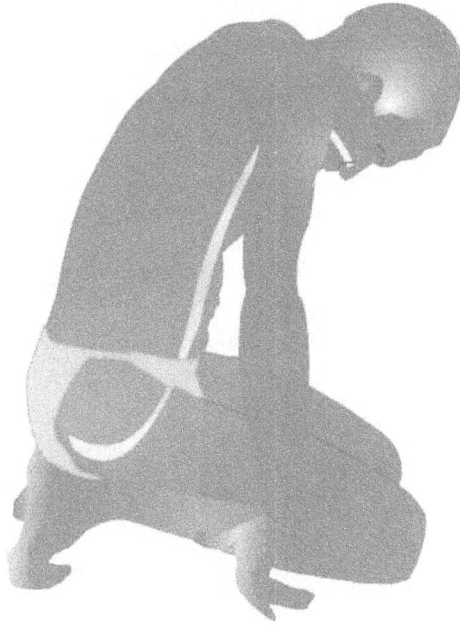

Regular Practice

The main instruction however is to do the daily practice, no matter what, no matter if kundalini rises or not. Do not train yourself to expect kundalini to rise as a reward for doing the exercises. Do not train yourself to be a pleasure-needing result-oriented yogi. If kundalini rises, that is acceptable. If it does not, the yogi should do at least one daily session aggressively.

Let me explain something else. When I came back from the Philippines sometime in 1972, I was at an air base in a place called Baldwin which is just outside Kansas City, Missouri. I learned the formal way to do postures while I was in the Philippines. This system was shown by Arthur Beverford. I realized that this procedure was not aggressive enough. It so happened that while I waited for discharge papers, I took a trip into the Kansas City. Near the university I saw a poster with Yogi Bhajan's Picture with a notice about kundalini yoga practice. When I saw that I felt that this was the thing I needed. This image is the picture of Yogi Bhajan which was on the poster.

I attended a class. When I asked if there was an ashram in Denver, the teacher said that there was but he stated that Yogi Bhajan was in California or New Mexico. When I got to Denver some weeks after, I went to the ashram. Later I lived there. Yogi was not there but his senior students were there, a man named Brian and another named Prem Kaur.

Needless to say, we awakened at 3.30am. We cleaned up and reported to the meditation hall. The exercises were gruesome. While doing *breath of fire* students did postures under supervision. In some poses a student had to keep breathing for about five minutes. It was aggressive but effective. Later Yogi Bhajan came to the ashram. At the airport, when we greeted him, he had a small bag. One senior teacher's wife, asked him to go to baggage claim for luggage. He replied, "Luggage? This is mine. I travel light."

Yogi Bhajan was simple but with exercises, he was strict. You had to do the exercises twice per day. There was no promise of happiness or even of kundalini raising. There was the commitment to do the exercise twice daily. That was it. After a session one did meditation then and there, either reclining on the back or sitting with spine balanced.

That is how I got this practice from him. That is how I share it with others. If one desires happiness as the main objective, this process is not suitable. If one reached a stage where one wants to influence the impact of kundalini on the psyche, this process is adequate. One must be strict. A person cannot bring kundalini under his thumb if he is not strict. Kundalini itself is a strict force that keeps everything in irons. To handle it one must be strict.

Kundalini will force one to have sex, to masturbate, to lie, to cheat, to be disagreeable when it cannot get its satisfactions, to be impulsive, to sell the soul and to betray anyone for some pleasure, to kick whatever or whoever to fulfill its desires. With an energy like that, if you are weak and if you cannot muster the strength to practice daily, it will not happen that one will ever get even some fractional influence over it.

Kundalini Tongue Loop-Back

The following diagrams are from kundalini practice. These are instances which may occur when trying to uproot kundalini from its base. At times kundalini deviates from its normal route in the subtle body but it will keep its route in the physical form. See how kundalini is configured in the physical body, coming up into the head.

In the next diagram you will see what kundalini did in the subtle body bending the head back and looping through the tongue and back to the base chakra avoiding its spread into the head.

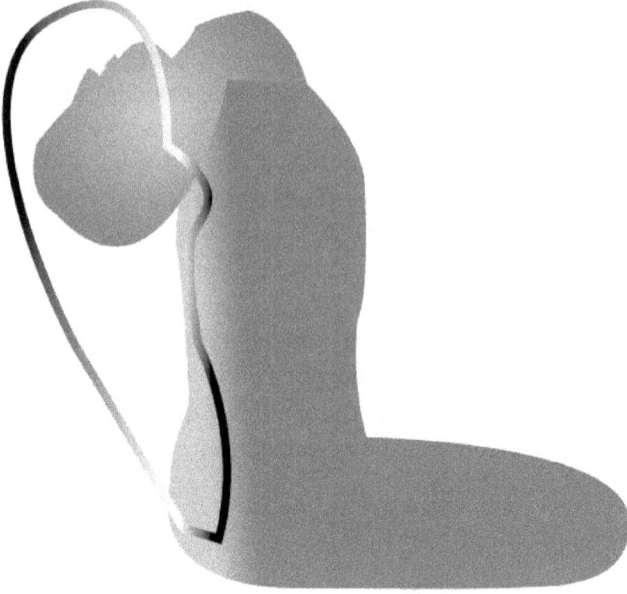

In this loop through the tongue, kundalini draws energy from the tongue and carries that energy to the base chakra, where it uses that energy to taste the base chakra. When this first happens, there is an astral electric shock.

In the next diagram, the subtle body is superimposed on the physical body showing both instances occurring simultaneously.

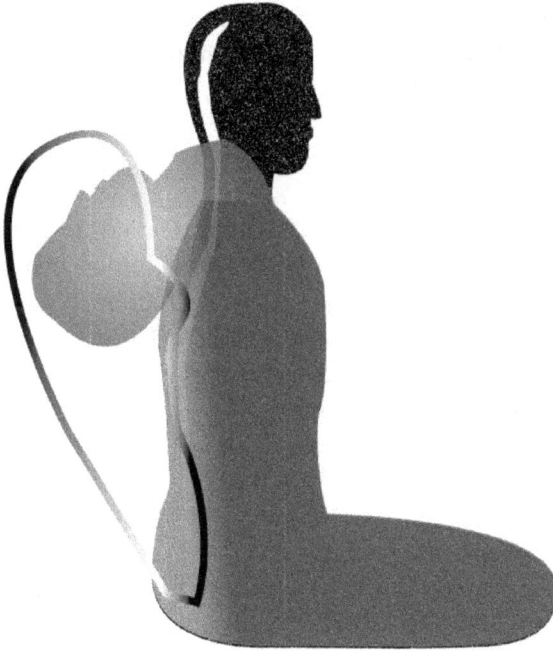

The subtle body is capable of postures, configurations and contortions which the physical one cannot display.

pranaVision

There is a type of vision which is vision through energy on the atomic and subatomic levels. Just as in science, images are created on the basis of atomic analysis, the human mind is also capable of detailed atomic vision.

One such perception is pranaVision, which is the ability to see the inside format of anything. The yogi is primarily interested in researching his/her psyche. In that case the application of pranaVision is to the various parts of the subtle body's anatomy.

During breath infusement, there may be the accumulation of energy in a particular part of the psyche. If the yogi keeps his attention at that location, he/she may get intense sensations which are felt and seen.

If something is heated, the force which provides the heat can see inside the heated object. If a part of the psyche is infused with breath energy *(prana)*, the coreSelf can see the inside of that part of the psyche.

pranaVision is important. The problem is to have confidence in it. If one has doubts, if one listens to the view of skeptics, that may erode the confidence which one would develop in it.

The best way to develop pranaVision is to practice the breath infusion daily, and to be attentive within the psyche during the practice. Do not let the mind wander outside the psyche. Keep the mind internalized. To keep the mind from being distracted by external light, use a blindfold during breath infusement.

Base Chakra Wash-Out

This morning during exercises, kundalini spiraled up both sides of the trunk. That was with a bliss energy which was like four-inch spikes of glass moving upward under the shoulders. I got an instruction. It was an order from a Buddha deity in South Korea. He instructed that I press on to wash out the base chakra. Rishi Singh Gherwal gave an estimate of a two-year practice to get that chakra fixed in the desired way.

There are numerous diagrams about kundalini. Some are from ancient yogis who left sketches. Some are from modern people who feel they know something about kundalini. Based on my experiences in the present life, I published strange diagrams.

Despite these illustrations, a yogi should have an open mind and not superimpose on kundalini some other configuration from a diagram published by me or anyone else.

Have an open mind, so that when kundalini moves, you can track its whereabouts and influences.

When working on the base chakra, I perceive it by subjective pranaVision. It was a brown energy which has the shape of a ⅜ inch disc which is about three inches across and which is like a brown cloud of energy. This is usually a dark brown or light brown energy. As I infuse it more and more, the energy dissipated. It was clear at the chakra.

Kundalini: What Is It?

Kundalini is the psychic lifeForce in the subtle body. To understand what it is one may study sexual climax experience and the rejuvenation-sleep mechanism which runs automatically in the body.

Something is regulating heart beat and breath functions. Something supervises healing in the body. That something is kundalini. The individual iSelf does not operate these features. Even when the self is not attentive to these functions, the functions proceed by an involuntary caring force in the body. That is kundalini.

When the body sleeps and the iSelf becomes unaware of the body, kundalini conducts the breathing functions, the heart beat and other aspects.

How to Enthuse Kundalini:

Kundalini is aroused in sexual climax. It expresses itself as overpowering sexual pleasure. In times of great excitement like for instance in war time or in emotional incidences, kundalini expresses itself as intense regret and as deep remorse or as intense loving feelings.

Raising kundalini up the spine into the head was done by yogis who used the breath infusion method, but there are cases of persons who aroused kundalini in that way by visualization or focus. A person named Gopi Krishna became famous after describing a spontaneous experience with kundalini.

Even though after the body reaches puberty, nature introduces one to sexual experience, nature rarely shows a method of making kundalini enter the brain through a sensational arousal. We can take it as a fact, that generally nature has no intentions of allowing kundalini to raise into the head but it does have every intention of arousing kundalini to energize the sexual organs.

Kundalini Arousal

Kundalini is part of the subtle body but it is not part of the divine form. In the divine body the coreSelf itself is the body, while in the case of the subtle body, the coreSelf is an inhabitant of that psyche.

This subtle body has kundalini and subconscious memory in its trunk. In its head, it has senses, conscious-memory, an intellect, a sense of identity and a coreSelf.

Raising of kundalini may result in kundalini going upward through the spine, jumping from one chakra to the next. If it reaches into the neck it may go further into the head. If it reaches into the head it may go through the crown chakra *(brahmarandra)* or through the third eye brow chakra *(ajna chakra)*, or it may pierce through any other part of the head.

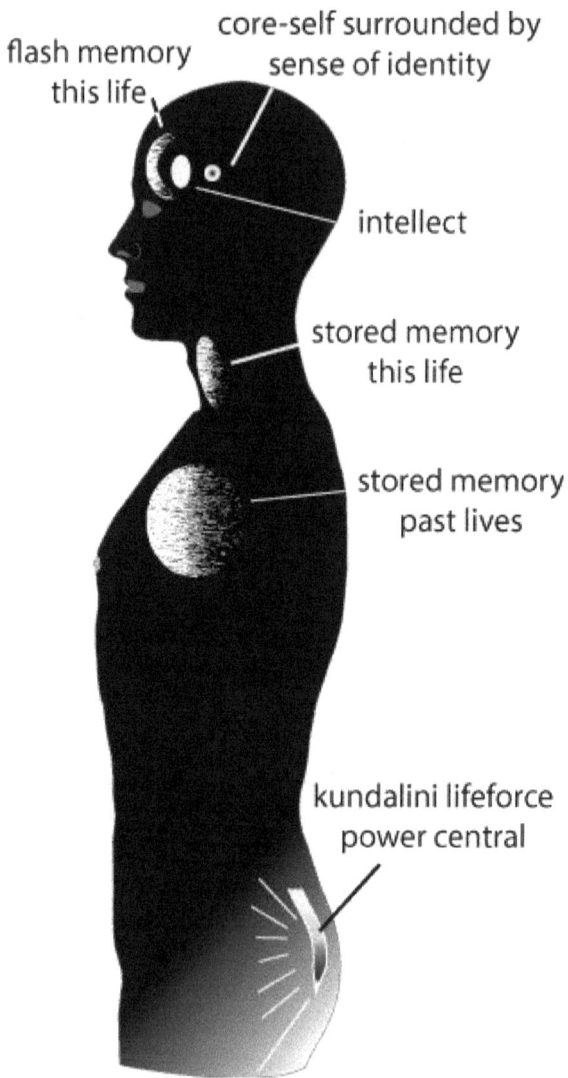

flash memory
this life

core-self surrounded by
sense of identity

intellect

stored memory
this life

stored memory
past lives

kundalini lifeforce
power central

Kundalini Base Infusion

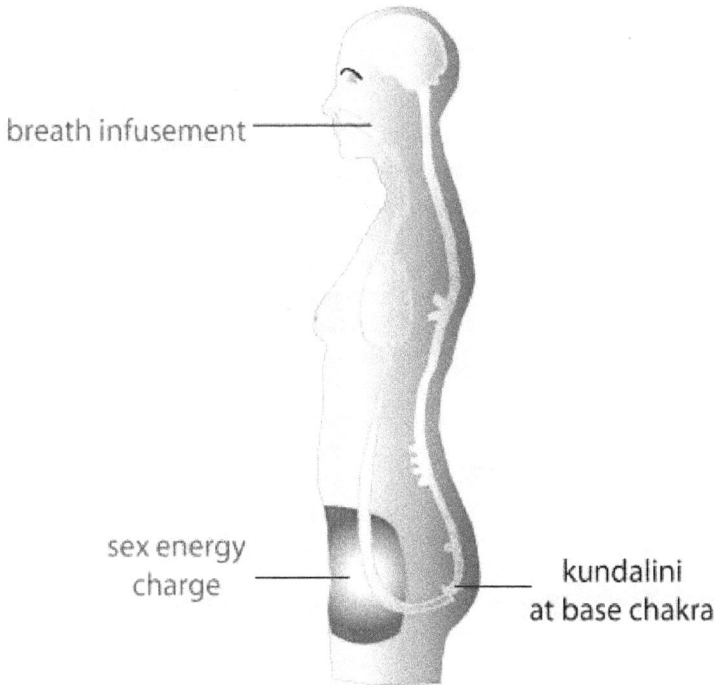

breath infusement

sex energy
charge

kundalini
at base chakra

When focusing on infusing the base chakra *muladhara*, there is a twofold approach. The first and the simplest is to infuse the base with energy so that it will have to move, to send out an energy bolt, or to spark to another chakra or another part of the body.

This system is already in place. We experience it in a very obvious way during sexual climax when the high charge of energy at the genitals, causes kundalini to jump to the sexual area. This is a spark procedure of linking, like in arc welding. Due to a power charge on one place of a metal, another place which has a low charge is attracted. In sex, the charge of lust attracts the kundalini, which jumps to become unified with it. That is interpreted emotionally as sexual pleasure.

In kundalini yoga the elementary way to charge the base chakra is to use the lungs, the navel region and the groin area to force kundalini to discharge itself in one direction or another. The combined lung, navel and groin energy fires itself into the kundalini and the force explodes.

To be an expert one should learn how to control that explosion so as to guide the aroused kundalini in a specific direction.

In the advanced procedure, kundalini is attacked in the same way but instead of firing the energy into kundalini, one fires around kundalini so as to unsettle it and to shift it from its base anchor position. While in the elementary practice, kundalini expresses a moving force of energy and still remains anchored at the base, in the advanced practice, it is the base of kundalini which moves.

Sometimes, when the base is energized in that way, it emits some laser shoots of white energy. If the yogi keeps the infusement and increases it further, kundalini becomes unhinged from its anchor position. Then the yogi can move kundalini here or there as desired.

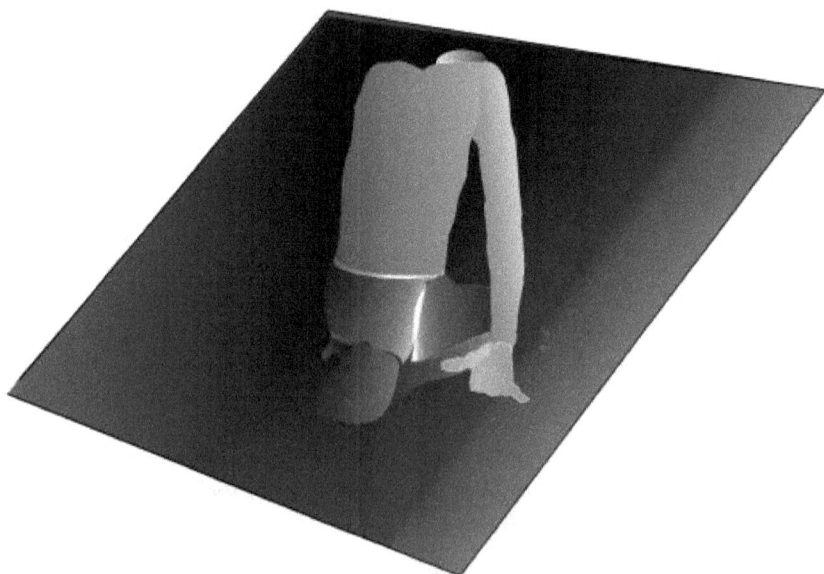

Buddha on Muladhara Attack

A Buddha deity gave an instruction about dealing with *muladahara* chakra. His idea is that the work done with kundalini pans out if *muladhara* chakra's rooting attitude is not dealt with through an aggressive attack to uproot it.

His details are:

Kundalini shakti *has the tendency to get rooted somewhere. To grow from that place it must spread itself, either as itself split into various parts or by branching out through giving access to other kundalinis which come under its subjugation because of needing to enter its establishment to get specific types of life forms.*

Kundalini's quest for form and pleasure is related to this tendency to root itself somewhere. A yogi must research this to get to the root of it and to understand that this is what he must eradicate.

Jumping kundalini into the brain is preliminary. That is stressed by Indian yogis but it is really nothing because so long as kundalini's root tendency is left unhampered, the yogi will again be compelled by it, to take another physical body, and that may not mean a human body. It could be any species, even an acquatic one.

A yogi should dive through sushumna nadi and research how kundalini is rooted in the present body. He should also go back into his time transit and see how his consciousness became rooted into the sperm particle of the father and then in the ovum of the mother, and then how through that root, the placenta developed.

This rooting system is done by kundalini. If one knows nothing about it, how will one become liberated. Kundalini will again dictate what the subtle body will do once one is deprived of the physical one.

When a man looks at a woman sexually, what does he see? What does he pursue?

Does the kundalini use the eyes for investigating if it can get itself rooted into the parent's sexuality? Even in external sensuality one can research this and realize kundalini's game plane, its primordial instinct.

Determination to Raise Kundalini

Since there is variation in the weather, and in the state of the psyche of the individual yogi, one must be determined to raise kundalini daily. Otherwise if one has a standard set time to practice, on some days, one will be unable to raise kundalini.

The weather changes. So does the energy content of the air we breathe, as well as the subtle air which the subtle body uses. This means that on some days, it will take a longer session of breath infusion to raise kundalini. On some days, as soon as one begins kundalini will rise, but on other days one may have to do a double or triple session to arouse kundalini.

There is also the factor of the energy which is in the psyche of a yogi. Due to low social or astral association, this energy may be depressive. The yogi must aggressively attack this energy and remove it from the psyche. This takes time, energy and attention.

An average full session of kundalini breath infusement takes about twenty to thirty minutes. But if there is low energy, it may take up to forty to sixty minutes. Immediately after the session, the yogi should sit to meditate.

In meditation one should note the effects of the infused breath. Such effects are:

- Energy coursing through some part of the trunk or head.
- Spontaneous hearing of naad.
- Spontaneous focus on naad.
- Visions of lights in the frontal part of the brain.
- Inward-outward movement of a disc of light in respect to the center of the eyebrows.
- Absence of thoughts and images in the frontal part of the head.
- Slow motion presentation of thoughts and images with ability to stop the presentation with very little effort.
- Presence of advanced yogis or deities (divine beings) in the subtle head of the yogi.
- Force of kundalini entering the head through the neck and going out of the head in some specific direction with a force of its own.
- Sudden descent of the yogi into the spine or into the trunk of the body.
- Appearance of scenes from the divine world in the mind space of the yogi.
- Appearance of scenes which are in the astral world, outside the astral body of the yogi, seen through a space which opens in the center of the eyebrows.

These events listed are some of the effects which one gets from doing the breath infusion before meditation. This is a jump start to meditation. The breath infusion is like using an elevator to go to a higher level in a building, instead of striding many stairs.

Kundalini Spark Jump

The basic process of kundalini breath infusion practice is that the pubic-pelvis area must be fully infused with fresh breath energy. Once that is done, there is a likelihood that the energy will develop a charge which will cause it to spark over to the base chakra.

To get some concept of this, we can review what happens during a sexual climax experience. In a sexual experience the sexual organs generate energy until that energy reaches a threshold. Then suddenly there is a burst of uncontrollable energy which is called a climax.

The climax takes place when the sexual organ charge increases to a certain level. Then there is a spark of energy where the kundalini jumps from the base chakra directly to that sex energy charge.

In the case of kundalini yoga, the charge from the sex plexus accumulates and then it jumps to the base chakra. The movement is in the opposite direction.

In sex the jump is from the base chakra to the sex energy. In the kundalini infusion process, it is from the sex energy plexus to the base chakra.

Reverse Course Taken by Kundalini

While doing breathing exercises this morning, I directed the infusion to the pelvic region. Then I retained the breath. After exhaling, there was a slight delay before kundalini moved, spreading throughout the limbs and body. Then kundalini reversed course and collapsed upon itself, moving into the heart region.

Re-ordering the Components of the Mind

When doing postures in combination with breath infusement, a yogi should practice the relocation of the attention energy, the intellect and the coreSelf

These three components are usually in the head of the subtle body, but they can be moved from their default positions. A yogi, must by all means learn how to relocate these and practice that extensively. If these are not relocated, their power or lack of power will continue unabated to the regret of a yogi.

For one thing the lack of power is something which plagues the core. The authority over the coreSelf is something which usually resides in the intellect. The sense of attention has a bad habit of doing whatever the intellect commands even at the expense of the core.

This can be re-ordered if the yogi practices to relocate the components. Postures help considerably for this achievement even though postures are physical.

If someone takes a large needle and suddenly plunges it into one's arm, the attention will go to that place immediately. However, it will not remain there. It will relocate back into the head. This jump to the puncture and then relocation into the subtle head, will happen so rapidly and reflexively, that one may not observe the shifts.

In yoga, the inability to trace the movements of the attention must come to an end. One can achieve that by a daily meditation practice in which one uses special techniques.

When doing the postures with or without breath infusion, always pay attention to the part of the body which is stretched, tensioned, relaxed, or seems energized. When you do so the attention and the intellect will attempt to relocate to those parts of the body. In some cases, the attention and/or the intellect may refuse to relocate. These subtle organs will resist and will remain in their default locations. In fact, the intellect may not simply refuse to relocate, it may insist that the attention be involved in whatever the intellect imagines.

In that case, if I do the bow pose, that would mean that my abdomen is arched. My back is under-arched. Still the intellect thinks of something else and engages my attention in that idea, such that my attention ignores the arched back.

I do the posture; people look on and think that I do it properly. Still within the psyche, very little attention is involved.

The intellect and attention should be engaged in the posture. They should be relocated into the tensing or relaxating of the stretch.

Breath Infusement Basics

The basic effort in breath infusement is to extract carbon dioxide from the lungs, while infusing oxygen. Carbon dioxide increase in the body has a negative spiritual impact and causes a decrease in psychic perception and an increase in physical focus.

It depends on the objective. If you want to increase physical focus, it would not be in your interest to increase the proportion of oxygen in the blood stream. In that case it would be beneficial to increase the carbon dioxide content.

A corresponding feature is there in diet, where a vegetarian diet will result in sharper psychic perception while a flesh diet will increase the physical prominence.

When doing breath infusion, the yogi should first make an effort to extract the carbon dioxide from the various parts of the body. By doing various postures while breathing rapidly, the blood stream in various parts of the body, collects the carbon dioxide from the tissues and by the pumping action of the heart, that is transported to the lungs and is expelled from the body, while oxygen is infused into the blood stream simultaneously.

During rapid breathing the heart beat increases to keep abreast with the transportion of the infused oxygen, and similarly the carbon dioxide is expelled from the system. Within about twenty minutes, most of the carbon dioxide is removed from the system.

On the subtle side, negative subtle energy is expelled from the system and an energizing force is infused into it. When most of the negative force is extracted, the kundalini acquires a charge. When this is increased, it sparks and jumps in one direction or the other. By the application of locks, the yogi channels this lifeForce power.

Initially the yogi cannot channel this force. It moves in an instinctive direction without his control. Over time, he/she gains some control.

Kundalini/Diet/Schedule

Kundalini practice is affected by changes in diet and daily schedule. Kundalini manages the physical body. Any change in routine affects it. A change in diet affects the digestive apparatus and the excretory system. These affect the energy distribution of kundalini. If one changes the daily schedule, kundalini must adjust to that. It affects practice.

More or less, one should know that if one changes the diet or schedule of daily social activities, the next practice session may be different. For example, yesterday my diet routine and schedule were changed. Subsequently when doing the morning session of exercises, I did more practice to cause kundalini to rise. In addition, the session was interrupted to evacuate the body. Whenever that happens one should return to the session and resume the practice.

One should make every effort to infuse air energy into the gap which is created by the evacuated matter. Stool holds energy. When it was evacuated, a deficit space created. That space should be filled with fresh air energy. In addition, for evacuation the kundalini used negative air energy like carbon dioxide, which should be extracted from the body by rapid breathing.

Kundalini Up Spikes

Kundalini rose with spikes from the spinal column. Subsequently it did not reach into the brain but stayed below the neck.

Kundalini is advertised as rising through the central subtle spinal passage which is called *sushumna* nadi. On the left side of that channel there is the *ida* track and on the right side there is the p*ingala* track.

However, besides these there are more channels or nadis, which are tiny subtle tubes. These are usually blocked so that subtle energy cannot course through them. Success in kundalini yoga means opening these tracks to allow the energy to continuously flow.

In the beginning years of doing kundalini yoga, one should remain focused on getting kundalini to travel through the central spine into the brain. This takes some effort of daily practice. Once it is achieved, one can divest the energy through the entire psyche.

When kundalini rose this morning, at first it hesitated to move because it considered that it would spike out instead of moving as usual upwards. The kundalini lifeForce has intelligence. It makes decisions one way or the other.

After that initial hesitation, kundalini rose promptly and spiked as per the diagram below.

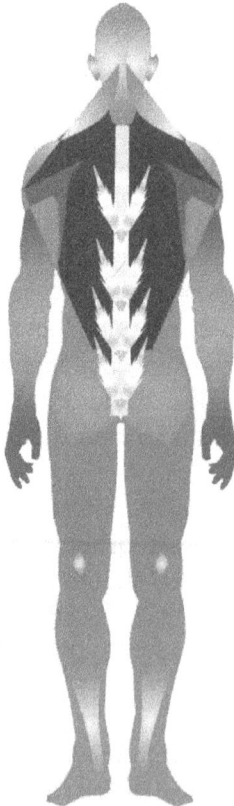

Kundalini delayed because of insufficient force in the pelvic area. That is not always the situation but it is frequently the most common reason for the delay.

Initially a yogi is fooled by this delay. He loses vigilance. Thus, when kundalini moves, he is caught offguard.

When kundalini rises into the head suddenly without warning, the yogi will lose control of the body. Actually, this is totally untrue because in fact, none of us have absolute control of the body. It is kundalini which controls of the body. We have a little say in this or that circumstance. Mostly kundalini cares for the body. We are pretend-administrators.

The reason why the yogi loses control is this:

Kundalini strikes the intellect when it is off-guard. Since that orb is the touch point between the coreSelf and objective consciousness at this time, the core also loses contact. The way the psyche is wired, the coreSelf is more like an accessory rather than being the auxilliary component, but it is the major power-supply of the psyche.

It is the intellect which should be protected from the striking of kundalini when it comes into the head. If it hits the intellect from behind, the intellect will lose contact with the body. The self will lose control even though what happens is that the intellect lost contact.

- Why does the coreSelf not maintain objectivity even when the kundalini strikes and stuns the intellect?
- What is the dependence of the coreSelf on the intellect?
- Why can kundalini disable the intellect on occasion when the orb is hit from behind by kundalini?

These are the questions which face a yogi.

One thing is certain. The delay of kundalini is usually based on a lack of sufficient energy during the breath infusion.

In the case of the physical world, we find that everyone knows his/her address, town or city and the residences of family and friends. But hardly anyone knows the kundalini, the intellect, their locations and relationship to the coreSelf.

Battle with Negative Forces

During exercises this morning there was a negative energy which discouraged the session just after it began. I ignored this influence and kept focused on completing the session. The energy remained in my psyche until about ten minutes before the session concluded. After that it dissipated. At one point I heard a voice in my head.

"Be sure to complete the session. Skip no postures."

That was Rishi Singh Gherwal. About five minutes after that I felt the presence of Yogeshwarananda. He smiled while he spoke to some persons. He gave a look of encouragement.

At one point during the session the retardative force pressed me to stop practicing. I ignored it but it kept asserting itself. When it applied maximum pressure, I practiced mainly because Rishi Singh Gherwal expected me to finish the session by doing some more postures with the rapid breathing. At that point kundalini rose into the throat. It invaded the throat chakra.

In the subtle body the throat chakra bloated and blocked the throat completely. The energy spread into the head and chest. It felt like twinkles with bliss energy spreading in all directions in crystal white snow flake configurations. The top chest area of the subtle body bloated. Some areas of the lower head which is near to the neck, bloated.

This bloating happened because I effectively applied the neck lock and restricted the energy to the throat chakra.

This practice session is an example of how a yogi should battle with negative forces in the psyche. It does not matter how these forces get into the psyche. The yogi must remove them. The main point is to do the practice and do it to the required extent, making sure that kundalini rises in a full way during the session. Kundalini itself which was bogged down by the negative force, and which discouraged practice, changes its attitude if one persists with practice.

Undoubtedly there is much negative energy which deters practice. A yogi should not be discouraged. The negative force will never end. It is omnipresent on this level. One should not waste time thinking of it. One should be committed to completing at least one daily session for raising kundalini. During that session one should continue until kundalini is aroused.

Yogi Afterlife

After repeatedly arousing kundalini into the spine, chest, torso and head, it tunnels through the thighs, legs and feet. Its arousal there is a bit different. When kundalini moves into the thighs, legs and feet (the lower extremities), it may feel like cramps with bliss feelings or as needles with bliss spark feelings.

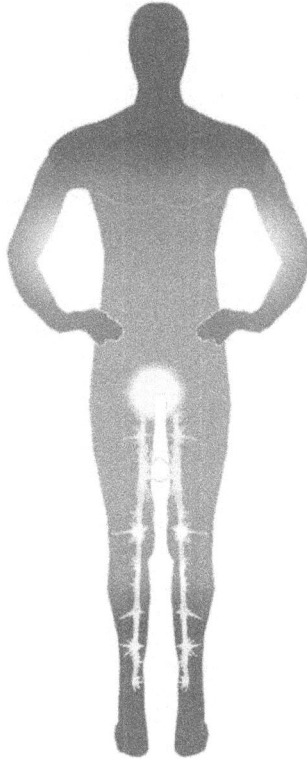

It is not as intense as when it moves up the spine or into the head. However, it is necessary to clear those lower extremities because they are parts of the psyche. If one is unable to clear those areas, one will be shifted to a lower astral world, after one reaches a heavenly world after death.

Rishi Singh Gherwal mentioned that using kundalini yoga to transmigrate to a higher dimension either in the subtle world or in the spiritual world, is like using an elevator to rise through a building in order to get to a higher floor; while using moral values and philanthropy as a means of elevation is like using a staircase which winds around a building and climbing that staircase from the outside of the building. Both methods are effective but the stairway is inefficient.

He said that a yogi can know how higher he will be elevated just by properly rating the kundalini yoga practice. The definite way of knowing is by gauging what dimensions he usually finds himself in during dreaming. It does not matter what his religion is, or what his process is, if his dreams concern mostly people using physical bodies who have little interest in advanced yoga, he will take another physical body on this planet or in some place which has a physical existence which is similar to this one. For such a person, the destiny after death is already revealed.

If on the other hand one reaches yogis and finds oneself practicing with them and associating with them during dreams, there is a chance that one will go to a higher dimension which is devoid of distractions. One will continue the progression in the astral world without having to assume another physical body as one did in this life.

Those rare yogis who can associate with divine beings in the divine world during dreaming, are assured of reaching those places after death of the present body.

Merely by checking the quality of the dream locations, one can know where one will go when one is deprived of the present body.

If it is left to the astral body, one will simply be pushed from a woman's birth canal again. This is because the astral body as it is, as it is unadjusted by yoga austerities, is prone to seeking sperm and ova for manufacturing for itself another physical form.

For general purposes and for purposes of traditional religion, there is physical and spiritual, which means gross physical like the body we currently use and whatever exists but is unseen due to subtlety. The gross aspects are considered to be physical in traditional religion. Things like light like sun light, radio waves, ultraviolet rays and so on are considered to be spiritual. A ghost is considered to be spiritual. In yoga, there is a third level, which is above the conventional spiritual plane

Mostly, a person who leaves a physical body, goes to the subtle world, not into the spiritual world. This is because the subtle body which we use, which is used in dreams and astral projections, is not a spiritual form. It is subtler than the physical body but it is made of subtle matter. Subtle matter is not a spiritual substance.

For yoga one should regard three categories, the physical, the subtle and the spiritual.

If a yogi fails with the yoga practice, and cannot consolidate it, he has no choice but to take recourse to the benefits which he accrued by his socially uplifting acts.

As a last resort, if a yogi cannot get his act together before he loses the physical body, he falls back on his consequential fate and makes use of that in the next life.

Both systems are not used. One can only use one of the systems. Social activities no matter how great and how approved and beneficial they are, will not help for yoga elevation. And yoga elevations will in turn do nothing for social upliftment.

These are two different currencies which cannot be swapped one for another. This is why we find that a person who is a great yogi may be in abject frightening poverty. It is because destiny thinks that he did not make a sufficient social contribution to derive social benefits like others who dedicated themselves to doing good in the physical world.

The astral worlds which are reached by those who amassed credits by favorable social activity are different to the astral worlds reached by those who perfected yoga practice. If a yogi did not complete the practice to a certain degree, it will not get him to the siddhaloka astral places where great yogis live. He will instead be routed to astral paradises where the pious people go. Then he will return to this world through the regular route of developing an embryo.

Part 2

Kundalini: Front Rise

Kundalini rose with intensity through the front of the chest and into the arms and forearms. This was with the intensity which is usually experienced when kundalini rises rapidly and suddenly through the spine and into the head.

When that happens if the yogi is not attentive, his/her body may fall to the ground, as when the kundalini strikes the intellect, the means of perception may become disconnected from the nerves in the brain which control the body. Then the coreSelf cannot give directions to keep the body standing or sitting. The body falls to the ground.

Over time after many sessions of practice the yogi learns how to manage the rise of kundalini and the supervision of the intellect, as well as the avenues through which the energy rises through the spine and floods into the head rapidly.

By repeatedly rising kundalini, the yogi reorients it to the head of the body. When kundalini comes up the front of the body and into the throat and head, it feels like trillions of tiny electric shocks of bliss energy especially in the chest and throat.

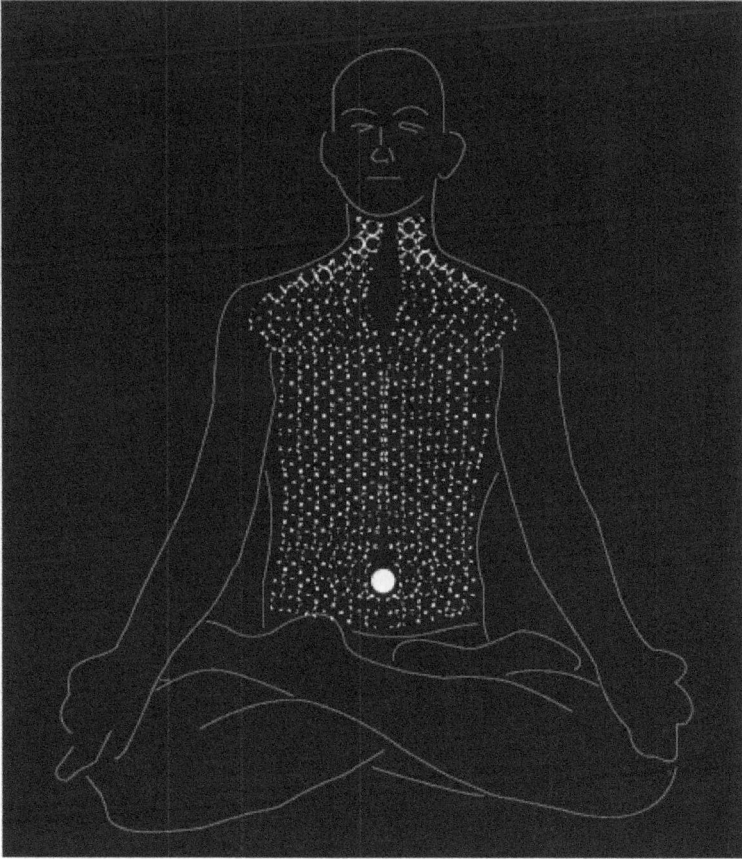

Kundalini Sex Control

Kundalini sex control is a complicated process consisting of getting various parts of the psyche to abandon interest in contributing to the storage of energy for sexual intercourse. The idea is to use the same energy for even distribution through the psyche and for reaching the brain.

Nature has it arranged for this energy to be channeled to the sexual organs but if one wants to adjust the system one should work to change this natural procedure. One of the areas which must be adjusted is the thighs. This area is a major contributor to the sexual hormone reservoir.

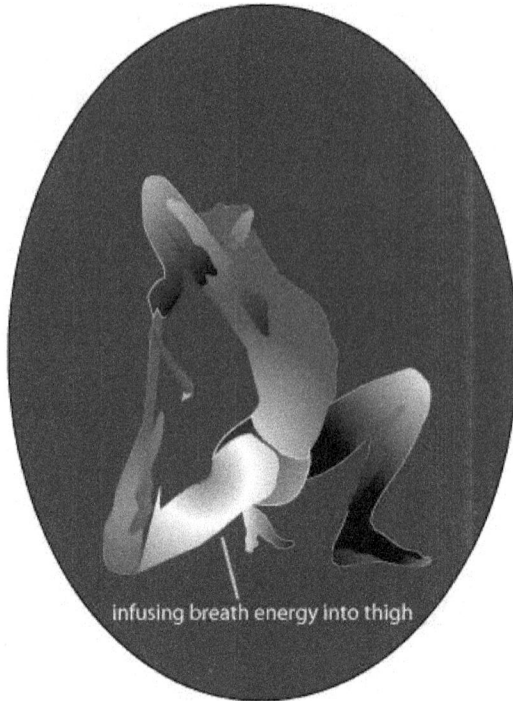

infusing breath energy into thigh

Jump Kundalini

Rishi Singh Gherwal gave notations about jump kundalini. It is a process used by yogis, to prepare for kundalini control at the time of death.

He said that sometimes a yogi cannot get his act together at the time of death. Death may come suddenly without the yogi being able to adjust kundalini just before it happens, Rishi said that sometimes certain incapacitating terminal diseases may cause a yogi to lose grip on kundalini during the last months or years of the body's life.

However, he said that if the yogi can master jump kundalini before the body reaches a bad state in which kundalini cannot be handled effectively, then when kundalini finally leaves the physical form and is free from being responsible for it, the yogi can use the method already developed to jump kundalini to a higher chakra in the subtle body.

Jump kundalini is the method of causing kundalini's base to jump to a higher chakra. Rishi said this:

Jump kundalini is not the same as kundalini arousal for any purpose, like kundalini arousal for sex climax or kundalini arousal for higher awareness. In those situations, the energy of kundalini moves from the base chakra but its base remains the same as muladhara chakra at the end of the spine.

Jump kundalini means that the base itself moves with the kundalini. When the yogi gets the base to move upwards from the base to the 2nd chakra or from the base to the 5th.chakra, that is jump kundalini. The yogi should practice and make the base jump upwards. He must attain the power to make it jump into the brain.

The yogi must get the entire trunk of the subtle body and the two appendages which hang down from the trunk (thighs, legs, feet) to be infused with a higher energy. This means in the subtle body.

Once that is done, kundalini's adhesive which keeps it at the base chakra is loosened. Kundalini becomes submissive to the suggestions of the yogi.

Kundalini becomes something that may float. It gets buoyancy. Otherwise, it is heavy and cannot be lifted.

Kundalini settles first into the semen of the father during the formation of the semen, as the root energy there. From that it creates for itself a tail which later becomes the blueprint for the spinal column. It is basically like a reptile, like an alligator, but with its brain connected to its tail.

When it is transferred into the mother's uterus, kundalini becomes the gravitational force which anchors the coreSelf for the formation of the fetus.

From its anchor point at the base chakra, kundalini conducts the growth and maintenance of the physical body. In the subtle body it is located in the same place basically at the base of the subtle spine of that form.

To unhinge it one should attack its grossness. To do so one must change its energy composition. That may be done proficiently by doing *pranayama* which is the 4th stage of yoga.

Some people use visualization and mystic exercise of willpower to command kundalini but usually kundalini ignores their attempts.

Instead of responding, it stays put at the base and directs them in getting pleasures like eating tasty foods and having sexual intercourse.

In the Upanishad period in India, some yogis came to the conclusion that the most definite way to upset kundalini was through *pranayama*.

The idea is to sabotage the natural way of kundalini and bring it under control so that one can be transited to a higher dimension. By itself as it is, kundalini is only concerned with existence in a physical body in any species. To upset that one must change its energy intake. An aggressive breath infusion practice is a sure way of achieving this.

For a beginner kundalini is deliberately raised by doing *breath of fire* or another effective breath infusion practice. After repeatedly raising kundalini once or twice per day, a student manages to flush most of the lower mento-emotional energy in the psyche. Due to that kundalini abandons many vulgar concerns. When the student exercises, he finds that kundalini's base may sometimes float to a higher chakra. Then a great yogi will appear. He may advise for more advancement.

Sex Organ Chakra Details

This morning I had several instances of kundalini rise during the practice of *breath of fire* mixed with postures. By doing *breath of fire* in various positions, one causes the infusion to go into various parts of the psyche. This gives the yogi firsthand knowledge about the layout of the subtle routes. He does not have to speculate or depend on diagrams of ancient yogis.

Many of the persons who become meditation teachers and who never did intense pranayama practice, give lectures where they describe the chakras and the nadis, even though these people never experienced the layout of the system in their psyche.

One cannot see this system just like that, just by sitting to meditate. In the first place, most nadis are blocked and are in a dark condition, such that they cannot be seen. It is only when they are infused by breath energy, do they become visible. Visualization does not open the nadis, neither does imagination.

At one part of this session, kundalini base energy changed into an orange color. Normally kundalini at the base chakra is a dark brown-black color, and in the darkness of the psyche it cannot be seen. In other words, if one were to go to the base chakra with a flash light, it would be so dark that even with the flash light one would see nothing. The darkness is so dense that it would absorb the light of the flash light. However, when there is a sexual climax, a spark of energy, like a lightning flash, passes from the base chakra to the sex organ chakra. Then a large explosion of energy occurs which is interpreted by the mind as the much-desired sex pleasure release.

During an intercourse there is a beginning point when the flash spark occurs and depending on the situation the large explosion will happen some seconds or microseconds after.

Since the spark energy leaves the base chakra and travels to the sexual organ chakra, one does not see it at the base but one sees it at the sex chakra and then there is a large explosion at the sex chakra which is seen by the entity through viewing it through the intellect.

Sometimes the energy is so intense that it burns the intellect and that orb jumps back into the head of the body.

This sex organ chakra is not the same as the sex chakra on the spine. The sex organ chakra is located at the perineum nerve junction.

After that intense explosion, the sex chakra turns black like coal and there is no visibility there, until another such explosion can be generated.

sex chakra on spine

kundalini
base chakra

sex organ chakra

Power not to Practice Yoga

Sometimes a yogi becomes plagued with an energy which prevents practice. The person may practice and then become dejected and hesitant, until at last practice stops completely. Then that person will avoid association with persons who practice.

Why does this happen?

The reason is the same as to why anything else stops which is that a retardative force enters the person's psyche and influences decisions. It transfers the person from a higher mental plane to a lower one, where the practice of yoga and the effort for self realization loses significance.

Many people do not realize that we shift up and down mentally into higher or lower planes, and are influenced by the energy of those levels. This is because of thinking that we are in control of the mental faculties. This thinking causes someone not to observe when he is shifted, because if he is in control of the mental faculties, then to him there is no question of being shifted here and there.

Once a person realizes that he/she is not a free agent and that he/she is controlled according to the mental level, it is easy to be objective and see the various forces which shift one mentally or emotionally.

Why is it that no matter what, one person persists with practice, while another person diverts from practice regularly and is not consistent?

The reason is simple that the person who cannot persist is overcome by a negative influence. In either case, that of the one who persists and the one who desists, the negative influences are there and are a reality. The negative influence is a sluggish force which causes the yogi to neglect practice or to cease it completely. The persistent yogi has a strong instinct for practice. Even if the negative force is applied in his/her mind, that person still does the practice.

The meaning of it is that association from more advanced entities is required. No limited person can resist all negative forces without taking help from advanced people. Telling yourself that you are powerful and that you are in charge of your life, and that no one can tell you what to do, is very good for building self-confidence but it is not a reality.

Here is a circumstance of the application of the sluggish force, which kills a yogi's practice. Last night I was in association with some persons in the astral world. Most of these persons are related to me physically. Some were friends from years back. In that association I had to relate to these individuals on their level of operation, which is a lower level than the one I am usually on. In any case, in this instance there was no way out, because of the pressures of fate.

By fate, we sometimes meet someone here or there. Then we are pressed into certain associations which may be counterproductive to self realization. Since these situations are pressed in by fate, one cannot escape them. In these situations, the best thing to do is to face the circumstance and perform as best as one can, with an intention to leave the association and return to the practice routine thereafter. That is what I did. There is one flaw in that approach however. In such associations, one may become infected with so much retarding energy, that one cannot re-direct oneself to yoga practice.

Usually I do not absorb much retarding force, but last night I did exactly that. Since that happened, I was inspired to write this entry to explain how to deal with it.

When my alarm rang for rising to do exercises, I turned it off. I remained reclined. This is the first sign of the success of the retarding force. It produced an attitude of carelessness in regards to the commitment for early morning practice. I did not rise for another two hours. Once I rose, I was busy doing practice, but before I practiced, there was a force within the mind which instructed the psyche to forego practice for the day.

I noticed that force, and was about to consider, when I said to myself. "We will practice. Forget the retarding influence."

It took ten minutes of practice, then I saw that force leave my psyche. It was shaped like a soup dumpling. It was of a light grey color. It was in the lower belly. Suddenly it left through the front by the navel. As soon as it left, all reluctance disappeared.

I traced this energy to one person in the group of persons whom I associated with the night in the astral world.

In yoga one must have three obligations

- to oneself.
- to the practice of yoga.
- to the yoga guru(s).

These three are required. One must have such a high value for oneself, that one honors the obligation to the self to elevate the self.

One must have so much respect for yoga practice and what it can render, that one desires to honor the practice by doing it on a daily basis.

One must have so much feeling of being accountable to the yoga guru(s), that one is terrified of having to face him/her, if one does not practice.

The three commitments are required. In Buddhism, there is commitment to the Buddha and the sanga which is the group of monks. There is also commitment to the process which Buddha established as the process of enlightenment. Essentially these three commitments are there in every type of spiritual discipline.

- It is you.
- It is the process of the discipline.
- It is the teacher(s) who inspires you.

Negative association does not have to be deliberate to deter yoga practice. It can be casual and unintentional. It is like a cold virus. If someone has it and unintentionally sneezes someone else may acquire it.

Thus, there is no sense in taking it personally. Understand that in any type of association with persons who are not aggressively practicing spiritual elevation, there will be a retarding energy which will put a damper on the practice.

Even though initially one cannot see the retardative energy, one can feel it. One should accept that the feeling can be visual in the advanced stage.

The part where one identifies with the thoughts is part of the kriya yoga practice to differentiate the components in the head of the subtle body. If the whole head is one thing and if one cannot differentiate the various parts, then by meditation one can develop clarity in that regard. That comes from practice over time.

Until one can separate the various components of the mind, one will be subjected to identifying with whatever thoughts or images the mind constructs. There is only one way to overcome that. It is the method of regular practice.

The word psyche means the psychological energy that a person has. There is psychological energy in the head. It is also in the toes. The psychological collection of energies of an individual self is called the psyche.

We stress the head but that is only part of the psyche. For instance, in the physical sense, the head is the most important part of the body. If the brain malfunctions, then one is out of it, even if the rest of the body remains in good shape. We stress the head but the human body is more than a head.

Since the attention energy, is in the head, whatever we perceive in the body has to be done through that attention. If one perceives something in the head, then since the attention energy is there, it does not have to focus far from its default location. If, however something is in the navel area or in the foot for instance, the attention must travel a little to get to that place, or a message must be sent via the nerves physically or through subtle nerves *(nadis)* to the brain or mind. That takes a little time, micro-seconds perhaps but it is still time.

The negative force will not leave of its own accord. It entered to become a permanent resident and to occupy the psyche, just as like when a virus enters the body, it multiplies and dominates some cells.

Similarly, negative energies, subtle forces, which enter the psyche come in to force it to do what those forces desire and to cause the psyche to develop for the benefit of such forces.

Hence if one can make the environment hostile or non-responsive to such negative forces, they will leave the psyche, or be destroyed in it or remain in it in a neutralized form, where they cannot hijack the mission of the psyche.

Kundalini Procedure

Rishi Singh Gherwal left a message which is a basic idea of how yogis leave their bodies commanding kundalini to go up through the body and out the head. Usually death of the physical body occurs by a shutdown of kundalini from the head downwards and from the feet upwards. Kundalini uses itself as the reference and pulls all energy into itself at the base chakra.

A yogi tries to beat that system by causing the energy to be retracted into the head. Just as in sexual intercourse, the head consciousness goes into the genitals to get pleasure satisfaction and bewilderment, the yogi makes an effort to pull kundalini into the head of the subtle body when death is on the verge of taking place.

Unfortunately, he cannot do this if he did not master it already in his day to day existence. As a creature of habit, kundalini does not respond to compelling instructions or imaginative visualizations which it was not conditioned to perform.

A yogi is a type of spiritual athlete. By repeatedly raising kundalini over many years while using a physical body, he/she can do the same at the time of death. His proficiency enables him to do this, not his religion, not his affiliation with a guru or any other factor.

Rishi Singh said that I should publish that a yogi has to use the jump process, which is when kundalini jumps from its base to other locations which it uses as new basis for its operation. The first jump is to the chest area or the heart chakra on the spine. The second jump is into the neck area. The third jump is into the base of the brain at the back of the head.

If the yogi can get kundalini to relocate that far, he is certain to reach the world where the siddha perfected yogis reside. From there he can practice further to reach the divine world. Rishi said that presently, it is near impossible for a yogi to go directly to a divine world after having a physical body. Thus, the practical accomplishment to aim for is to go to the *siddhaloka* places where great yogins reside, and where one can get further instruction and more association to reach the divine places.

The first jump location is the chest area or the heart chakra on the spine. The yogi must get above the navel. So long as he is unable to move kundalini's base above the navel, he is condemned to another haphazard rebirth, which means despite his aspirations, his psyche will remain with the interest in sexual indulgence and nutritional accommodation.

Even if by the grace of nature, in old age of a physical body, a yogi gets away from sexual indulgence as a result of impotence or as a result of not having youthful sexual forms in availability, still the yogi will be captured by nutritional accommodation, because it so happens that the primary interest of kundalini, its instinctual need, is for nutritional accommodation.

What is that?

That means fat and muscle, especially fat. Kundalini looks for nutritional accommodation. If it can find that, it can live in the physical world and gain sustenance. Thus, it is attracted to male musculature and to female fat cells which lump in certain parts of the human form.

The conquest of the navel is a downward push, but to reach the heart there has to be an upward push. First there is the downward push, and then there is the upward push. That is the procedure.

Kundalini in Balance

Sometimes when doing kundalini yoga practice, one may find that the kundalini comes up one side of the body and does not ascend the corresponding other side. Some persons come to a yoga class with the queer idea that everything should be and will be put into balance by meditation and yoga.

They feel that the odd left side or hanging right side will come into position and they will forever from then onwards, be a perfect equal on either side, never ever to go out of balance.

In the human species, there is imbalance in the body since the heart is hung more on the left side and the left lung is smaller than the right one. Is this unnatural? If it is, one has an argument with nature.

If one does kundalini yoga, and suddenly during the exercises one finds that kundalini rose on one side only, just take it as it is. Do not try to put nature through a measure. It may have good reason to do what it did. Observe what happened. Do what you can to cause kundalini to go further down whatever right or left channel it enters, by a side stretch for instance, by applying muscular locks on the particular side, by wiggling or whatever intuitive action or focus one feels will cause kundalini to go further up or down the particular channel which it opened.

Usually when kundalini rises on one side from a stretch on a particular side after breath infusion, I usually observe it. Then I move to the other side and check to see if kundalini will course on that side. If it does not, I observe that and continue practicing. I never stop to question it nor to put it into a balancing act.

Yoga Objectives

Yoga is listed by Patanjali as having eight parts. Posture or *asana* is one part as the 3rd stage in the eight segments of yoga. Higher yoga is called *samyama* by Patanjali. That is the three highest parts, when done as a sequential practice.

In English, *samyama* has the meaning of meditation but its precise meaning is complete *(sam)* restraint *(yama)*. People are mostly concerned with meditation and not with the preliminary parts of the process as listed by Patanjali. Some people are concerned with postures but only for the purpose of physical health and beauty.

Yoga is for transcending ourselves as physical systems and finding everything else which is the self. In other words, besides the physical body, what am I?

Yoga is an escapist process. Those who feel confined in the physical world, like prisoners in a max-security prison, may try for yoga. With yoga we escape from this dimension and research other places, trying to find something which we are agreeable with. In meditation *(samyama)* the yogi researches other dimensions in the hunt for something which suits his needs.

If he finds a dimension which involves the use of a temporary body or which is connected to a place where temporary bodies are used, he is not interested. He keeps looking.

The highest stage of yoga, is called *samadhi* which is mostly tripping out from this place and keying to other dimensions and other types of beings, divine beings.

Why? Because a yogi realizes that if he has a connection to someone in a divine place, he may migrate there.

To find what a yogi investigates in this and other dimensions see chapter three of the *Yoga Sutras*. There is a list of those achievements.

Yoga is not concerned with straightening kinks in this environment, nor in becoming harmonious with it. On the micro level among the bacteria, a yogi sees that this is a survival situation. The yogi has no hope of harmonizing with this or of causing this to harmonize with the self.

Our idea is to abandon this and to find an already-existing place which is devoid of the survival profile.

Social Issues or Yoga

For me social commitments are a waste of time. Still, they are necessary. In the Bhagavad Gita, Krishna explained to Arjuna that the physical world was insubstantial. Then Krishna told Arjuna, that he (Arjuna) should complete duties perfectly.

Arjuna was confused. He asked Krishna to clarify what to do, either to be involved socially or to focus on self realization. Krishna told Arjuna that both things were required, the social involvement and the self-realization puzzle but he insisted on Arjuna's completion of social duties.

When Krishna spoke to Uddhava in the *Uddhava Gita*, Krishna discouraged access to social duties and family concerns. He pivoted Uddhava in the direction of self realization on a full-time basis.

This means that what one does for spiritual success will vary according to one's position in relation to the social world. For the most part we are involved socially because of having desires which can only be fulfilled through social involvements.

A guy went to meditate in the forest just outside a village. After a while he began to think that he would have to eat. An old man whom he spoke to told him that if he wanted milk, he should acquire a cow.

He got the animal but it was miserable, because there was no pasture in that part of the forest. This guy was advised to acquire land. He did that. The cow got pregnant. After the calf was born, the guy was happy. Milk came from the udders. He later became doubtful about the situation because of the time it took to milk the cow and procure its feed.

He was advised that he needed a wife to assist. He got married. After sometime, his wife showed some irritability. When he asked elders about that, they said that a wife needed to have sex which would produce the bonus of children.

One can see where I am going with this. Social involvements will multiply and utilize the time required for spiritual life. Therefore, each yogi must draw a line as to how much involved they will become. It begins by reducing desires.

Patanjali wrote that desire energies are eternal. If we believe what he wrote, it means that the elimination of desires is out. Learn to side step and avoid desires. If something is a permanent reality, one cannot think it out of existence.

A yogi should learn to evade desires. Once a desire possesses someone, that person is urged to fulfill it. A yogi must resist and hide from desire energies, otherwise he/she will have no time for self-realization.

I remember other existences and previous lives in physical bodies on this planet. For me I am desperate to get away from this. I took this body for a specific purpose which has nothing to with the social situations that were necessary to produce this body. I tried to settle with nature for using this body, to settle with ancestors for using this body. Otherwise I stick to the reason why I took it.

Most people have no idea of a past life. They have no idea of a reason for taking a body. For them they are the bodies. For me I am not the body but I had to assume the body to do what I wanted to do physically.

Still, with that came the obligation to parents, relatives, teachers and government officials who contributed to the creation of the body.

The trick is to meet these obligations efficiently but not to expand them. If they are expanded, they will encroach on the time which could be used for self realization.

I raised a family. I have four children. I am done with that. I served some relatives in a fair way. For me there is not much to do other than self-realization. I do not have many desires. The main desire was to author books for giving information about meditation.

Other desires do not attract me because I can see that in the end, they will fizz out to be nothing, or worse, fizz out as unwanted obligations in this or in a future life. Those who cannot see anything outside of this life have to fulfill desires without knowing where it will lead in this or a future life.

If you think that self-realization is or should be your main concern, you should meet social obligations head on in an efficient way, where you fulfill them but do not expand them. At the same time, you have to use every bit of spare time to push on with self-realization.

Be clear about it. This body will die. One will be deprived of it regardless of if one wants to relinquish it or not. The father of my body was not ready to give it up when he laid on a hospital bed and was in the last day of his life. Do not be like that. This body will be confiscated by nature.

Once you see that you must ask yourself, "Then What? Where will I go? Who will I be? How should I prepare for that?"

All social issues pale in their significance if one keeps that in mind at all times. I needed a body to write information in English about self-realization. I pledged emotionally, to beget children and that I would do this and do that. I signed.

I had social obligations. I met them head on. Was it a hassle? Did it affect my spiritual life? It does not matter because an obligation is just what it is. It does not have to be something that one likes.

Taking a body is a business contract. Once you get that in your head, it will be easy for you to know how much time is for social and how much is for self-realization.

Kundalini Charge Preliminary

When doing the kundalini exercises, one will first do the preliminary charge. This is a four-stage process. If this is done successfully, kundalini will rise immediately after if one continues to increase the charge. This is because kundalini will have no choice in the matter, but this does not mean that one will direct where kundalini will go. It will move in some direction, but which direction is left open because that depends on the yogi's proficiency in practice, on the blockages in the psyche and in the type of charge force which accumulated.

I will describe the four-stage process:

Stage One:

Charge the lung and heart fully with fresh air infusion through rapid breathing. This involves an aggressive use of the diaphragm. In fact, all of *bhastrika* or *kapalabhati pranayama* breathing involves the aggressive use of the diaphragm. The diaphragm is the main muscle involved in rapid breathing. *Bhastrika* is when there is rapid breathing with focus on both the in and out breaths. *Kapalabhati* which is easier is when that breathing is done with focus on the out breath, with the in breath occurring just as a reflex of the forced-out breath.

This stage one of charging the chest region of the body (breast and rig cage in women), is the first stage because that is just the way the breathing is designed to enter the nostrils, feed down the neck and be absorbed into the lungs or be expelled from it.

Once that is done and those cells are filled with fresh air, they will allow the rest of the body will benefit from the infusion.

Stage Two:

stump kundalini

This is infusion from the chest to the navel area. This causes blockages in the navel to be shattered by the force of the breath infusion energy. These energies are directly above the navel. They flow into the navel but they lock there and do not flow out easily. When one does the infusion and the infused energy reaches this blockage, it forces its way through. It pushes the old energy downward.

If you were to see this psychically, you would notice that the energy reaches a dead end and cannot go beyond the navel. There is the increase energy push from the infusion. The energy twirls around the navel vortex. Then it flows downward.

Stage Three:

stump kundalini

In this stage the energy which twirled around the navel goes downwards in a hurry. It meets the reproductive center. It rushes there. When it gets there instead of reaching a dead end, it enters into the reproductive area in a flush and mixes with the sexual energy. As a result of this mix, the nature of the sexual energy changes. That energy loses its lusty charge. This energy then flows upwards a little. Then it turns down into the genital region.

Stage Four:

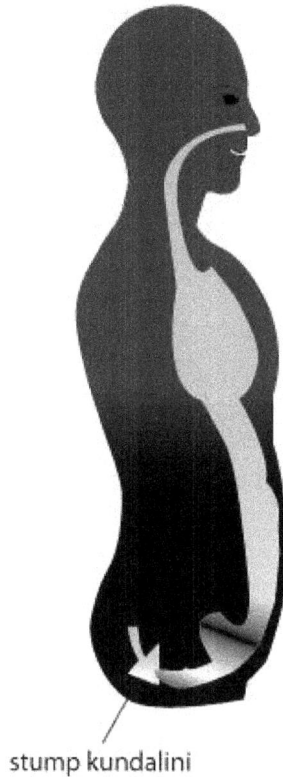

stump kundalini

This is the last stage of the preliminary practice. This is where the energy which was mixed with the sex energy, goes to the base chakra. It tries to strike kundalini but at first, kundalini expresses a rejection energy in order to repel that force. The matter would end there with that rejection being effective but if the yogi continues the infusion, the charge becomes more potent. It attacks kundalini. It mixes with kundalini. The explosive mix causes kundalini to move from its position.

These are the four stages of preliminary kundalini rise. During each session one must go through these stages either rapidly or gradually according to the intensity of practice. A novice does this. The proficient master does this as well. The difference being that the master can complete this preliminary stage in the first five or ten minutes of practice, and the novice may take twenty or thirty minutes.

Recall Chambers of Memory

During exercises, kundalini rose on one side, when after an infusement of breath energy, I intuitively stretched that side. After that I repeated the infusement again by rapid breathing and then stretched to the other side, and kundalini rose with the same impetus.

In some cases, when one practices like this, kundalini does not rise on the other side. Or it may rise only partially in reference. The main effort is to practice without worrying about this. The more one practices and the more one clears various tiny tubes in the subtle body, the more kundalini will invade every part of the system in a satisfactory way.

If kundalini blasts out one side of one part of the body, say the left side or right side, if one keeps doing that, kundalini will finish its infusement of that side and will of its own accord begin attacking the polluted energy in the other side. Thus, one should not waste time considering why kundalini did not rise in a balanced way.

During this session after doing the breath infusion for about twenty minutes, kundalini rose evenly through the front part of the body, coming up around the navel and then into the rib cage and then into the neck. This felt like tiny frost sparklets, twinkling like energies with micro charges.

I made an effort to file these experiences in the recall chamber of the memory. If I do not do that, I will not report it since there would be no memory of it.

In some cases, when the recall chamber of memory is filled, I scribble a notation and then return to complete the exercises. Failure to make notes or to transfer records of these experiences into the recall chamber would result in my not writing these books.

There were many great yogis in the past, who made no notes. They took no time and effort to transfer their experiences into the recall chambers of memory. Thus, we have no record of their progress and cannot benefit from their experiences.

How to get Energizing Energy in the Thighs

During exercises, kundalini rose with aggressive force several times into the trunk. Once kundalini came under the armpits on either side, as a spike energy which was condensed bliss force. It then shot through the arms.

During the practice, Rishi Singh Gherwal discussed the importance of working on the lower extremities, which are the thighs, legs and feet. He felt that a yogi should keep the feet in tip top shape in as much as in yoga the head is stressed.

Rishi said this:

"The thighs are used by kundalini primarily for the creation of reproductive hormones. That area is usually off limits to the yogi. The yogi should do stretches in postures where the thighs are targeted, so that the accumulation of blood and energy there is distributed through the body and is not collected for genital expression is sexual intercourse.

"In its natural state, the thighs are the enemy of celibacy. Therefore, a yogi should spend some time reforming the energy which is created in the thigh.

"As the body get older the legs and feet become starved of oxygen. A yogi should note that and make special efforts to get the polluted blood in the extremities back to the lungs for a recharge of oxygen. The psyche is one mechanism and even though in yoga, there is focus on the head mostly, a yogi should service the other parts of the subtle body.

"Even though the physical body is a different form, its neglect causes unwanted alternations in the subtle form. A yogi should care for the physical form in so far as the subtle one will mimic the physical behavior."

In compliance with Rishi's statement, I took care to push air into the thighs especially through their central bones. This is done by doing rapid breathing in a posture which stretches the thigh muscles, and keeping the attention of the mind in the thighs during the breathing. This keeping of the attention in the thighs causes subtle air to be pulled into the thighs. This fragments the subtle sexual energy which is stored there. It courses though the entire body instead of being channeled into the genitals.

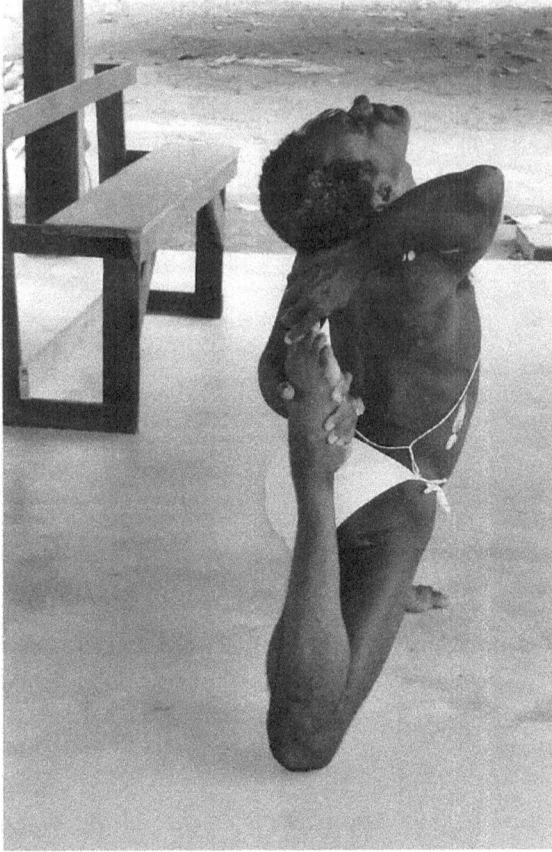

Inspiration from Higher Planes

Kundalini rose today several times during the exercise session. It penetrated the flesh and nerves in the neck, feeling like micro bubbles of bliss energy.

After that occurred, Rishi Singh Gherwal appeared in my consciousness. He explained that to have kundalini rise through the spine is insufficient for getting a yogi to a higher *loka*. The word *loka* is Sanskrit for existential zone. It is pronounced as loak or loaka, rhyming with the word cloak.

Existential zone means a place where one can exist with others who are in the same frequency range. For example, on this planet there are demarcations or borders in countries, communities and cities. In some areas, there is high security. One cannot enter without permission. There are also prisons which are designed primarily to keep people confined but which also serves the purpose to keep unconfined people from entry.

On the whole on this planet there are tight restrictions, some of which are enforced by nature. For instance, one must have a certain type of body to live at the bottom of the Atlantic Ocean. Even if one is the greatest engineer, still one cannot live there using just a human form. All the same the creatures who live on the bottom will not survive for long if they were confined to a land space where humans feel comfortable.

In the hereafter, there are many existential zones. A yogi is carefree in everything except where he/she will go after being deprived of the present body. He/she wants to go to the highest dimension possible, to be with divine beings, abandoning the social associations we currently have.

The problem is that to get there, one must have a suitable subtle body which vibrates at a corresponding frequency. On this planet, sometimes even though one has friends in another country, still one cannot get a visa to go there. It is the same in the hereafter. I may know a great yogi who reached a high plane of existence but that in no way gives me the right to go there. He can come to a lower plane where I am located or he can send a telepathic message to me but for entry there, my subtle body has to be up-energized.

What happens with a yoga guru is this. After a disciple practices for some time and realizes the situation of these higher dimensions, he/she inquires of entry to those higher places. Then one is told, "You will have to do this practice and that practice, to get the subtle form to change to a suitable frequency."

Sometimes, a yoga guru graduates to such a high plane, that the disciple is unable to contact him for techniques. Then what happens is that a message is found in the subtle world about how to qualify. That message may be sent by the yoga guru, or he may have left it on a subtle plane or from his existence when he was on that plane, a vibrational energy was left which gives that message.

The method of transmittance is not the issue because as soon as the student makes enough effort and advances, the message becomes evident. In cases where a yoga guru was unable to leave a message and where there is no energy anywhere which would inspire the yogi on the required methods, the yogi guru usually descends from the higher plane and gives instructions into the mind of the student.

Such a student has to be non-argumentative, non-critical, and very respecting of the guru, otherwise the student's attitude itself bars the student from being inspired.

Pleasure as Reference

After kundalini rose through the neck, through the flesh, nerves and spine, not just through the spine alone, Rishi Singh Gherwal said this,

"When one begins to do yoga, the idea about it has to do with physical existence and the exposure one had in that particular body, especially sex desire and other pleasure experiences.

"The infant's first idea of pleasure is twofold, based on feelings and based on taste. What is the infant feeling initially besides its own body? That is the mother's body. What does the infant usually taste at first after birth? That is the mother's milk. Thus, these two experiences, the sense of touch of female form and the liquid from female breasts are the essential experience. From this the other experiences gradually become evident.

"If you take the infant away from the mother, the infant cries. If you deprive the infant of the mother milk, the infant protests.

"Later the sex urge develops. The mother loses significance because the infant finds that it is attracted to other bodies of similar age. This is designed by nature but the infant feels as if he/she crafted it.

"In all respects the infant is a nobody initially, a social nothing. It cannot contribute service to society. It is worthless. The parents give some value to it by training it in how to behave and function usefully.

"The child must attend school to increase its worth to society and to achieve status for the family. All along the way, it is distracted by pleasure, especially by sexual pleasure. The two most demanding compulsive organs are the tongue and genitals. Both of these organs rule the entity with an iron hand, saying, 'Eat this, eat that, unify me with this, unify me with that.'

"Thus, when the entity comes to yoga, these organs try to control the practice. Since there is really little use for the sexual organ in yoga, the entity is perturbed about how to get sexual pleasure through the exercises.

"Kundalini is the root cause of sex desire and of taste impulse. One must come to terms with that reality by raising kundalini and causing it to abandon its sex development. To do this kundalini must be trained to go upward instead of going downward through the pleasure nerves in the genitals.

"Nature's way is to taste and then create sex hormones from what is tasted. Then use those hormones in sexual expression. Let us review that passage. First the tongue and mouth, then the intestines, then the sex hormones are manufactured, then the sex pleasure is derived. That is the natural way.

"Let us review the yogic method. First again there is taste, then there are the intestines to extract energy from what is tasted, but then the sex hormones are manufactured and then what? Then the energy is made to go upward, abandoning the passage through the genitals.

"However, if one was introduced to yoga after having much sex fulfillment, one is tormented by the memory of that. One has a difficult time changing the habits of kundalini. At first when kundalini rises, a person may be surprised to find that it could give pleasure in another way by going upwards as contrasted to the natural way of going downward through the pleasure nerves of the genitals. Later as one practices, one is accustomed to the upward rise and the bliss energy that is expressed when that happens.

"As one advances one must leave aside the attachment to this bliss energy. One should focus on distributing kundalini evenly through the psyche.

"Why should kundalini only pass through the spine, leaving the rest of the psyche without a sufficient infusement of higher energy? The entire psyche should be infused. When one passes from the physical body, there is a chance that one will go to a higher dimension. One may be lucky to be with divine beings like Krishna and Shiva. Otherwise, one may have a vision or a sudden experience at death, but it will be a flash then one will find oneself again entering the sexual energy of new parents on earth, and coming again as a helpless baby. What has God to do with it? It is the natural way."

Laser Kundalini

During exercises this morning, kundalini rose in an unusual way which was up and then down. First, I raised kundalini through the trunk of the body evenly. This happened because under Rishi Singh Gherwal direction, I did this for the past six months. His instruction was to work with kundalini in the trunk and defocus from getting kundalini into the head for a time.

This instruction was to force kundalini to find the nadis in the trunk and to cause it to flush through those passages, instead of avoiding them. The entire psyche must go through a transformation from lower energy to high energy. If just the head of the subtle body is energized, the rest of the system will degrade the head anyway. Thus, the whole system must be energized for success to relocate to higher planes.

A person can wait to see what will happen at the time of death of the physical body, or he/she can work industriously to move the psyche to a higher plane before the physical body passes in order to be sure that the transition occurs.

When kundalini arose in a strange way which was a little up and then down, I lost tracked of the movement. This carelessness occurs when one is distracted. There are basically two types of distraction during kundalini yoga practice. One is external stimuli. The other is internal stimuli.

In this case it was an internal thought which came into the psyche from an external source. Sometimes there is an internal thought which is created by the psyche. In this case, this was a thought from someone outside the psyche. It penetrated the psyche. When it did so, it caused the memory to activate other thoughts from within the memory. These psychic movements cause one to advance slowly. Over time, one can get this under control.

I tracked the downward movement of kundalini which was a movement downward from about four inches in the centre of lower trunk downward though the reproduction chakra of the body. This took place in the subtle body. As kundalini moved down it took the form of a white laser beam which splintered and sparkled. It emited blue white microscopic sparklets.

After this kundalini rose into the trunk evenly but it was like shattered windshield glass moving upwards with bliss energy.

These actions of kundalini are vital for the removal of polluted subtle energies which keep the psyche in a dull-energy state of subtle mass ignorance.

Kundalini: Lack of Sensitivity

Sometimes during kundalini yoga practice, one fails to note the various paths the energy takes. For one thing, unless one developed a high degree of psychic sensitivity, one will miss most of the small charges and movements of kundalini energy.

Even in routine actions of the physical body, there is involvement of kundalini that goes unnoticed. Take for instance if one should urinate and one fails to do so, the bladder is distended with liquid, until a point comes when one must urinate. One is compelled to do so, regardless of if one is at the proper location or not. Then there may be a burning sensation or an electrical sensation in the bladder of the body. That is a feeling of kundalini.

During sexual discharge, during sexual arousal, there is kundalini energy surging, accumulating and discharging like the arc of a spark plug, but can one realize that as kundalini's movement.

A lack of psychic sensitivity makes it impossible to know what kundalini is unless it discharges and acts with sensation such as in sexual climax and in its rush into the head of the body during kundalini yoga exercises.

Kundalini Research

The study of the nature, work and influence of kundalini should be one part of meditation practice. This should be done even when one does not practice yoga. Raising kundalini should be done daily, at least once per day. This will cause kundalini to find easy routes through the entire psyche and will give the yogi a chance of becoming familiar with the one psychic energy which controls the creation of physical bodies and which itself is the repairing agency in the body.

But besides raising kundalini and observing its spread through the psyche during yoga practice, a yogi must also observe kundalini when it is not aroused by yoga. In other words, one must note how kundalini behaves in the normal consciousness of the body. One should note its habits, its powerful influences over the psyche and its command of the body.

Who/what controls diet? Who/what controls sexual attraction? Is it the coreSelf? Is it kundalini? Who/what heals the body when it is diseased or wounded?

Yogi Attacks Thoughts

Sometimes during a yoga practice of postures and breath infusion, one notices thoughts in the mind. Some thoughts have little power to command the coreSelf to view them but some have the authority to do so.

During the exercises, one usually ignores these thoughts or one becomes distracted by them. This is because it is not practical to study the nature of such thought-energy, while doing the exercises. Still one should note the thoughts. Then later, during meditation, study those ideas, regarding how they arise in the mind, who was their source and how did they derive power to command the self to view them.

During the session if one can raise kundalini into the head, one will find that certain thoughts disappeared of their own accord because of the infused energy which entered the head of the subtle body, but some other thoughts after losing much of their commanding power, may remained in the subtle head.

These remaining potent thoughts should be attacked with the infused energy. While in some meditation practices, the thoughts are observed dispassionately or they are ignored or tracked even, in this practice, thoughts are attacked or assaulted aggressively with the breath infusement energy. The yogi directs the accumulated energy to the mental place where the thoughts occurred.

Anesthesia Effects on Kundalini

After observing how anesthesia affects the kundalini, I can say now that medical drugs which affect consciousness should be avoided. They may used if absolutely necessary as in surgery. It is best not to use drugs for recreational use because one never knows what it will do to the operation of the kundalini in the long range.

It took two weeks after getting anesthesia in the lower spine, for the kundalini to resume the normal way of operation during the breath infusement practice. Kundalini was paralyzed from the waist down for about six hours after the anesthesia was injected, but it was still affected for two weeks after. The chemicals are not purged from the body in one or two days. The same thing can be said about the subtle part of the chemicals and their effects on the subtle form.

Even though there are many involuntary actions taken by kundalini in the physical and subtle bodies, most are in the interest of the well-being of those bodies. If kundalini is disabled by chemicals, it cannot render services.

In the daily maintenance of the body, the main maintaining force is the kundalini. It is not the intellect. It is certainly not the coreSelf. One should take steps to help kundalini in the chores of maintaining the body. As human beings, we become vicious and defensive when the tongue is not allowed to taste whatever it desires and to say whatever suits its fancy. But if we detach ourselves from the sense of taste and are reserved and considerate, we will appreciate the services rendered by kundalini.

Monks Discuss Yoga

Last night in the astral world I was with some members of the Hare Krishna Movement. Some of these individuals were disgraced in the society and lost senior positions as leading monks.

I was with a set of persons who were either sannyasi monks or teachers of the school system of the society. I was a teacher in the system where I lived in the ashram regiment.

Some teachers and sannysis had homosexual inclinations. Some were practicing homosexuals at the time, except that it was proven later that they sexually abused boys in the boarding school system which was set up by the founder of the society.

The Hare Krishna Society is a case study about human nature, how people take a religious leader and then cannot find fault with the leader or with themselves. Instead, they are condescending to everyone else.

There are two parts to this. People either find fault with the leader and cannot find an advantage in finding fault with themselves or they find no fault with the leader because if they do, it would imply that their decision to follow him was flawed. In either case it is an effort to protect the self of the follower.

Finding fault with a leader does not in any way take care of the fault of the follower. In this life one must make do, which means one has to use what is available, even if what is available is not perfect. Actually, one must see that what is here is here. One can only put things to use or leave them aside.

In South American, there is a Creole saying that if one cannot find the mother, one should suckle the grandmother. Usually the infant cries because the look of the shriveled breast of the grandmother is a hellish sight.

As I conversed with those former Hare Krishna leaders, the senior said this, "I do not know why he did not have a system for yoga exercises in the morning. It would have taken about half hour. Many sexual problems would have been non-existent."

It was a stupid question because we all knew why. The reason in that in the lineage of teachers, over time, the system of yoga which is described in the *Bhagavad Gita* in chapter six, became outlawed. The founder of the society simply did as requested by his predecessor. In that sense he was blameless in the matter.

In India, in the spiritual lineages which are called *sampradayas*, or spiritual societies which advocate a certain doctrine and practice, one must do as instructed by the predecessor. It is similar to the commercial franchise in a developed country, where one can buy into a franchise but one must represent the product in a stipulated way.

One other monk said this. "*Urdhvareta!* That is the secret. It was attained only through yoga austerities. Otherwise the stuff flows down. Then we are bound to have sexual problems either with the same or the opposite sex."

He spoke of the idea in the Indian books about semen flowing upwards into the brain, rather than flowing downward through the genitals. *Urdhva* is Sanskrit for upward flow and *reta* is Sanskrit for semen.

Interestingly these persons were the very same people who gave me strict warnings about not doing yoga when I first entered the Hare Krishna ashram in West Virginia. Before I got there, they knew that I practiced yoga. They were sure to inform me about the rules of the lineage. They were afraid that I would influence others to do yoga.

During the morning session of exercises, these persons came. They checked to see how the energy flow is altered in the subtle body as a result of breath infusion. One of them said that it was such a simple logical practice, that anyone could do it.

I said nothing to him. There are tons of social resistance in spiritual groups and in the normal society which goes against yoga practice, especially against anything that interferes with the genital usage of semen.

The practice may seem simple enough but the establishment of it in one's life only occurs if one can get over that resistance. Yoga practice with the upwards flow of semen even if done proficiently does not free a male from family obligations nor from obligation to participate in the reproduction of baby forms.

Crippled Yogi

In spite of a superficial surgery and the limitations that put on my exercise session, I got some air infused into the subtle body. As this body gets older the time may come when the postures cannot be done. Who knows, this body may be destined for a crippled state anyway?

As I did the breathing, I observed that some persons who are either disinclined from exercising the body or who just cannot do it due to pain in the joints, can do the breathing exercises. That would rely on a willingness to exercise the diaphragm. One would also have to be willing to give the lungs vigorous usage.

Doing the postures are an added benefit for getting the infused energy to spread throughout the physical and subtle bodies, but if one cannot do the postures, one would derive a benefit by doing the breathing only.

Subtle Head Space

This morning I did a few postures with stretches. Then I did some *pranayama* breathing in a seated position. It is not much breathing, but I filled the base chakra region. Then I applied the abdominal lock.

Kundalini then typically rises up to the head or spreads out into various parts of the body, with greater or lesser intensity.

This morning, kundalini went into the subtle head. There was golden and white energy, bouncing back and forth in all directions in the subtle head space, rapidly. This went on for five to ten seconds before the energy calmed and diffused in the subtle head space.

The calming was partly due to a mental force applied by me to resume normal consciousness.

When I became aware of the physical body again, there was some concentration of energy in the chin, cheeks and upper frontal throat areas.

This experience, indicated that the subtle head space is a *container*. Kundalini was enclosed. It rebounded within the contained space.

Rishi Singh on *Padmasana* Lotus Posture

During the exercises, when I was almost finished with the session, Rishi Singh Gherwal appeared in my head. He instructed on what he termed to be the proper way to sit in *padmasana*, lotus posture.

His idea is that the muscles and ligaments which connect the thigh to the torso should be so relaxed that when one sits in lotus posture, there is no strain. There should be a perpendicular axis of the pelvic bucket-shaped region in reference to the floor. He said that this is the best posture for meditation but if a person does not have that relaxed musculature, still the person should sit comfortably and not be in a pose which causes the mind to drift to muscular aches and pains during meditation.

Bubble Body Information

During the exercises, I got a notation from Siddha Swami Nityananda. It was that the bubble body he uses was created by breaking the genitals from it.

I do not know when he left that notation in my psyche but I recall wanting to ask him about the details of how that body type is achieved. It is a special body which is developed out of the present astral form. While the astral form has no limbs, that body has none. It is like just a head and a trunk which are both ballooned.

The value of such a body is that one can prepare to go into causal existence. One becomes exempt from the astral worlds.

In breaking the astral genitals, it is not an act of breaking those organs even though that is mentioned. The act is one of stopping the astral hormones from being expressed through the genitals. In the angelic worlds, there is sexual indulgence between astral forms, but if one is a successful yogi, one may get away from those situations, since really if one is engaged for sex in the angelic kingdoms, it means that eventually one may resume as a physical being, as a mammal, and will again be on the physical plane as a human or animal of some sorts.

To break the astral genitals, one does not remove them. One causes the sex chakra to be involved in energy distribution in all parts of the astral body except for the astral genitals. This may be hard to imagine if one is accustomed to sex acts, but if one can go back mentally to being an infant and to being a toddler, one can get some idea of gender without sexual polarity.

Kundalini yoga if it is successful will eventually cause a sealing of the passage which is from the sex chakra to the genitals. When that happens, there is a sealing from the inside of the trunk of the subtle body. The genitals lose sexual interest.

Our Pleasure Needs

This morning kundalini rose after doing rapid breathing in the bow pose and then stretching to the left and to the right in turn evenly. The energy was a compressed cooling force, like pressed tiny pearl droplets of bliss globules.

In sex experience one is impulsively focused on the pleasure. This is why most mammals (humans included) do not understand kundalini even though they experience kundalini during sex experience.

The same lack of proper focus can occur when doing yoga, except that in yoga one has more objectivity. The bliss expression of kundalini during yoga, allows for a more detailed observation. It is the clearing action of the aroused kundalini that is to be noticed and not the bliss aspect of it.

It does happen though that when a person begins to do yoga, he may crave the bliss aspect as a replacement for sex pleasure. If one was preoccupied with sex before doing yoga, and then one practices, one will want to find a similar pleasure. As such when kundalini rises, if it does, one will expect a pleasure.

A living being is pleasure crazed. That is the situation. It takes years of practice to wean the self from cravings. Let us consider a simple dietary aspect like sugar. How many of us can voluntarily cease consuming it?

Some people even though they may lose teeth, even though they may be under pain in the nerves of the teeth, even if they are afflicted with diabetes, will not cease eating sugar.

This is a challenge for yoga students. If they sense that it will cause curtailment of pleasure needs, they become reluctant to continue the practice.

Reproductive Game of Nature

This morning kundalini looped around the pubic area. It began at the base chakra. Then it looped around the pubic area and went into the navel and disappeared.

This is the reverse of the normal route used in the genetic system which we were graced with by nature, a system which sponsors sexual indulgence for the purpose of reproduction and which carries a high psychoactive energy which we usually interpret as a much-desired pleasure.

For the purpose of yoga, that special gift of nature for reproduction, must avoided. If one is successful with this, there will be a reversal, such that the reproductive mission of the body will change into a self containment inner circulation.

Instead of energy moving down in the body, pooling in the pubic area, and discharging in sexual flushes of energy, the energy will be recirculated in the psyche without sexual charges. The psyche will lose interest in reproduction.

It so happens however that even if a yogi can complete this practice, he/she is still not in the clear since if the yogi becomes lax nature will reestablish the reproductive intentions.

What is unnatural is that only. Unless it is maintained, what is natural will be reasserted.

A yogi will be in the clear when his subtle body changes into a *yogasiddha* form, otherwise he is always in danger to regressing and acting as a human animal, which means he will again be involved in the reproduction game of nature.

Kundalini Downward Arousal

This morning during exercises, kundalini rose into the chest area as pearl-like drops of bliss energy in the chest. These were like tiny pearls in a glistening white color, giving a bliss energy to the area.

During another rise, kundalini went downward from the base chakra. It emitted sparks while it shot a laser-like beam of energy through the center of the body and into the head.

Base chakra arousal in a downward direction, is not encouraged in kundalini yoga but when it happens with a bright energy like a flash of lightning on a dark night, that is considered favorable for practice.

There was one persistent intrusion thought which entered the head of the subtle body during meditation. It was from a person who asked if I would agree to give lessons in bhastrika *breath of fire* practice. I replied as follows:

"Lessons can be given, but that is not the issue.

The teacher is not the problem. It is the student.

The teaching is not the problem. It is the student's practice of the teaching.

I can teach but will you practice? Will you consistently endeavor?"

The Sexual Route

During exercises this morning kundalini came into the cheek bones. That felt like little molecules of bliss energy moving there and then moving in the cheeks. I checked for the route from the base chakra. It came up in two energy streams from the base, then to the front part of the body, then to the front left and right side of the neck and then into the cheek bones. This meant that kundalini did not use the *sushumna* nadi central spinal passage.

At one time during this session kundalini arose and crisscrossed by jumping from the left to the right and to the left, from the lower pelvic area into the rib cage. Usually kundalini moves up the right or left or right and left simultaneously or just the center. It rarely crisscrosses.

When this happened, as I looked into the subtle body, Swami Rama said, "Show the sexual route."

I then looked for it but it was not in the pubic area. He remarked, "Where is it? How has it disappeared?"

I did not answer the question. There was no trace of it. The only hint was a memory impulse which showed a small string like object dangling in the pubic area.

Masters of Death

This morning during the exercises there were comments of Swami Rama who showed the ins and outs of the *agnisara* practice which is supposed to give a yogi the upper hand at the time of death. The idea is that when it gets close to death, within hours or days, the lifeForce becomes more loosely connected to the energy mechanisms in the physical body. At that time, the yogi can take steps to kill the body by forcing the lifeForce out of it.

Usually the lifeForce wants to possess a diseased, damaged or old body until the very last cell in that body dies. At a certain point a yogi is supposed to make a decision to remove the lifeForce and not to allow it to stall for time.

If the lifeForce is permitted to do death in its own way, the subtle body will be de-energized, short of energy, exhausted as it will be. Then the yogi will depart from the body and descend to a lower astral plane. From there he may be lost and may even forget everything about yoga and yoga teachers, just as when a person finds himself/herself in some parallel world in the dream state and realizes later that he/she totally forgot his/her social identity and got involved in that world as if there was no other place.

In talking about creating a pathway for kundalini to take at the time of death, Swami Rama described that in a round-about way. This is what he said,

"After birth, one's kundalini gets possessed of the need for food and especially through the sucking impulse it gets a greedy attitude about breast milk. Some of our mothers had difficulty weaning us because we were greedy about it and protested by crying and behaving badly when we were transfered to other foods.

"Then again as toddlers we were attached to sweet foods. The parents either deprived us of it or serviced our needs and supplied every whim.

"But then again in the teen years, after sexual desire becomes evident, we wanted to have sex, even immorally, even if we did not understand what would happen if there was a pregnancy or if there were emotional complications for the parents. Then we rebelled and did things which our parents prohibited or discouraged. We did not care about our parents. Our main concern was to satisfy the sex urges which were in fact, the path that kundalini took through the lower part of the body.

"Some of us were married. We became obsessed with having sex in a bedroom but we also wanted status, as a house, job and salary. These were avenues of expression of kundalini.

"For a yogi these aspects of social life are diversions from the real issue which is how to master the departure from the body at death. From the time a yogi gets a body from a woman's reproductive system, that yogi should work day and night to know how to master leaving the body. Birth is the flip of death. The two go together.

"The yogi must whittle out a passage and cause kundalini to get used to that route and then use that at death. But it has to be done when the body is healthy, not just at the last minute, like some who when they have terminal diseases go to a pilgrimage and pretend that they will master death and attain salvation."

Fated: The Usual Course

This morning during exercises Swami Rama appeared. He mastered *pranayama* practice during his youth. When it was near the end of his body, he pushed his lifeForce out through the sushumna passage and through the crown of the head. In explaining that action, he told me that it has to do with teaching kundalini a new route for its passage.

There was a conversation like this:

"What is its old route Swami?"

He replied,

"Sexual access and excretion passage is its old route. It prefers sexual access but nature dictates that it become more accustomed to excretion as a matter of routine. In a dying body, a person may become occupied with either constipation or diarrhea. Due to that, kundalini takes the route which it runs food through on a daily basis. That road or highway ends at the anus.

"It has nothing to do with religious affiliation, superstition or a person's philosophy. Suppose I am a great philosopher. I figured the by-ways of human activity. Or suppose I am the leader of a religious sect. Will I be spared constipation or diarrhea at the time of departure from the body? Will I keep my mind from becoming occupied with health problems when the body is near its death?

"Have I stopped kundalini from getting used to the highway that ends at the anus and the one which runs through the pleasure-yielding nerves in the genitals?

"If I have not done that, kundalini will take the lower passage out of the body. The attention of the self will follow kundalini through that passage. Where will it emerge? Into which dimension? Into a dark astral world or into one with full light?

"I will still have my philosophy, religion, creed or belief but where will I be?

"In yoga there is this solution which was bestowed by ancient masters like Gorakshnath, whereby we train kundalini to forget the lower highway and to learn how to use the highest highway which leads to the top of the head and beyond in higher subtle dimensions.

"There are two ways of mastering this process of controlled departure of kundalini at the time of death. The first and best method is to master the process of kundalini yoga in the youth of the body before say about 16

years of age. I did that when I had my last body. This is the best way but it is not an easy achievement because it hinges not on your decision in the new body but on the decision in the last life and providence's cooperation. If in the last life you mastered yoga to a great degree and then you pass on, and if providence cooperates with the plan and sets you into a birth environment where you can begin yoga practice in childhood, then you can use this first and best process.

"However, since providence cares very little for anyone and regards someone as a mere straw blowing in the winds, it is usually the case, that a yogi has to master yoga later, after childhood, after he leaves the parental environment.

"Agnisara is a separate process but it is part of bhastrika pranayama *and* kapalabhati. *As part, one should practice and make sure that the navel area no longer holds energy. Why do you think that the navel keeps some energy? It is not for itself. It is because kundalini instructed it to do so. Everyone likes to hoard energy for use to enjoy.*

"If I like to gamble, I will hoard any money I get for use in the casino. Kundalini likes sex. It instructed the navel chakra to hoard energy hormones, for use in sexual pleasure. One must stop the navel from doing this. Let me put it this way, if one fails to stop the navel, if one fails to change this natural construction of the psychic mechanisms in the psyche, one will be fated to take the usual course when leaving the body."

Part 3

Kundalini in Toes

During the first stage of exercises this morning, none of the advanced yogis were present but there was an instructive energy left from the presence of Rishi Singh Gherwal. That energy was activated. It rendered a message explaining that I was to get kundalini to go into the finger tips and toes such that each nadi which reached to those places was electrified with fresh subtle energy from the breath infusion practice.

If Rishi was there in person, he would have said this,

"Before the yogi sits to meditate, the kundalini shakti should be used to infest every nadi with fresh energy. If this is not done, the energy of kundalini will be used inefficiently in those parts which are not infused. The result is that kundalini may rise into the head but due to dark energy in other parts of the subtle body, the yogi will be restricted in where he can go and how he can perform in the higher dimensions.

"Mahayogin Gorakshnath gave the process of hatha yoga for the purpose of a complete energization of the subtle body, for the re-conditioning of every part, not just the head. In your physical body, suppose there is a poisoned chemical in all parts of it except the spine and head, what will be the result of that? Consider this in terms of the subtle body.

"Even though the subtle body is junked by an advanced yogi who completes what is required, that form must be purified first before the yogi can eliminate it. No one can become liberated with an impure subtle body."

During the exercises I followed this instruction and brought kundalini to the tips of the fingers. When this happened there is no sensation of kundalini rising into the brain. When kundalini goes into the fingers, there is a sensation of it spreading under the arm pits and then shooting to the finger tips. This feels like needle cramps under the arm pits and into the arms and finger tips but this feeling has a bliss aspect. The same feeling is felt when kundalini reaches the toe tips with needles cramps in the calves and ankles. On may be inspired to stretch the arms or to wiggle them during the infusement.

Breath Rate

I was disturbed by two persons during the exercises. One was a disgraced monk. He lost religious authority. The other was his assistant when he served as a monk. Both persons are politically inclined. Their religious affiliation was saturated with political power concerns.

Dealing with such persons in the astral world is a set-back for a yogi. Somehow, by the force of providence, one is sometimes forced to relate to such people. One must patiently bear with their corrosive view points.

In the middle of the exercise session, Yogeshwarananda appeared but not in a miniature form which is usually used by yogis to enter the psyche of a student. He appeared as an invisible presence. He said this,

"Denounce those yogis who say that a person can advance spiritually by decreasing the number of breaths, by slowing the breath rate during meditation. Those who state this are dishonest yogis.

"During the winter months when they hibernate, bears and other creatures have decreased breaths but it does not increase their spiritual perception. In fact, what is their spiritual perception? The correct way to regard decreases of breaths for a yogi, is to consider that if you infuse the subtle body with sufficient energy then due to that influx, the subtle system may not need fresh air for a time. During that time, there will be a decrease in the breathing rate. Thus, if one meditates just after infusing the body, then yes there will be a slow rate. That is different to when a person does not infuse breath and experiences a decrease in the rate.

"First they should infuse the air and then meditate. Do pranayama as the 4th stage of yoga. Then do the other four states which concern introspection immediately after. That was the definition given by Patanjali. That is classic yoga.

"For a beginner the 5th stage which is pratyahar *sensual energy withdrawal will take up the meditation time, but for an advanced person, that stage may be completed in a jiffy during the meditation session. He/she can proceed with the other three advanced stages which Patanjali named collectively as* samyama, *the complete restraint of the mento-emotional energy."*

Focus During Meditation

This morning session had many instances of kundalini raising. So long as one does not consume the sex hormones, there is a likelihood that kundalini will raise on a consistent basis as prompted by the infusion of breath energy. After practicing for some time, kundalini should remain in an aroused condition continuously but our life style may prevent that. Thus, it is necessary to practice daily to prod kundalini.

As usual there were thoughts which distracted. I dealt with those in the usual way of confronting them or infusing them with breath energy during the session. These thoughts are tiny instances of mental invasion but nevertheless they have a power to disrupt practice by causing the focus to shift away from wherever it should be applied. The thoughts are demanding. They represent the social demands being made to the yogi.

A yogi cannot legitimately avoid all social demands. We read that when Arjuna wanted to side-step warrior duties, Krishna pressed him to complete them. Even vicious work which is a duty should be performed or it will bring unfavorable consequences. Just the other day somebody criticized violence to me. However, we cannot make spiritual progress without discipline. In fact, in human existence violence will be committed. It must be used in some instances if we want to bring about permanent change. One such permanent change is to raise kundalini. If you can raise it by talking to it nicely, by loving it or by any pleasant method please do so.

A yogi should promptly take care of social demands. If he/she does not, these demands will have the power to distract one during the exercises and during the meditation session. Some demands are not mandatory. Those can be dismissed by one method or the other but the ones which are legitimate cannot be nudged by any means except by execution of those social functions.

During the last twenty minutes of the exercises, I focused on the head of the subtle body. More or less kundalini yoga is an effort to work on the base chakra and cause kundalini to move up the spine, all the way up or just partially. If one is successful in moving kundalini into the head, once or twice or thrice during the exercises, one can shift the focus and work on infusing energy directly into the head of the subtle body. With kundalini being in the head, the infusements will operate to cleanse the mental or emotional energy which is from a low plane of existence.

When I sat to meditate, naad sound was barely audible. I noticed that it sounded different. It was distant like if it came from a billion miles away. It barely reached where I was. I tried to situate the self in it but that was not possible because it was too distant, like something in a galaxy which is seen as a pin point through a telescope. I did however place the coreSelf as near to it as possible. A faint energy came in through the right top of the head. I positioned the coreSelf there.

I immediately looked forward after doing this, because the head of the subtle body was free from thoughts and any other types of mental and emotional low energy forces. When I looked forward, the third eye formed an *in and out* energy moving with a purplish brownish hazy energy which seemed to form behind me and then gather and move towards the center of the eyebrows and then collect in a circular shape, recede away from me and then disappear. This kept happening for ten minutes. This stopped. The third eye space was stable with a misty haze.

I did not stare at the haze with a sharp focus because if one does so, it may disappear as if it does not desire to be observed and has the power to stop one's perception of it. In doing so one stares but removes the investigative interest from the staring energy.

I did this for ten minutes. This is a practice which is recommended in many of the kriya yoga lineages. It is said that if one does this, a bright star will appear but it does not always happen as stipulated and hoped for by some yogis. Rishi Singh repeatedly explained that the yogi should work with breath infusion to put the psyche into the desired dimension where supernatural perception will be possible. The yogi should not impractically and stubbornly remain in a low dimension and imagine that he can change his psyche or make himself go to a higher plane.

Light Behind a Coal Mountain

The exercise session this morning was good with a few thought interruptions. It is amazing how just one or two thoughts can be just as disturbing as many of them. It depends on the power released in the thoughts and the energy which was embedded in the thoughts force from its source person.

One thought from one person was persistent. It hung in the mind like a jelly fish floating beneath the waves in an ocean. It took some infusion of breath energy to dissolve it.

During the exercises I saw a few advanced yogis like Swami Shivananda and Rishi Singh Gherwal. Swami Shivananda was far off. I was only in contact with him for a short period when kundalini arose into the head, and gushed through the back top. He said nothing but he looked in my direction casually, just as when one hears a bird among some bushes and one looks to see what it is.

Because kundalini rose in a specific way and with a certain forceful pressure, it propelled me into the dimension the Swami resided. I became perceptible there for about fifteen seconds. Kundalini however subsided. Even though it raised again it did not propel the psyche into that specific dimension.

When I sat to meditate, it took fifteen minutes to reach naad sound. A question of why arises. The reason was that the thought force which disturbed me during the exercise session damaged some mental energy which kept me distracted for fifteen minutes until I got everything aligned properly in the head of the subtle body. Naad sound was not in the usual place which is near the right ear. It was at the top back of the head. It was quieter than normal. In any case, I tried to go into its influence but I was unsuccessful.

I tried five times. Each time, I would enter naad and then find myself in some other part of the mind. Then I would return to naad but for some reason, I could not remain in its influence. After this I entered naad again. Then I stayed in the back of the head but did not hear it even though I was in its influence.

Sometimes, it happens that one enters naad, remains in it and does not hear naad even though one is in it. This is because at sometimes when one enters naad the subtle hearing sense tunes out. This is okay in this practice, provided one still remains in the zone of naad.

As I stressed repeatedly, much of meditation practice has to do with location, psychic location, mystic location, supernatural location, call it what you will. It is not direction-less. It is not vague. It is not void with no sense of up or down.

After being in the naad zone while not hearing naad, things seem to settle in the psyche, especially in the frontal part of the head. Thus, I took the action to look forward. Suddenly there was a light glowing in the front but it was like a sun rising behind a large round mountain. It was as if the mountain was as black as coal and then that light was rising through a hazy atmosphere. That was there for a while. Then it disappeared. A flattish rectangular misty light appeared.

Rishi Sing Gherwal was not there. He left an energy for explaining that light. It meant this:

"Perception of these lights are determined by the amount of energy which is infused into the psyche. That energy causes the psyche to reach a level where supernatural perception is possible. Perception of these lights do not come about by desire to see the lights, nor by making efforts to force the lights to appear. One sees the lights when one reaches a dimension in which the psyche used in that world, has the perception capability.

"Thus, the whole effort to advance in yoga requires a re-figuring by the yogi in regards to what he desires to achieve. Suppose you are in the astral world as a ghost being without a physical body. Then just trying as hard as you can to be a physical being will never make you physical. But if you enter a physical being's feelings then you may come out as a physical being in the physical world as that person's child. Similarly, if you

develop an existence in a higher dimension, you will have the supernatural perception which is natural to that environment."

Special Note:

Some advanced yogis leave instructions in the astral world for students. This is similar to leaving written instructions for someone or leaving a will. A yogi who does not want to remain on a certain astral level for someone, can leave a message for that person. That information will then be activated when that person reaches that level and needs the brief. To correctly read the message, one must have a mind that is free from disruptive energies.

Enter the Intellect

This morning the exercises session was great with kundalini rising into the chest on the left and on the right side alternately. It rose and went through the buttocks, electrifying that area.

To make kundalini go to the right side and then to the left side, one has to do certain stretches as soon as one stops infusing the breath and one feels that kundalini will move. By making a stretch to the left, kundalini became pulled to the left side which is termed *ida nadi* in Sanskrit, and moving to the right caused *pingala nadi* to be affected.

When kundalini moves into an area it flushes stale subtle energy and causes the region to be filled with light. Kundalini usually remains at the base chakra and conducts its operations for the maintenance of the body from there. When it rises it usually does so by spreading its power through the sexual organs. This causes sexual arousal.

When it spreads into the chest region, one interprets that as affectionate feelings, as love.

In yoga, the idea is to cause kundalini to electrify the entire subtle body not the sex area and human social affection concerns. Kundalini has access to every cell in the body. This may be realized by persons who are sexually involved and who can take some time during sexual experience to note what happens when there is sexual climax, when cells of the body are induced to contribute energy for sexual experience.

It is difficult however to make this observation because of the intense feelings which we interpret emotionally as pleasure. This pleasure bars us from making an objective assessment of what kundalini does to cause the intense focused feelings of pleasure with the genitals being the main focus of the experience.

When I sat to meditate, it took three minutes before I linked to naad. Why is that? For one thing it was a successful session because kundalini rose several times and I directed it in the proper channels. I infused the intellect. I also infused the third eye because I was aware that it was affected when I infused it. Thus, why did it take a full three minutes to be aware of naad?

The reason is that somehow or the other there was a persistent thought which entered the intellect, a thought from someone else. It penetrated the intellect and did not budge even after the intellect was infused.

I had to deal with that intellect for those three minutes. I entered it and challenged the thought force. I confronted the thought head on. It disappeared.

Usually the coreSelf is outside the intellect but in this case because of the persistence of the foreign thought, I entered the intellect. This is like entering a bubble which is dark inside but which is spacious and which has a subtle object inside which is like a small jelly fish.

After getting rid of that thought force, I got out of the intellect and went to the right back of the head to be in naad sound.

After fifteen minutes with naad, I looked forward and noticed light where the intellect was located. It was like when there is a moon in the sky which is on the other side of the planet and hence cannot be seen, but which lights a cloud with a glow in the night sky.

Kundalini to Crown

Email Inquiry:

It is said that once the Kundalini reaches the crown chakra, one experiences self-realization or enlightenment.

MiBeloved's Response:

That statement is like the statement which is told to some girls as soon as they reach puberty, where it is said, "If you have sex with a boy, you will get pregnant."

But some of the girls find out that if they have sex, they get pleasure and there is no pregnancy, at least not on the first involvement.

Or it is like the female tourist who was in London. When she got near Buckingham Palace, the tour guide pointed to the large stone structure and said, "Whosoever lives here is the Queen of England."

The touring lady then developed a desire to move into Buckingham Palace. She applied for a work permit and then applied for a job as a cleaner. It was the perfect thing because she thought that if she could occupy the building, the whole of England would honor her as the queen.

In the description of the job there was a statement to the effect that the cleaner was given a special room in the building. She applied and was employed. On the day when the employment began, she was greeted at the entrance which was a large metal gate. A man who was the Master of Servants led her into the Palace. He showed her the small room which was reserved for the cleaner. Seeing that the room was small the lady suspected that something was amiss. In a sarcastic tone she spoke to the Master of Servants, "It seems to me that this is quite suitable for the Queen of England. Would you mind informing the butler that I am here? And please, your lordship, instruct the chambermaids to report with my linen."

But the Master of Servants being an expert diplomat merely bowed to the lady and left in a haste. When he got to his office, he called the security and asked them to escort the lady from the palace grounds.

What am I saying?

Well, not everyone who has a kundalini experience at the crown chakra becomes enlightened in the way Buddha was enlightened or in the way that Paramhamsa Yogananda was enlightened.

In fact, someone may lose objective consciousness when his/her kundalini rises and hits the crown chakra. Instead of becoming enlightened that person may experience nothingness and come back to this world with no memory of the experience and no objective understanding of what occured.

In Yoga, there is *jada samadhi*. *Jada* is Sanskrit for stupid or dumb. There is an experience in which a person goes to higher awareness but does not have the objectivity to understand what it is and has no coherent memory of the experience.

Most beings in this world evolve upward. That means that if one shifts a rattle snake into the human species, that entity would be vicious and would be in a prison shortly. One cannot successfully elevate a person way beyond his/her instinctive evolutionary behavior. One will not take an alligator, put the spirit using that body into a human body and suddenly get a Mother Theresa or a Mahatma Gandhi because one caused its kundalini to rise into the crown chakra.

The problem one will have if one relocates that spirit into a human body is that it will carry with it, the same kundalini which it used in the snake body. The kundalini would carry with it, the vicious tendencies. It will make neither head nor tail of a crown chakra experience.

Value of *Pranayama* Practice

This morning meditation session was intense but there were people from India who were present. These were five persons who are sannyasi monks. Some are deceased. They argued about a process of spiritual discipline which did not work to give them the results intended after leaving the physical body.

I kept doing the exercises as they conversed about different methods of spiritual advancement.

My exercises lasted fifty-five minutes. Then I sat to meditate. In the meditation the intellect was quiet by virtue of the infused breath energy into it. The coreSelf moved up into the crown of the head but the crown chakra and the brow chakra were absent. This was a silent meditation practice where the energies were quiescent.

No thoughts or images arose. Off in the distance those swamis chatted. They mentioned incidences which occurred when I was in their association some years ago. It was useless to discuss anything with them about *pranayama* practice because when a person does not do *pranayama*, that someone has no confidence in it and cannot comprehend its value.

Navel Clearance

During exercises, a Tibetan yogi explained that while in the India system of the chakras, there is much focus on the sushumna nadi spinal passage, in some of the Tibetan traditions, especially the one which came through Marpa, Naropa and Milarepa, the stress is simply on one chakra which is the navel center in the front of the body. This is not the navel chakra because that chakra is on the spine.

This system is concerned with the spread chakra which emanates from the spinal center. Rimpoche said this,

The spinal chakras are more like the prime minister and other officials of a government. These people have intelligence, charisma and managing power but they cannot do anything by themselves. Can you imagine what the prime minister would be if there were no other persons surrounding him, carrying out his wishes? In some cases, the prime minister of a country cannot defend himself if he were challenged to a fist fight. But if his bodyguards are nearby, no one dares to attack him.

We discovered that without their accessory expansive influences, the spinal chakras are merely hollow authorities. Rishi Singh Gherwal asked me to speak to you. He said that you would publish this information. Others can use it in the future even after you leave the body.

It is good that you have such a clairvoyant and clairaudient ability. That is rare with so much trash-chatter in the minds of human beings. From our view point and we are perhaps the most advanced yogis in terms of flushing the subtle body, the main issue in the physical body and in the adjacent subtle form, is the frontal navel chakra. Destroy that and you are free. What did Patanjali say about that chakra? I heard he said something to the effect that when that center is shattered, the yogi gets intimate knowledge about the layout of his psyche.

We looked at your translation. Ha! You did a good job of it. Even though you are not an advanced yogi, there were hardly any mistakes in your work. Anyway, you said the word kaya *means body. Well I do not know what dictionary or intuition you used but it means psyche not body. What does body mean? To some it means the physical system, to others it means the physical and the subtle body combined.*

Let us use your translation except for that word. Translate it like this:

नाभिचक्रे कायव्यूहज्ञानम्॥ ३० ॥

nābhicakre kāyavyūhajñānam

nābhi – navel; cakre – on the energy gyrating center; **kāya – psyche, body;** vyūha – arrangement, lay out; jñānam – knowledge.

By complete restraint of the mento-emotional energy in relation to the focusing on the navel energy-gyrating center, the yogi gets knowledge about the layout of his psyche. (*Yoga Sutra* **3.30)**

Our lineage declares that if a yogi changes the construction of the navel area, so that the energy ingested does not coalesce there, and instead goes straight to muladhara without having interest in the sex-reproduction apparatus, the struggle for liberation is over.

Produce these drawings to illustrate this:

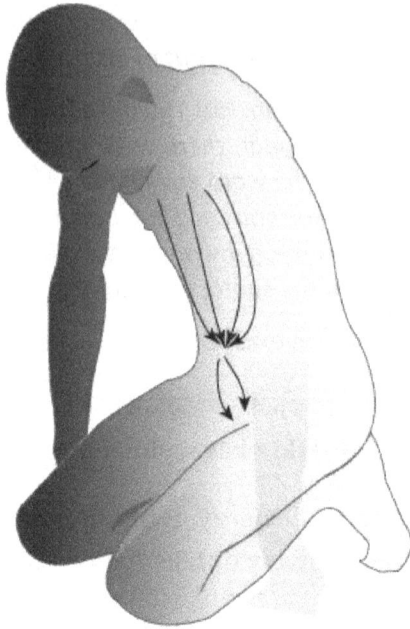

↑   breath energy
going from lungs to navel to pubic area
and then to base of spine

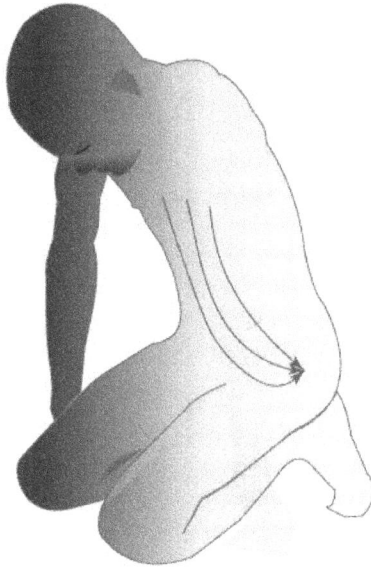

↑ Breath energy
going from lungs through navel area
unobstructed and not retained,
going directly to base of spine.
Navel hold power is abolished

Special Note:

The Sanskrit word for the complete restraint of the mento-emotional energy is *samyama*. It appears in verse 3.16 of the *Yoga Sutras* and applies to many verses which occur after verse 16. Please see the verses before 16 in chapter 3 to understand term samyama. It directly means the highest three stages of yoga combined as one practice.

Effectiveness of a Method

This morning Rishi Singh Gherwal sent one of his yogi friends (Rimpoche) to speak to me. At first during my exercises, I saw the two of them in the distance like seeing two ants from afar. Suddenly the other yogi appeared in my subtle head.

He checked my practice. During the session, he showed an arm-shoulder shake and said that the idea was to be sure that the whole system was energized. Every part of the subtle body which kundalini services should be properly energized. The old prana, old subtle energy in any areas should be flushed.

As if to make a joke, he said,

"You cannot expect that God will clean this for you. You must do it yourself. If it is something that you can do, then for sure know that the God will not come and do it for you. You must do it yourself."

I said to him, "These are aggressive practices. People want something passive." He replied,

"This is not for everybody. Those who require other methods may find other systems. We use these because these give the results intended. There is no controversy about methods. It depends on what you want to achieve and how far you are willing to go to accomplish that. One more thing, tell people that what they do not experience will not be desired by them. Once you experience higher states, you may be willing to work to attain those, otherwise if there is no experience, if providence does not reveal a certain level to you, there will be no reason to do practice for those accomplishments."

"A human being no matter how great he is cannot force a high experience, but some people get experiences through taking hallucinogenic drugs. But the higher levels which are off limits even through drug use cannot be experienced or even dreamt of unless providence allows one to access those planes."

Soon after he left. Rishi came but he was silent. I resumed the naad location meditation and then came forward in the subtle head to see if the intellect misbehaved or not. It was silent as if it did not exist but the third eye opening was activated.

Why Practice Yoga?

The question as to why one should practice yoga may arise from time to time. Especially since one will not get transcendental experiences during each practice session, why should one do this? How should one urge oneself to practice if one feels that one should practice but one is discouraged by the yoga itself.

Yoga may be a cause for discouragement because it does not always yield transcendental experiences or meaningfull realizations.

Again, why practice?

If one practices to please oneself or to live up to an ideal or aspiration how will one continue if the ideal does not manifest. If one does not achieve from yoga what one set out to accomplish, why should one do it, especially since other activities, bring immediate benefit in real time?

If one practices to please a teacher, why should one continue if the practice does not yield results or if the results are hard to come by and are rarely experienced.

If out of a year of practice, one will only get about 7 or 8 meaningful realizations and transcendental experiences, is it worth it?

In my own case for instance I may have three motivations. Any of these is sufficient for me to continue with or without satisfaction and a sense of accomplishment.

Those three reasons are:

- Obligation to yoga gurus to comply with their request for practice.
- Sense of purpose to myself, feeling that the practice reinforces myself.
- Sense of duty to others who need the information which I share as I practice.

Kundalini and Intellect Fusion

Rishi Singh Gherwal explained that just as the natural way is for the kundalini to express itself through the sexual orifice as its highest pleasure, and while doing so to bring the intellect or thinking mind to the sexual location for indulging in that pleasure, so the yogi must over time when he becomes proficient in raising kundalini into the head on a regular basis, cause kundalini to meet with the intellect in the head.

When a yogi reaches this stage where he can cause kundalini to fused with the intellect in the head of the subtle body, that yogi crosses most of the territory that stands between a beginner and full proficiency at Patanjali's idea about ceasing the *vrittis*.

From kundalini yoga which concerns the chakras, and the nadis of the subtle body, a yogi graduates to *brahma* yoga practice, which begins where he is focused on causing kundalini to come into the head to be directly focused on the intellect and not on the chakras, not on the 3rd eye brow chakra or on the crown chakra.

To do this the yogi must be proficient. He should raise kundalini through the spine on demand by whatever way he chooses but by a method that works and not by an imagination which in fact does not budge kundalini. Once that method is perfected and it is a sure thing, the yogi should divert kundalini so that it rises with intention to reach the intellect.

Rishi showed a passage that kundalini will eventually take to do this, where it courses through the middle of the body, enters the head and then fires at the intellect. The value of this practice is that if it is done to proficiency, the yogi will be in a position to comply with Patanjali's no-*vrittis* method. He will reach the culmination of yoga.

The most rebellious, most resistant psychic organ is the intellect. Some think that it is the sense of identity but actually, it is the intellect which influences the sense of identity to adhere to the numerous psychic and physical objects and energies which degrade the coreSelf.

Patanjali was aware of the sense of identity and still he identified the intellect as the culprit for keeping the core hog-tied in physical existence. He insisted on its purification.

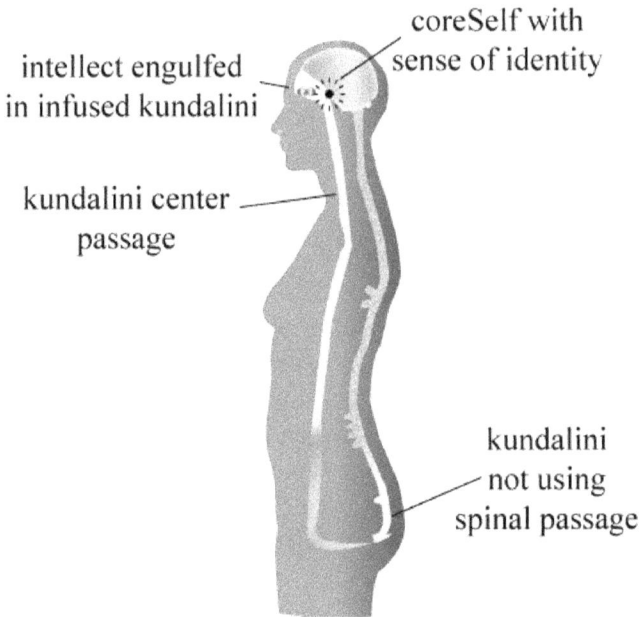

intellect engulfed in infused kundalini

coreSelf with sense of identity

kundalini center passage

kundalini not using spinal passage

Root Chakra Purification

Eating healthy and exercising would have direct effects on the navel chakra which is sometimes regarded as the 3rd chakra. The root chakra is hard to target through exercises unless one does special postures which affect it.

To find if an exercise affects the root chakra, make a test by jotting down the time of the main daily evacuation or bi-daily or tri-daily main evacuations. Then go through a two-week routine of doing the exercise, if the evacuation does not happen hours sooner than it normally does, one does not affect the root chakra.

There are other things one can do in the mental and emotional areas. For instance, the root chakra sponsors survival skills and competition. If one decreases aggressive and competitive attitudes, that would affect the chakra.

Curtail the Intellect

Rishi Singh said that meditation on the brow chakra really means meditation on the intellect. It does not mean meditation on the brow chakra. In real terms in higher yoga the concern is as described by Patanjali which is the shutting down of the random habitual activities *(vrittis)* of the mind. Most of these activities are done by one psychic organ which is the intellect.

Rishi Singh said this,

"The reason why the focus is said to be on the third eye is this. The brow chakra is there. The intellect usually focuses through that chakra to express its intentions. However, the real problem is not the chakra but the intellect. This is evidenced by a carefully study of the Yoga Sutras. *The second sutra means one thing and one thing only but that is the silencing and removal of independence of the intellect which constructs mental and emotional ideas.*

"A yogi must get the intellect roped in so that its independence is nil. That is the gist of yoga.

"How to achieve that?

"Can it be done by drinking a glass of water?

"Then do that

"Can it be done by urinating?

"Then do that.

"Only in advanced meditation levels can one see a psychic organ. In the meantime, one can recognize it indirectly by its functions or vrittis *which are listed by Patanjali. To curtail something that is invisible one may curtail its obvious operations. Because the operations are real, it is not a matter of blind faith. They are manifest as psychological operations which one experiences."*

A Yoga School or Institution

During practice this morning Arthur Beverford suggested that I begin a formal school for yoga practice. He said this in the presence of his teacher Rishi Singh Gherwal. For his part the Rishi made no remark. He thought of my doing a translation of the book by *Swatmarama* which is *Hatha Yoga Pradipika* and some of the literature of *Gorakshnath*.

More or less I am done with translating Sanskrit books but I will do something if a teacher instructs that it be done. The reason is that the instruction should be adjusted because of our current cultural condition. Now we have the acceleration of technology which imposed a different way of looking at life, and which will make the Sanskrit books more and more irrelevant unless the translator can remain loyal to the original idea and also match the meanings into the current culture.

Translating Sanskrit books is not easy. Writers use these books to endorse their ideas by hijacking the authority and name of a previous teacher.

To translate loyally is difficult. Even if one can do it, if one is not badly motivated, one has the added responsibility of making it culturally relevant. These are not easy achievements. I struggled with this with the *Bhagavad Gita,* the *Uddhava Gita, the Anu Gita,* the *Yoga Sutras* and the *Markandeya Samasya.*

Instead of translating more books, I should invest time in practice so that I can advance as far as possible before fate confiscates the body. While practicing I should leave notes of what I did so that others in this time, place and culture, can get some idea of what can be achieved.

Regarding beginning a school, I am disinclined but if providence facilitates that I will comply. Personally, I am not interested. I wrote books and will publish a few more if providence permits more time in this physical body. The books which I produced so far have enough information to get anyone on a sure footing for meditation practice.

Arthur Beverford did not establish a school for yoga. Even though Rishi Singh Gherwal wrote books, and gave formal classes while he used his last body, he did not establish a school either. Beverford put his energies into establishing a school for Japanese martial arts. I was his main student for yoga. He wanted to establish a school but there was not sufficient interest. He found that people were more interested in martial arts. He hoped to use that as a stepping stone to yoga, especially since that was the idea of the Bodhidharma who first brought Buddhism to China.

If anyone wants to set up a yoga school, I would assist the person as much as I can. That is what I will do. Right now, I am cashed out for time. I have barely sufficient time to get myself in order because fate strikes to take this body.

Fate is impartial and does not care one hoot if I run out of time while teaching. It will give me not even one second extra to complete my practice merely because I am involved in a yoga school. A friend of mine once said that there is no use in writing the books if I will not train someone.

That is his idea. He is focused into the physical world, into social life of human beings. His attention is trapped there. He does not understand that the guillotine of time will soon decapitate him while he carelessly attends to the human affairs and neglected the self interest.

It is really hypocritically to go on focusing on helping others when in fact one is afflicted with the very same diseases one sees in everyone else.

Meditation: The Best Time

Someone called yesterday about the best time to meditate. Regarding this, everybody has his/her opinion. My proposal is simple. Try doing meditation at different times and then discover which time is best. Of course, the lifestyle and employment schedule cuts into the use of the daily 24 hours.

Be reasonable with yourself. For me the best meditation is between midnight and 6 a.m. Rising early for meditation is practical if one rests early in consideration of the body and mind getting sufficient release. If one stays up for this or that reason, getting up early for meditation is not practical. The mind and lifeForce will be reluctant to provide encouragement. One will struggle through mental and emotional negativity while one practices.

Usually in ashrams, one must rise early around 5 am to meditate. Usually one must do postures in a group session. Then one sits or reclines to meditate.

In advanced ashram environment, each student rises and then practices postures and breath infusion with or without supervision. Then one meditates in isolation. The reason for this is that each student is at a different stage.

Doing practice under the supervision of a teacher can be disagreeable, in the sense that one must do what the teacher says regardless of what one desires. Even though I check students practice periodically, I do not stand over students.

If I teach a student, I lose track of my practice. That is not good for me.

When one becomes a teacher, one loses grip on one's studentship under the more advanced teacher. I am never eager to be a teacher. Still, teaching duties are there. They must be administered no matter what. The students too must submit.

One person said that my teachers are not physically present. But there is no difference between an astral teacher and a physical one. In fact, the astral one is more of a nuisance because he/she is more subtle and direct. There is a tighter discipline which is required when one deals with astral yogis but somehow people think that I do not have to comply with a teacher.

If you want to find out if someone is under the control of a great yogi, check to see if that person makes advancement. Yogic advancement does not come from laying around and doing as one pleases, doing what is convenient, doing what one feels will please the mind. It comes from application of psychological disciplines on the components of consciousness.

Advanced yogis do not spoil disciples. They do not have time to spend with cry-baby disciples or with disciples who are into mental fantasies and who are lazy due to lower emotions.

When should a student rise to do practice?

Ask a question:

How important is yoga? What do you hope to get from it?

People accept hardships, but for what?

People will go out of the way to get certain things and will even go against people who really have their interest at heart, but why?

Underneath everything is motivation.

We are nothing when compared to what motivates us. Whatever motivates, that is the controller of the psyche. That will dictate the urges and endeavor.

Yoga Practice

Yogeshwarananda made a remark about the lack of yoga practice in spiritual aspirants.

This is what he said:

"Considering the benefits of meditation and the example set for its practice by great people, even by Krishna, the generator of a Universal Form, who claimed to be the Supreme Lord, it is a wonder that human beings do not practice yoga in greater numbers.

"The cause of lack of practice is inertia which in the Gita is listed as a dulling psychological force, as tama guna. *This attribute of physical nature influences everyone but it persists in the human society to cause the neglect of yoga. It is an emotional force, which when expressed in the psyche brings on an attitude of 'I do not feel to do yoga.' or 'Yoga is too strenuous.' or 'What is the benefit of it anyway?' or 'What is liberation?' 'Who needs it?'*

"However, there are people who do yoga in part through meditation practice or through setting aside times during the day for prayer and contemplation efforts. These persons avoid the physical practice of yoga. Higher yoga uses physical practice. The difference is that in higher yoga, the physical practice is done in order to enhance meditation.

"Stated differently, 'To effectively avoid the physical practice, one must first do it and put the physical system and the subtle system in order in their most efficient and highly charged states.'"

People are usually surprised to hear that Krishna did yoga. Some people have this idea that since Krishna is God, He could not do yoga.

Does it make sense that a God would kill others? Why deny Him the right to yoga and assert him the right of righteous warrior?

In any case check three occurrences of Krishna with yoga.

- His training under Sandipani Muni, where he was trained in the use of narcotic drugs. Also check to see if he ever used pan or betel nuts. Check the active ingredient in that product.
- His training in samadhi when he went to perform austerities because one of his wives insisted that he approach Shiva before begetting a child. He studied and trained under Upamanyu Rishi. As a result, he had an interview *(darshan)* with Shiva and Devi.
- His final departure from planet earth. Both the *Mahabharata* and the *Bhagavata Purana* accredit both Krishna and Balarama with doing meditative absorption *(samadhi)* before leaving their bodies.

When Narada visited Krishna in Dvaraka one of the observations was Krishna sitting in meditation.

In the *Bhagavad Gita*, Krishna said he instructed ancient yogi kings in the hoary past in how to use yoga while ruling kingdoms (karma yoga).

Learning Breath Infusion

The bigger challenge today is finding clean air to breathe. Bigger cities are so mired in pollution that breathing is a hazard no matter where you are. An interesting point is that *breath of fire* speeds the flow of blood through the body. It is similar to the fight or flight response but after, the breath slows to meditate.

Initially in charging the system with the infused breath, there is an acceleration of energy and blood movement (heart beat). But if one sticks with it to a certain point, that ceases. There is a switch, where one perceives the energy moving through the system. At this stage one should push on with the practice, to push the energy through the system. There is another switch where the mind suddenly jumps to a higher level.

During that final stage, there is no rapidity. The mind and its apparatus either come to a stop or one perceives supernaturally.

Let me itemize the stages which happens during a successful raising of kundalini through rapid breathing *(bhastrika/ kapalbhati pranayama)*.

- Acceleration of the breath transfer in the lungs, causing speed increase of the heart beat due to the heart's natural response to the rapidly infused breath.
- Infused air is coursed rapidly through the blood stream with concentration in the chest, intestines and pelvic areas.

- Infused air makes its way into the lower genital area and the buttocks. From there it begins to affect the sacral pelvic bones. The result is that it goes up the spine if the yogi continues to practice. If the yogi stops, he/she will experience accelerated thinking and mental rapidity during the meditation which occurs immediately after.
- Kundalini moves up the spine. The mind jumps to a higher level because it comes under kundalini attack when it is electrified with the increase breath energy.

If the yogi continues the practice to this stage, the meditation will be such that the mind either slowed to where thoughts come in slow motion or they do not manifest, or the yogi finds himself/herself on a higher plane where there is objective perception of supernatural persons or environments.

At this stage, yogis who reside in higher worlds may suddenly appear in their miniature forms and give instructions, holding informed conversations.

A more regular occurrence at this stage is that the yogi gets crystal-clear realizations about the location, size and operations of the various components of the mind. Or the yogi gets skills in how to control and operate the intellect.

Sometime around 1972, I made the comparison and experimented with several types of *pranayama* just to see their various effects on meditation and to judge their worth. Arthur Beverford once showed alternate breathing *(aniloma-viloma pranayama)*. He never practiced it before meditation in my presence.

What he would do is sit on a couch and then close his eyes and meditate. He did not give details about what happened in the mind. He never mentioned psychic organs as I do. He requested that we rub White Flower Embrocation between the eyebrows before we began, since that cooling sensation draws the mind to the meditation point of the third eye.

He stressed focus on the third eye and said that a person has to find the *primal creative cause,* the factor from which this creation initially emerged.

Beverford from all indications, from numerous conversations, seem to feel that the *primal creative cause* may not be a person but was the ultimate source of this manifestation.

When I asked him about Krishna, he smiled and said, "Yes, Rishi Singh Gherwal told us about Krishna and about the experience of Yogi Markandeya who was swallowed by a Baby Krishna who floated on the waters of dissolution and also about Krishna's foster Mother being sucked into Krishna's existence through his mouth.

(Rishi published a booklet which was his translation of the part of the *Mahabharata* which related the experience of Markandeya.)

White Flower Embrocation is an oil that comes from Asia. It has Camphor (8%), Menthol (15%), Methyl Saucylate (40%) Eucalyptus oil, Lavender Oil and Peppermint Oil.

Since Beverford never practiced alternate breathing in my presence, I did it to see what it does and to find if it would accelerate meditation. My conclusion is that it does but unfortunately it takes hours of concentration to get results if one's nadis are polluted as many of us are.

I did it after doing *bhastrika.* My conclusion is that one should do *bhastrika* or *kapalbhati* rapid breathing before doing a session of alternate breathing.

Why?

Because if you do alternate breathing only, it will take forever, at least 2 or 3 hours of practice before one can attack the nadis. All the while one has to keep what's called a 2:4:1 count. It is mind racking to do that. If one loses count one must repeat a sequence. If one does rapid breathing first, one can do the alternate breathing for fifteen minutes, if one likes and it will take one to a higher plane.

Persons who are interested in detailed description of the various *pranayama* breath infusion techniques should get *Light on Pranayama* by B.K.S. Iyengar. His book is detailed.

I insist that we respect the literature of the ancient yogis. They went further than we can ever know. The fact that they did *pranayama* should not be underrated or ignored. The question we should ask ourselves is this:

Why did Patanjali do it if he could have sat and meditated?

Yogi Bhajan is my friend because he freely without asking one to be his disciple, shared the rapid breathing process.

Once to my surprise within the last 6 months, I saw Yogi Bhajan talking to Rishi Singh Gherwal. It was in a way where I felt that Rishi was instrumental in getting that practice to Yogi Bhajan. I did not question them about it because with such yogis, if one questions, they disappear.

Yogi Bhajan sees me as a disciple but only because I practiced. Otherwise he has nothing to do with me as far as he is concerned.

Once in the astral world when I got to a certain level of proficiency where the nadis were cleared and glistening with crystal clear energizing energy, Yogi pointed to me from where he was with some disciples. He stated that I was an example of what it means to be a yogi. Despite this, his relationship is based on practice. If I stop practicing, that is the end of it. He did not appraise my practice for my benefit but only to prompt others to get more serious with the practice and to motivate themselves to raise kundalini during each session.

I practiced various *pranayama* methods previously but I learnt what was called *breath of fire* from Yogi Bhajan. He did not use the Sanskrit names initially but later I realized that his process was *kapalabhati* for beginners and *bhastrika* for advanced yogis.

When I came back from the Philippines sometime in 1972, I was discharged from an air base near Kansas City, Missouri, at a place called Baldwin.

Anyway, once when I left the base and went into Kansas City. I saw a poster with Yogi Bhajan's photo and a sign about kundalini yoga practice. I went to a few classes and an ashram in Denver. I headed to Denver because my mother lived there.

After being in Denver and attending classes, I joined the ashram and went through the rigors of ashram life. As a result, I learnt as much as I could. I traveled to Los Angeles, California and Taos, New Mexico where Yogi Bhajan was resident.

Later after I was no longer in those areas, I continued the practice. Here is the gist. One should be shown the practice physically to begin with but by viewing videos, one may get enough ideas to begin the practice without being shown.

Mostly one begins with *kapalabhati* and then progresses to *bhastrika*. There are variant descriptions of these practices in India. Presently the authoritative book on the pranayamas was written by B.K.S. Iyengar under the title of *Light on Pranayama*. He does in that book not encourage those two kundalini practices. However, that is the general attitude of the gurus in India.

Yogi Bhajan never said that *breath of fire* was dangerous. He taught it to anyone without formality or discrimination.

The beginner's way is like this:

Use various postures which you are familiar with. Do rapid breathing thrusting the breath out with as much force as your body can apply. In this which is *kapalabhati pranayama*, the focus is on thrusting the breath out forcefully. There is little or no focus on the in breath. Yogi Bhajan taught that you did it as rapidly as possible.

Why? He never explained as far I am aware. However, I feel that if you do not do it rapidly, the system does not accumulate sufficient psychic charge to affect kundalini.

This charge is accumulated in the sense of a tire which is enlarged because it has a valve which retains the air which enters it. If one removes the valve, the tire will still take air but it will not retain it. The idea is to retain the psychic charge which increases. Cause that charge to head in the direction of the base of the spine, where kundalini is based.

A question arises as to how it is possible for a psychic charge to manifest from physical air. The answer to that question is this: The physical air has a psychic counterpart. While the physical body absorbs air, the subtle body mimics that action with the psychic air-energy.

One can do this sitting on a chair. One does not have to be in a yogic posture. If one sits and does the rapid breathing one can also rise kundalini just as a yogi would in a yogic posture.

As stated above initially the main focus is on the out breath. In the advanced stage, a teacher recommends that the student focus on both the out breath and the in breath with special focus on the in breath. Some students however graduate even without being advised by a teacher.

The only difference between *kapalabhati* and *bhastrika* is that in bhastrika there is the focus on the in and out breaths.

Besides that, there are locks. They are many of these but the three mandatory ones to learn are the sex/anal lock, stomach lock, and neck lock. There is one mental lock initially which is the focus of the attention to the third eye.

The stomach lock means to pull the abdomen under the rib cage and to pull back the navel to the spine in a joint pull.

The neck lock is the action of pulling the chin back to the throat without tilting the head forward.

The sex-anal lock is when the anus is pulled up into the body the way a horse pulls in its anus after it passes manure. In fact, the Sanskrit word for this lock is *ashwini mudra* (*ashwa* is horse). The sex lock is when one releases urine and one stops before the bladder is empty, one contracts a certain muscle.

Initially the sex/anal lock is a joint muscular action but as one advances one realizes mentally that these are separate muscular actions.

Why the locks?

The actions of the locks are mimicked in the subtle body. They cause the charged force to go to specific locations. If these locks are not performed it will be impossible to control kundalini if it moves from its native place at the base of the spine.

The locks are applied as soon as one stops rapid breathing during any session. One begins the rapid breathing. One continues until one feels that lungs no longer absorb air, and until one feels a burning sensation in the lungs or navel area. Then one stops the breathing and applies the locks. One holds the concentration at the center of the eyebrows. When the air dissipates, one will feel that one should breathe out and breathe in. One does this and begins the rapid breathing again. This is done repeatedly until the subtle body is sufficiently energized.

Shaking: Kundalini Yoga

During a call this morning there was a question about the shaking during kundalini yoga exercises.

During exercises when kundalini raises or moves into another part of the body, one may be inclined to shake or to straighten a certain part of the body so as to facilitate kundalini's movement through the subtle form.

Why is this necessary?

It is not necessary but it would facilitate one's efforts and would cause certain clogged *nadis* (subtle arteries) to be cleared.

It may be compared to running water through a kinked garden hose. If a hose has several kinks, certain kinks will straighten by the water pressure which courses through the hose. When those are straightened the hose will move but those kinks which are more resistant will not be released.

The gardener can handle the hose to release those kinks or he may yank the hose to do the same thing, just as a yogi may shiver the body or shake a certain part to cause kundalini to flow unrestrictedly through the subtle form.

Why would a yogi not use visualization or will power to release the kinks?

The answer is that some kinks do not respond to will power or imaginative commands.

Kundalini / Sex Organ Chakra

This is to clarify the various energies involved in rising kundalini, especially the link between sex energy and kundalini. In this system the chakras are on the spine and are not in any other part of the trunk of the body. However, these spinal chakras express themselves through the body. It conditions various organs there. In effect the spinal chakras spread their influence to other parts.

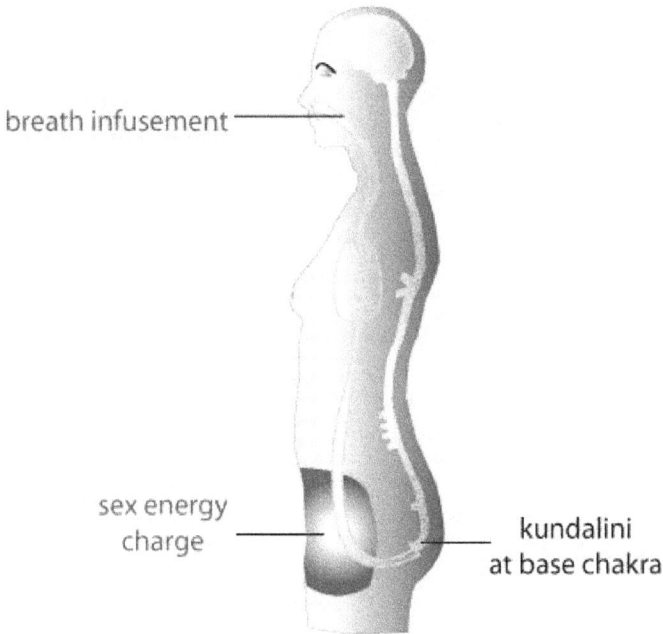

breath infusement ———

sex energy charge ———

kundalini at base chakra

Look at this diagram about the infusement of breath. As it passes through the pubic area, the breath is surcharged with sexual energy from the sexual organs which are the testes and ovary mechanisms. Picking up a charge there, a psychic charge, the breath-infused energy which is in the blood stream, directs itself to the base chakra.

Look at the next diagram in which the sexually charged infused breath energy in the blood stream causes kundalini to spark. Since it was hit by the infused energy, kundalini explodes but it does so at the base chakra and does not move up the spine.

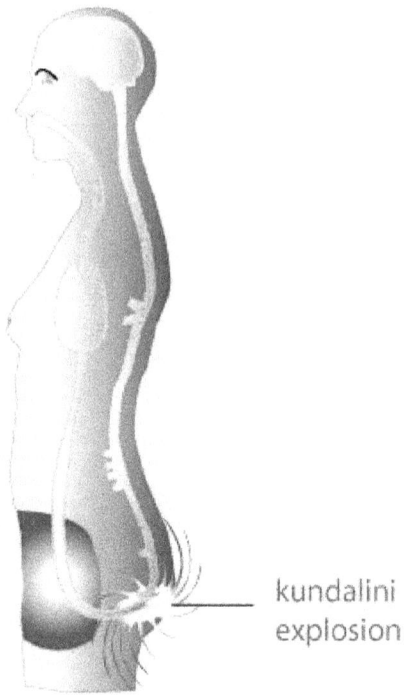

kundalini
explosion

Look at the next diagram in which the pubic sex force is dissipated by the infused energy. The sex charge in the pubic area disappears. Kundalini did not move up the spinal column. It maintains its explosive charge. It is fed more energy by the breath infusement which the yogi does during a session of exercises.

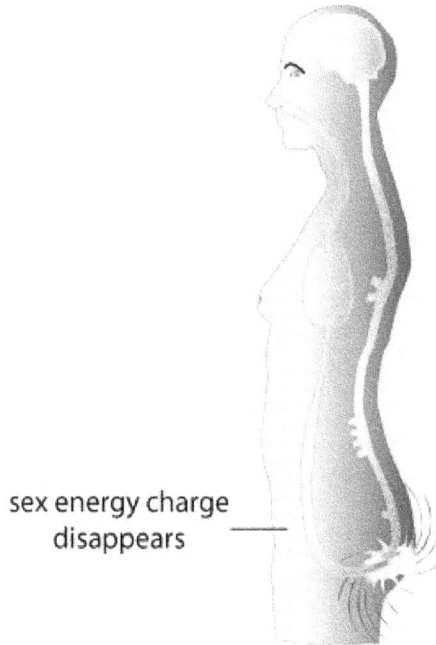

sex energy charge
disappears

Look at the next diagram. Notice that kundalini began to move up the spine. It reached a little above the 2nd chakra which is the sex chakra. There is a dark color above the chakra because that area has a dense energy which kundalini has not vaporized. Thus far kundalini vaporized only the energy in the two lower chakras

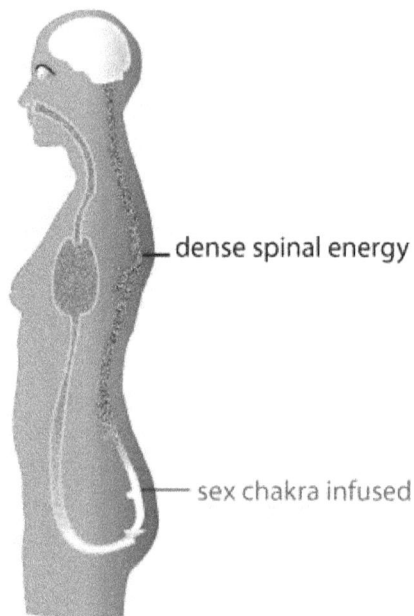

dense spinal energy

sex chakra infused

Let me stress that the sex chakra is on the spine itself. The sex organ chakra is in the pubic area and in the gonads (testes). There is a difference between the sex organ chakra and the sex chakra. In kundalini yoga, the sex organ chakra has value in its delivery of energy to the infused breath energy. It has no other value. But the sex chakra on the spine is different. It has value as part of the conduit passage of kundalini. When ascending the spine, kundalini passes through it and when coming down the spine, kundalini passes through it in reverse.

Kundalini is least concerned with the sex chakra on the spine but it is very much addicted to the sex organ chakra in the pubic area. During sexual climax, kundalini runs up one notch on the spine to the sex chakra. It shoots out of that chakra and hits the sex organ chakra. This gives an intense sensation which is contrasted with *brahmananda* which is the pleasure felt when kundalini hits the crown chakra.

Kundalini and Energizing Subtle Energy

Is raising kundalini the same as stimulating subtle energy in the psyche?

Just as blood or plasma is a term for the red liquid which moves through the arteries and veins, *prana* is a general term for the energy which moves about the subtle body.

Just as there are different kinds of plasma in the body depending on the location of it and on if it expended its useful charge or not, so there are different kinds of *prana* or psychic energy in the subtle body. *Prana* is the charged subtle energy. *Apana* is the unwanted subtle energy.

Prana is to kundalini as gasoline is to an automobile. The vehicle moves when it extracts energy from the gasoline. Kundalini moves if it is infused with *prana* or subtle energy. Kundalini is not *prana* but it uses *prana*. It is infused with *prana* in the kundalini yoga exercises.

Kundalini is the same force which causes sexual expression in the form of sexual pleasure in the body. Since most of us are familiar with the sex drive and its basic operation, we can study how it operates and uses that information to predict and assume what it will do when it rises through the spine.

I sat in the park reading a book. I was out for a stroll to see what the trees bloomed and what the birds did. I had no ideas of sex arousal.

A lady passed by the park bench. She wore a short skirt and a low-cut sweater. As soon as I saw her, I experienced an arousal. How was that possible since I had no thought of sex and I did not know the lady?

Obviously in this case there must be at least three forces involved:

- A sexual energy latently stored in my body
- A mechanism which converted that energy into an active force
- A trigger or switch which was activated by my sight of the woman

These three aspects can be listed simply as:

- sex hormones
- kundalini
- sensual impression

What happened?

The visual sense absorbed energy from the woman. This energy was transmitted to the kundalini, which took that energy as a signal to activate the potential power of the stored sex hormones.

If I used a todler's body, the kundalini would not use the visual energy in that way. There would be no stored sex hormones which it could activate in the body.

Now let us see how this fits into what occurs when one does pranayama or an aggressive kundalini yoga practice.

The infused breath mixes with various types of hormonal energies. It strikes kundalini. Kundalini then absorbs that energy and rises through the spine where it may or may not raise high enough to enter the brain.

I used the term hormonal energy because in that case it occurs in the physical body. But simultaneously it happens in the subtle body. In that system it is energizing subtle energy, psychic force.

The infused air mixes with other types of stored energy, (especially with sex energy). That combined energy strikes kundalini which becomes activated. Once it is activated it will try to spread through the subtle body. The idea is to make kundalini spread through the spine primarily and then go into the head.

In the example of the woman and the park bench, the sight of the woman was the trigger. In other words, the visual information of the woman's form which entered into the brain was the trigger.

In the case of kundalini practice, the infusion of the breath into the lungs was the trigger.

For directing an aroused kundalini, a yogi uses locks which begin with the anus contraction, sex lock, stomach lock, neck lock and third-eye focus mind-lock. But there are other inner body locks which come into play as one advances in the practice. These deprive kundalini of its ability to spread itself through various parts of the body to pursue mundane existence.

In the advanced stages, along with these locks, one restricts kundalini's interest. For instance, it has an interest is sex. It has an interest in retaining stools in the body. It has an interest in over-eating. It has an interest in less breathing so that it can stock pile carbon dioxide. It has an interest in bodily emotions so that it can better promote social existence in the physical world. It has an interest in speech for the purpose of defending itself and laying out plans to expand physical existence.

The interests are varied. The yogi must sabotage these interests of kundalini. When those avenues of expression are closed, kundalini remains trapped in the base chakra and has only one way out which is to go into the brain.

If you position yourself in the brain in the central place where the iSelf usually remains, and if you then try to call kundalini into the brain by will power or by visualization, 99% of the time kundalini will ignore you. It is for this reason that we do aggressive breath infusion in kundalini yoga. This system infuses fresh air and hormonal energy into the base chakra. This stirs kundalini and forces it to do something. As soon as it tries to use that infusement to go into its favorite channels, it is blocked by the yogi. It is forced to go upwards because it has no choice.

There is no doubt about it, kundalini yoga is a forced process. Those who do not want to force kundalini has the option to sit to meditate. They may induce kundalini to come up by willpower, by uttering sounds, by music, by visualization, by ingesting drugs and any other method.

After or during a fall, some persons experienced kundalini suddenly rising into the brain. Others experienced it while meditating, others while dreaming, others while listening to music. Of course, the usual method of kundalini experience is given to us free of charge in sexual stimulation. Sometimes when one bends over or when one gets up from a chair, suddenly without warning, kundalini rises into the head.

One should have the energy circulate through the physical and subtle bodies with such efficiency that the least amount of kundalini's energy is used for bodily concerns. If that portion is used most efficiently then a greater quantity will remain for spiritual practice and for enlightenment in the subtle head.

Concentration of kundalini in the lower trunk, which is at the anal, sexual and nutritional chakras, is a no-no for yogis. This concentration should be diverted up the spine into the head.

The convention of nature is to compile nutritional energy for sexual purposes. A yogi has to violate the convention by restricting the sexual access of the energy. Unless one begets children and intends to raise that progeny responsibly, a yogi/yogini should divert the hormonal energy from its sexual functions. Needless to say, this is unnatural but unless it is achieved, yoga success will not happen.

Yoga like everything else hinges on what you desire and what you must to do to achieve that. If one wants full success and especially if one wants to go to higher dimensions, one must qualify for that. Raising kundalini on a daily basis is a must for those persons who want to go to the *brahma* level of existence, the spiritual plane where everything is spiritual, the people, the environment, the vegetation, everything.

Just as there are forms in this world and all the forms are made of physical energy, so there are forms in the spiritual dimensions where there are spiritual environments. To go to such a place permanently, one must elevate the psyche by some effective method. Patanjali gave the formula for transiting to higher dimensions.

जात्यन्तरपरिणामः प्रकृत्यापूरात् ॥२ ॥
jātyantara pariṇāmaḥ prakṛtyāpūrāt

jātyantara = jāti – category + antara – other, another; pariṇāmaḥ – transformation; prakṛiti – subtle physical nature; āpūrāt – due to filling up or saturation.

The transformation from one category to another is by the saturation of the subtle material nature. (*Yoga Sutras* 4.2)

That means that for my psyche to change into that of a celestial or spiritual being, I must cause a saturation of the energy from that higher place in my psyche by some effective method.

Suppose my idea is to go to a heaven where a particular deity resides. I should know the type of existence and feelings, which the bodies have there. Once I identify that, I must change my psychology to that type of nature. Then that heaven would be available at the end of this physical form.

Yogi Bhajan: Attacking Sushumna Nadi

I was in communication with Yogi Bhajan for the last four days. He said that once a yogi can consistently raise kundalini on a daily basis, and after this was done for some time say for two years, the yogi should forego that practice and strive for a different goal which is to flush *sushumna nadi* central spinal passage, at least once per day, preferably twice per day.

This is not a mental process. One uses inhaled breaths to do that. This is not visualization. This is an aggressive process of infusing air into the system and causing it to accumulate to the extent that it enters *sushumna nadi* and flushes the used energy which lodged there.

When the yogi achieves flushing of *sushumna nadi,* the naad sound is heard in the back of the head. It seems that there is a long cylindrical tube going down into the body. This tube seems to be grey-misty inside. Or it may appear to have a black or dark brown light within it.

Sometimes it appears to be clear, full of light or bliss energy.

Yogeshwaranada gave the instruction for raising kundalini to the crown at least once per day but Yogi Bhajan said that the raising of kundalini to the crown may give a yogi a false confidence unless the yogi understands that such raising should be done to the extent of having a completely flushed-out *sushumna nadi,* where kundalini remains exposed from the top and is not allowed to cover itself with dark energy again.

This instruction brings to our attention the fact that when kundalini moves into the head, its tendency is to immediately resume its position in its favorite location which is the base chakra. When it does that it pulls a dark energy over itself.

To stop kundalini from doing this and to cause kundalini to abandon its natural tendency, one should strive in *pranayama* breath infusion practice to keep *sushumna nadi* clear.

Sushumna nadi will not remain clear on its own accord, nor by mere willpower. That is not its tendency. If a yogin wants to keep it clear, he must strive daily for that achievement. To say that one's kundalini remains at the crown chakra always, is like saying that one's teeth remains clean always. That is an impossibility. Yogi Bhajan wanted to alert yogis, not to get fanciful ideas about what they can do to kundalini by willpower.

There should be a change is in one's interest. Initially the effort for raising kundalini is in part an effort to substitute kundalini's climax in sex experience with kundalini's climax in the brain. Once a student gets beyond that motivation, he/she can work on the spiritual task.

Initially one does spiritual practice to escape the hassles and inconveniences in the physical world. Later, when that fades one does spiritual practice due to attraction to persons who live on the spiritual level. The motivation switches as one progresses.

Kundalini Outside the Body

kundalini spread outside subtle body
attention oriented outside subtle body

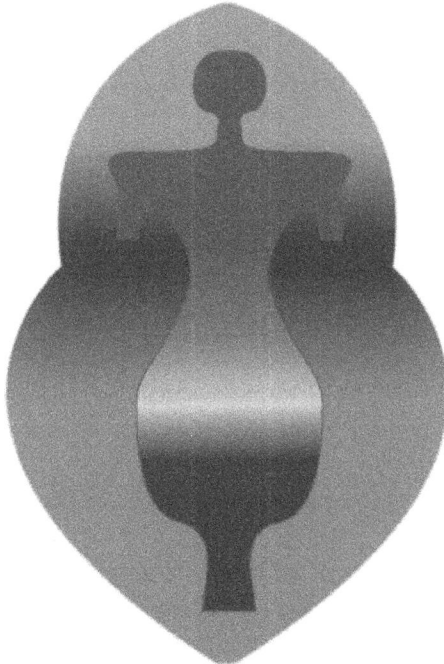

For this present body kundalini begins in the sperm of the father. There it is an urge energy. After a time, it influences the protein energy in the mother's body to formulate an embryo. This formation takes place around kundalini. It encases kundalini which then lives in the formation.

Even though it lives in the formation, kundalini expresses itself or its energy through the formation. We experience that as consciousness of the physical body. Because of that energy spread, we feel pleasure and pain in the body.

From the start kundalini designs the system so that it can spread through the body and go outside the body in a particular way. That is the original design. It is not that kundalini has to do something to cause this. This is inherent in the original design.

There are blockages but these are put there by kundalini itself. From its perspective they are not blockages but conveniences.

If you plan to build an apartment building of six stories high, you would create a piping system so that some water can reach the 6th floor. You would install the required pumps. Some areas for instance the bottom floor may have excessive water pressure. You may increase the pipe size to cause a reduction in pressure flow. In the same way, kundalini designed the psyche for its convenience.

Yoga is for adjusting what kundalini designed. The question is not why or how the kundalini goes out of the body in all directions but how can a yogi do what is unnatural and channel kundalini to the central spine and brain.

Kundalini Arousal Failure

If you find that you do rapid breathing *(kapalabhati/bhastrika pranayama)* and still you are unable to raise kundalini or that kundalini only rises on the average once per week even when you do exercises daily, it means that you have to intensify the practice.

How to do this?

These are some methods of intensity:
- Do two sessions in a succession.
- Commit oneself to continue a session until kundalini is aroused and courses though the spine into the head.
- Make a commitment to the teacher, that you will continue rapid breathing with or without varying postures until you sense that kundalini is aroused and enters the head.

Doing two sessions rather than one, means that the usual sequence of exercises is repeated twice. Usually each student has sequences of exercise which consist of postures and breathing. Do the usual sequence. Then begin the sequence again. This means that if the usual session last for twenty minutes, one begins that session again and continue it to completion which may take at least another fifteen minutes.

You will find that in the second session there is less resistance to the energy which you infuse. Kundalini will, more than likely, be aroused.

Committing yourself to continuing a session until kundalini is aroused is a difficult method, because usually when you finish the usual session, the mind assumes a reluctance to continue. This reluctance may convert into a depression energy which will cause one to feel negative if one tries to continue. This negativity may prevent the student from practicing.

However, if he is strong in the objective to raise kundalini, he can use this negative energy as a force to help him to push on. This would mean that he protects the mood energy so that it does not come in contact with the negative emotions which are generated in the mind.

One may also make a commitment to the teacher, but this a very difficult way to handle this. A kundalini yoga teacher is not the same as other types of trainers who are overly concerned about the progress of students. A kundalini yoga guru will accept such a commitment but will not pressure the student to complete it. The student must apply pressure himself/herself.

It is different if one lives in an ashram, where all members are committed to complying with certain rules of life style.

You can commit yourself to a teacher about raising kundalini into the head, but then the whole task will rest on your determination. No one will be there to enforce the commitment.

Actually, in the higher stages of yoga, we continue the practice with a commitment to the teacher. We complete this because we are desperate for success in the practice and want to migrate to the subtle world in which our teachers reside.

Kundalini Enlivens the Body

If kundalini leaves the physical body, that physique is a dead one. Kundalini is the aspect which causes the body to live. It is not the individual self, nor individual mind which causes the body to live. It is the kundalini. In fact, in a coma when the individual is deprived of the ability to manipulate the body, the kundalini keeps the body alive. As soon as the kundalini is disconnected the body dies.

The one thing that keeps the body alive is the kundalini. This does not mean that the coreSelf has no value. Take the example of a car. Does the driver keep the engine running? It depends on how you look at it, but actually we know that the engine runs more or less on gasoline. Gas alone is not an engine but without it even if everything is in place, including the driver, the pistons, the spark plug, the initial blast of electricity from the battery and the starter, still the engine cannot operate.

Kundalini is the factor that runs the body. It heals the body when there is damage. It is subtle lifeForce. It is the thing around which a new body forms in the next mother's body. It will design that next body according to its tendencies which for now one assumes are one's tendencies.

Yogis want to scrap kundalini because it endorses and forms all the lower transmigrations in lower species of life, in all sorts of queer physical and subtle dimensions. Scrapping kundalini is an absolute must if one is to go to the spiritual side fully. The question is: How to do that?

Sex and a Depressed Kundalini

Kundalini takes energy from the physical and psychic hormone systems in the body. This system is greatly taxed in formation of sexual fluids. Still, if we understand nature's viewpoint that generation of bodies is the most important thing, we can understand why nature designed the psyche in such a way as to give most of its budget of hormonal energies to the sex function.

As it is, once puberty is developed in a body, that sexual system draws most of the hormone energy into the sexual area for the manufacture of sperm or ova. This is both a physical and a psychic reality.

Hence in sexual climax, kundalini's stockpile of hormonal energy will be diminished, such that little energy will be left for any other purpose. Kundalini will then have to stockpile more hormonal power. That may take a day or two.

This system will suffer a depression if much energy is expressed in the sexual blast of energy in the genital area.

On the other hand, if the kundalini's energy is blasted into the head, one will not feel that depression but may otherwise feel an elation. Nor is there a physical expression of fluids as in sexual climax.

Spiritual Relationships

The social relationships which develop for this body are not necessarily spiritual connections. In fact, many social roles are inconsistent with the spiritual one which would be if two persons, for instance, were instantly transferred into a spiritual environment.

What is a spiritual environment? That is where you live in an environment which is indestructible, which is free from deterioration.

Last night in the astral world, I was in a dimension where I met an old version of the subtle form of a relative from this life who is now deceased but who assumed a new body and lives in the United States. The person's astral form even though it uses a young adult body, assumed a look like the person's old age body from the immediate past life.

Even though that person has a new body which looks different from the old one which died, still the subtle form assumed a look like the old body which died about sixty-five years of age. This person, who was a social senior in her past life, made demands on the basis of our relationship in the past.

Somehow at the time, we both found ourselves in a hellish astral place, where there were men scattered about on the ground with crushed limbs. Sometimes even though one did not perform enough criminal or anti-social activities to spend some time in a hellish place, one may have done enough to warrant a visit to such places to see the ghastly conditions of those who reside there. It is like having to visit a prison or war hospital.

In any case, we did not stay in that place for long. Soon after that old relative began to badger me about continuing the social relationship which was from the past life. I explained that the previous social role was temporary and was not my priority. I assumed this body to fulfill other purposes.

The physical body influences the subtle one to feel that all beneficial relationships formed should continue forever and again, but that is not possible. A yogin must learn how to facilitate the social relationships formed in each life and also fulfill his/her mission for spiritual purposes.

If we adhere only to social relationships which depend on having a certain body in a certain place and time, we will restrict ourselves to a struggle against time in the effort to keep those relationships over a span of many lives. Of course, time will not honor the requests? That will result in disappointment and anguish.

Physical nature is flexible. With it, I may have a *father to son* relationship with an entity in one life and then a *son to grandfather* relationship with the same entity in another life. Which is the self relationship?

From the spiritual angle, am I the person's father or grandson?

One way to look at this is to consider all relationships as being flexible and to feel that there is a potential for any type of relationship with anyone else. The relationship energy can take any form, one may surmise. However even though that assumption may work in the physical social world, it will not do in the spiritual social situations.

In my experience the interpretation of oneness with the object occurs due to a lack of detailed sensual distinction on higher planes, just as when a person comes out from a dark cave where he resided in isolation for a time. When he first emerges, he is blinded by the light and cannot see. To him for all practical purposes he is one with whatever is there. Factually, he was restricted in sense perception in the new environment.

That has to do with environments.

There are also higher experiences with divine persons. There is the story which Markandeya told Yudhishthira in the *Mahabharata* how he (Markandeya) was lost in Krishna's cosmic body for eons. Then he was thrown into another atmosphere in which that cosmic body resided. Even though it may be said that he merged, Markandeya, as a great yogi and favorite devotee of Krishna, was aware during his travels in that body that the cosmic person was distinct from himself.

Has a fetus merged with the entity who is the mother using that pregnant body? Superficially, the fetus is merged but it is distinct.

Spiritual sense perception is a reality but normally we do not develop it. When we enter spiritual zones of consciousness, we experience that as mergence without distinct sense perception. But that is the beginning of the spiritual journey.

What is sad and what is something we should cry for daily is the development of supernatural and spiritual sense perception. Its attainment is almost completely out of reach.

Third Eye Focus Update

The original instruction which Beverford gave to both myself and Sir Paul Castagna way back in the early 1970's was to sit to meditate and then focus on the center of the eyebrows. This instruction originated with Rishi Singh Gherwal, who was Beverford's yoga teacher.

I adopted the practice and discovered methods of improving it. In any case, Beverfold gave this update:

While meditating on third eye, slowly locate the optic energy and retract that into the coreSelf.

Why was this update given? Well I did not ask Beverford for the reason. But it is this:

Sometimes while focusing on the third eye the practice proves to be counter-productive since the focusing energy may energize the thought-formation powers of the mind. There may be an increase in thoughts and ideas because of the increased focus in the frontal part of the brain.

Beverford says that this problem is solved by retracting the optic energy while doing third eye focus. That implies that the optic energy is the main trigger which activates impulsive thinking during third eye meditation focus.

Optic energy retracted

core-self

Third Eye Energy Focus

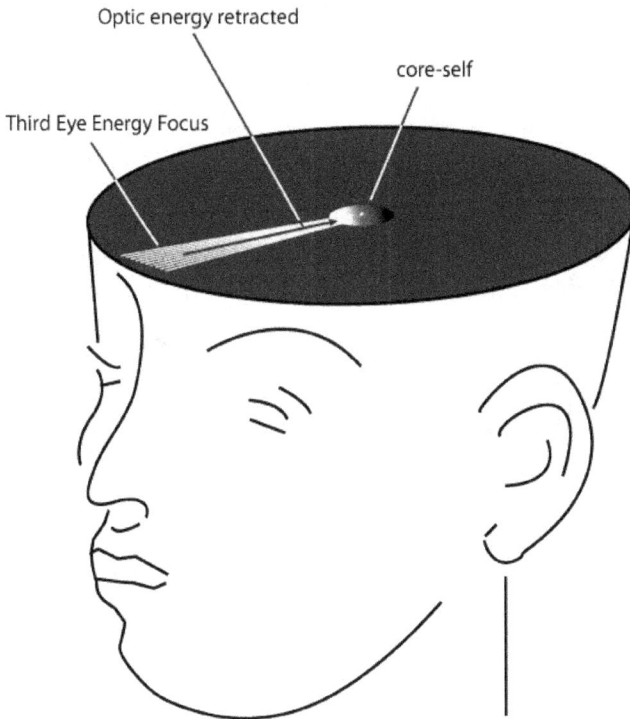

Notice the black arrow which points to the coreSelf. That represents the optic energy going to the core.

Notice also that the third eye focusing energy is spread. That is the way the energy is usually fanned out when it is directed to third eye. Ideally, this energy should be made with a single ray of attention energy but this ideal is not usually the case.

Part 4

Back Support - Meditation

Sitting up to meditate can be a chore. Many teachers advocate a straight spine. That is the ideal advice. However, one should work with one's back and negotiate its curvature.

According to ethnicity spines vary and no amount of yoga will change that. Still one can come to an agreement with a faulty back by learning how and where to brace it during meditation.

In the diagrams below, I show a method for bracing the lower and upper spine. Both areas need support. When the upper back is comfortably against a surface, the lower back is usually not touching the wall. That lower back needs support because the chest cavity, head, and neck bear down on it.

Nature's solution to this problem is to kink the back, to curve it so that the weight is transferred to the lower wall. To help nature in this effort one should use a wedge support which prevents the spine from curving backwards.

If one sits in lotus usually at least one knee will float above the ground. If this knee is not supported at the onset of meditation, it may distract the mind.

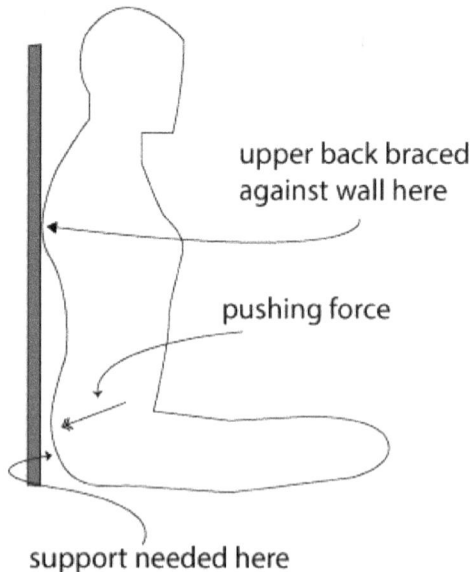

upper back braced against wall here

pushing force

support needed here

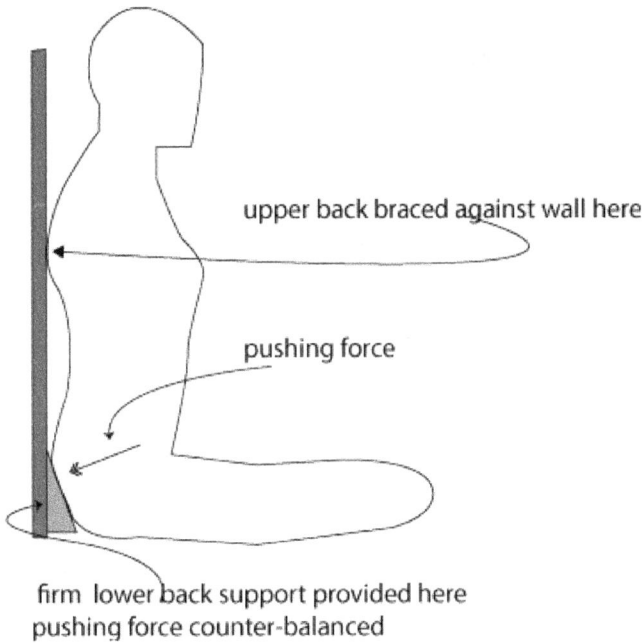

upper back braced against wall here

pushing force

firm lower back support provided here
pushing force counter-balanced

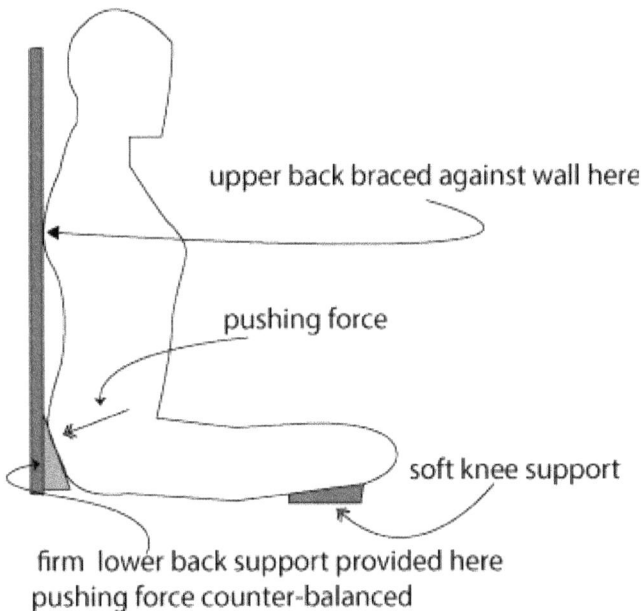

upper back braced against wall here

pushing force

soft knee support

firm lower back support provided here
pushing force counter-balanced

From a side view if the middle portion of the back is not curved something is out of line. From the side, nature did not invent a straight back. What one should achieve is balance of the weight of the back. To make it straight and to keep it in that form would require tremendous concentration which would circumvent the meditation as the mind would remain focused on keeping it in that position.

From a side view, there should be a space between the central back and the wall if the back is in a balanced position. Look at the diagram below. See how the weight travels down the spine. It flows through the neck, then shifts forward. To counterbalance itself and follow the skeletal frame of the body, it shifts back. When it makes that backward shift, it should be given support as shown by the wedge shape.

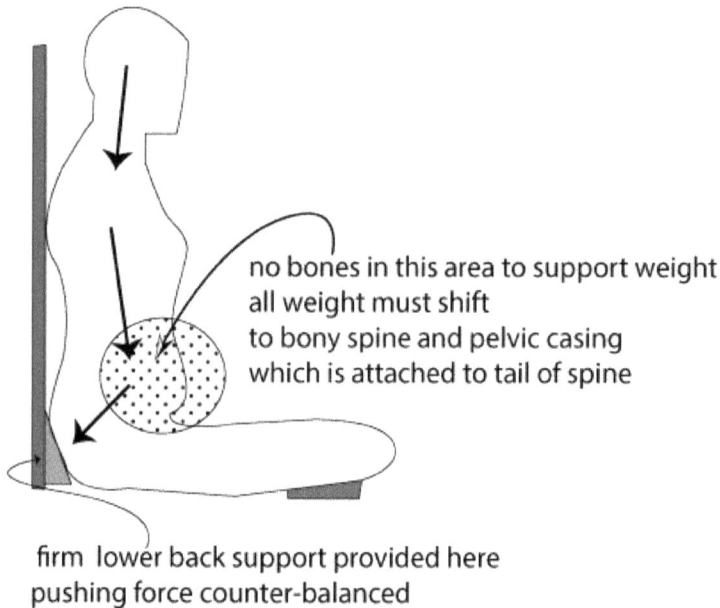

no bones in this area to support weight
all weight must shift
to bony spine and pelvic casing
which is attached to tail of spine

firm lower back support provided here
pushing force counter-balanced

To understand the forward shift, study the side profile of a pregnant woman. In her body when the weight of the fetus is off-centered from the pelvic region, the spine pulls forward but its tail piece stays backward. A pregnant woman finds it necessary to pull her shoulders back to counter balance the fetus and pull it over the pelvic region.

Submission and Yoga Practice

Willingness to practice yoga is directly connected to the willingness to be a nobody.

For the practice of yoga, it will be necessary to submit to someone who is advanced. It is not that the teacher needs honor and superiority. The process of learning itself, with or without a teacher, requires submission. Even in cases where a person discovered yoga techniques without the presence of a physical teacher, that person submits to revelation or inspiration.

For genuine submission one must be willing to take a student's posture. It does not end at some point in the future, since as one advances one must submit for higher instructions either from the same teacher or from another.

Many who come to study yoga do not want to submit. They have the notion that yoga is a process which is free from the need for submission.

Yoga Authorities

Two authorative texts on yoga, are the Yoga Sutras and the *Bhagavad Gita*. In the sutras, Patañjali gave a definition which has a total of three major parts. The objective in the final part is the reunification of the coreSelf with its purified highly energized psychic perception.

In the first part, Patañjali suggests there be no mental modifications for prolonged periods in meditation. That brings about a distinction between the coreSelf and its perception equipment. When this distinction is gained, the core is instructed to remain separate from the equipment. This separation or segregation is called *kaivalyam*.

The objective of yoga for Patañjali is *kaivalyam*, either as coreSelf being separated from the impure perception equipment or as the coreSelf being unified with the purified perception equipment

Krishna on the other hand lists the purpose of yoga as being *atma-vishuddha* or the purification of the coreSelf and its psychology. This amounts to the same as Patañjali, except that Patañjali gave a more detailed exposition.

Traditionally in India, Shiva is said to be the founder of yoga. His wife *Durga* is listed as his first student. It is written that *Matsyendranāth* learned yoga from Shiva only because *Devi (Durga)* was instructed in it by Shiva. *Matsyendranāth* who used a fish body, listened as Shiva discussed it with Devi by a lake.

However, Krishna is also accredited as the founder of yoga, as in several incarnation he instructed others. Krishna also claimed to be the founder of the karma yoga process which was used by Arjuna after Arjuna heard the *Bhagavad Gita*.

Kundalini to Crown Chakra

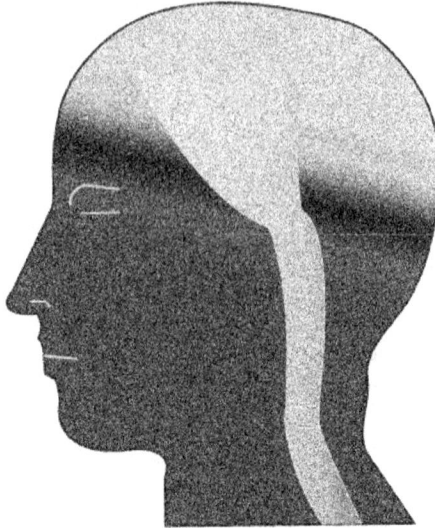

Kundalini attacks crown chakra directly,
by passing all psychic components in subtle head.
coreSelf may lose its sense of objectivity.

When kundalini attacks the 7th chakra, the crown or *brahmarandra*, it may do so from any angle. If it is a direct attack, kundalini will bypass any energy gyrating center *(chakra)* in the subtle head and reach the crown directly. This will put the intellect out of commission. The core will find itself in a bright golden light or in a shimmering energy, being pushed upwards by a mystic force.

The coreSelf relies on dense subtle energy for objectivity. Thus, when it finds itself in the shimmering energy of kundalini at the 7th chakra, the core may lose objectivity and become subjective, to such an extent that it cannot differentiate itself or anything else.

Some persons marked this as an advanced stage, as oneness with the Absolute. Some yogis however who transcended the need for dense subtle energy, are able to retain objectivity in this advanced *samadhi* state.

Marijuana Yoga

Marijuana and yoga were used together for centuries in India. Some yoga sects regard Shiva as the God of ganja. They feel that they worship him by smoking pot.

I do not recommend marijuana, since eventually if one's subtle body becomes addicted to it, one will go to a cross world in which the people there live in ganja vegetation. Some reach a stage where their subtle forms become grafted into ganja plants.

In the *Srimad Bhagavatam* there is a description of a parallel world in which men are kept in addiction to smoking ganja and are used as sex slaves by the females who manage the environment.

As far as Shiva is concerned. There is more than one Shiva. Some do not use ganja. But there is a Shiva who is the patron deity of the ganja plant. He is a supernatural being.

Kundalini Strikes 3ʳᵈ Eye

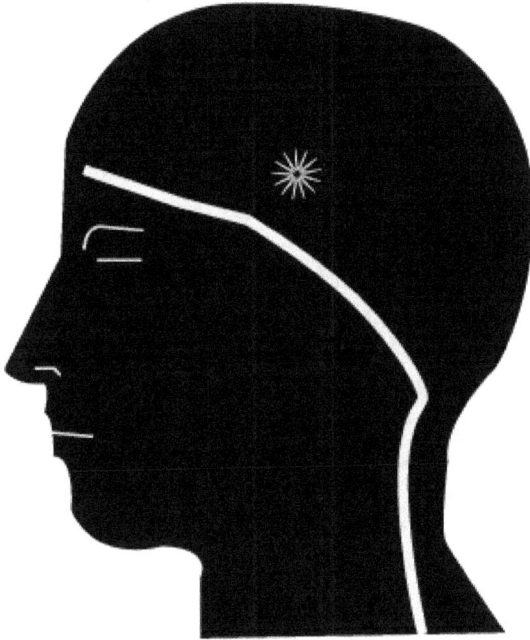

kundalini attacks third eye directly
bypassing all psychic components in subtle head

In this diagram, kundalini reached through the neck into the head. It tilted to the third eye. It bypassed the components in the subtle head. It bypassed the causal body which is located in the chest of the subtle body.

The coreSelf may or may not be aware of kundalini's passage. In some cases, where a yogi is sensitive, he/she can sense the rise of kundalini from the base of the spine but otherwise some yogis do not realize kundalini until it strikes the brow chakra or third eye.

This comes as an experience of sensations at the third eye. It forcibly attracts the attention to that area. Kundalini may or may not pierce through the third eye, but it will usually spread through the *nadi* out-rays in a spatial way.

What are the components which kundalini by-passes?

They are the coreSelf, the sense of identity and the intellect. The coreSelf and sense of identity are in a deep love affair like two love birds who cannot be separated and which are fused together as one. They are not one in fact but for the time being, the core cannot distinguish itself from the sense of identity.

The intellect is also fused to the coreSelf but indirectly only, through the sense of identity which surrounds the core spherically like the skin of a watermelon which covers the pulp. Thus, it is not such a difficult feat for a yogi to segregate the coreSelf / sense of identity fusion, from the intellect.

As soon as kundalini strikes the 3rd eye chakra, the intellect becomes aware of it and instantly alerts the coreSelf / sense of identity fused combination. This alert causes the core to become aware of the strike of kundalini upon the third eye.

One can get some idea about the *nadi* out-rays by pressing the eye lids on the eyes in a dark room, and then using the finger tips of each corresponding hand to put a gentle push-in pressure on the eyeballs. As one does this one will notice lights on the inside of the head. After a time, these lights will form into a round or doughnut shape. That is the depiction of the chakra energy.

When kundalini strikes the 3rd eye chakra it runs through the *nadi* out-rays just as when one turns the ignition of a car, electric power travels down the electric wires from the battery into the starter and then a specific distribution of power is initiated. In a car it is not haphazard. In the subtle and gross bodies, it is defined by *nadis* and nerves respectively.

One can see the *nadis* on occasion but usually one feels them. That is something like in the physical body where you feel a nerve pulsating or hurting as in the case of a tooth-ache and where you do not see it. It does have a visual value but you cannot see it except in an X-ray image.

Kundalini Burst Without Sex Charge

Sometimes one finds that kundalini lacks a sex charge due to the sex energy being dissipated in a physical or astral sexual encounter. Then one should still make an effort to raise kundalini.

Kundalini always has a sex charge but it does not always have a full charge. It can have a minimum charge which is in effect no charge. Kundalini derives a sex charge from whatever nutrients is taken into the body as well as the psychic energy taken into the subtle body.

The basic kundalini is only a survival mechanism, like a most basic organism which only tries to survive, like a virus for instance. Its main business is to survive; it is not concerned with anything else initially. Later when it is feels secure the reproductive urge develops. It splits into more than one virus body. Those new forms repeat this behavior.

At first kundalini is in the father's body. There it wants to survive. It finds however that it can do that and nothing else in the father's form. It moves into the mother's form for further development for a more sophisticated means of survival.

In an adult body kundalini maintains this primal survival urge but it develops interest in reproduction. For that it takes help from the 2nd chakra. As kundalini develops it moves from mere survival to reproduction, then it moves to expanded nutrition then it moves to distribution of energy at the 4th chakra, then it moves to expression at the 5th chakra, then it moves to refined perception at the 6th brow chakra, then it moved further to cosmic sensual detection at the 7th chakra crown of head.

It is influenced by and influences in turn each chakra and its related energy mechanisms.

It is not a matter of needing a sex charge. It has to have that as it develops from a mere survival impulse. Suppose I say that a hibiscus plant has a charge of energy from its flowers. Then if someone ask of the necessity for flowers, that would not be a good question. We understand that at a certain stage the plant will bear flowers as a matter of course. Kundalini carries a sex change as a mandatory expression. In one sense a plant feeds it flowers. In another sense the flowers feed the plant.

Even though kundalini produced the sex urge as it developed, that urge feeds kundalini. Kundalini feeds on the urge.

Usually in kundalini yoga, sex energy is the main way of charging kundalini but in some special process, one avoids that energy and raises kundalini without it.

There are occasions when for one reason or the other, the yogi finds that the body has no sex charge. When that happens, he/she may work longer in the exercises to arouse kundalini. Then when it is aroused, the yogi should take note of the nature of the energy just to understand what sex energy does to kundalini when it infuses kundalini as the main cause of it rising.

These observations are required if one is to advance into higher states. For instance, suppose a yogi gets addicted to raising kundalini with infusion of sex energy. What does that mean for him as far as where he will go when the physical body dies.

Will he go where great yogis who eliminated the sex charge in their psyches reside? Can a yogi be satisfied in a dimension where the sex charge is totally absent?

There is no breach of celibacy unless one reached a stage in practice where sexual expression proves to be a setback.

Patañjali listed celibacy as one of the required practices. So did Krishna and other masters of the masters of yoga, but still unless one reaches a stage where one can notice what sexual expression does to one's progression, there is no breach.

In kriya yoga there is no one standing over a student telling him to do this and do that or not to do this or do that. The most the teacher will do is bring it to one's attention that perhaps a certain lifestyle is counterproductive. Yoga as Patañjali defined it is not for people who need to be propped by peer pressure.

The whole thing is more like a school affair and less like a guru-savior process, because the student must learn the method, practice it and get checked by the teacher to see if the practice was assumed correctly.

Some people think that study is not required. They are correct, except that they are not talking about Patañjali yoga, because Patañjali was a bookish practical yogi. He wrote instructions for yoga and its accomplishment.

Breach of celibacy means that I observed what sexual expression does to my practice and I do not like those results. Hence, I took it upon myself to attain celibacy. Due to that my practice accelerated. My teachers were appreciative of the advancement made. But then the sexual urge reasserted itself. As expected, my practice suffered. There was a lag in advancement. I felt as if I regressed. I checked my psyche. I saw that it was due to the breach.

On the other hand, we should not try to make a martial law about celibacy. There should be no intimidation for people to cease sexual expression. It would be easier to stop the Milky Way from spinning, than it would be to stop sexual expression. One man or woman in millions may do it.

There is no difference for men or women because it is the same sexual energy in differing moods as per the gender. The kundalini uses that energy in either gender. Unless one figures in ancestral energy, one's calculations about sexual expression are flawed.

A man cannot see a woman in a sexual way as a means of penetration and reception unless someone somewhere somehow penetrated the man's psyche and needs a body and then becomes attracted to the woman for the purpose of getting an embryo.

As soon as one strips away man's interference with the process of nature, one is left with sexual acts between a male and female which more than likely will produce progeny. Nature gave the sex urge for reproduction not enjoyment?

The progeny is there at the end of the sexual act of a fertile couple but the progeny is there at the beginning as well.

Erection and its related mechanisms are designed to get semen into the woman's tubing for the purpose of reproduction. We humans have interest in the pleasure, and it appears that nature does not mind, but still nature's intention remains reproduction. In so far as nature will allow us to take human forms, we may ignore nature's purpose and stick to the pleasure part of these attractions but the truth is that nature will prevail sooner or later.

As a departed soul needing a body, one perceives the profile of the parent's subtle body. If that subtle form exhibits sexual potential, that is all that one sees. One sees nothing else. Like that time when I took a body from a woman who was not married and who was raped by my father. Or that time when I took that body from my teen-aged mother who was not married to my father and who was stigmatized because she lived in a community in which unmarried sex was taboo. From the realm of the hereafter the taboos are not considered.

Kundalini always has potential for survival, acquiring nutrition and then using the stored nutritional energies for reproduction. In yoga we train kundalini to use the energy for promoting increased clarity in psychic perception.

Since kundalini's basic outlay is survival and reproduction, that potential will always remain intact, even though a yogi may re-focus the system.

Kundalini has no concern with celibacy. That is unnatural for it. If one checks the instructions in *Uddhava Gita* one reads about the *sutram* sexually charged cosmic force. It was there in the beginning. It has supernatural power. A limited yogi cannot abolish it.

Our existence as we know it now came about after that sexual cosmic charge was initiated by the Supreme Being. It is not possible for us to upset it at any stage.

A yogi may ask the Supreme Being for an exemption from the influence of the cosmic sexuality but it is hardly likely that it would be granted to him. Sometimes, a great yogi gets an exemption. Then his/her highly purified subtle bodies maintain neutrality towards sexual influence. But that is rare.

More or less, so long as one is in these physical worlds and their adjacent subtle worlds, one cannot be absolutely celibate. Still a yogi should strive for that but he/she must be reasonable and accept the restrictions which are imposed by fate.

The trick is to locate loop-holes in the natural sexual and reproduction system and use those but it must be something legitimate which is approved by the Supreme Being or it will result in abject frustration.

Swami Shivananda passed from his physical body long ago, in the 1963. He stays in the astral world. Recently just last week he transferred to the *brahma* world. He is out of the influence of the *sutram* cosmic sexual force. Until one reaches that place one cannot be totally exempt from sexual interplay.

Because kundalini is innately attached to sexuality, one has to make a daily effort to twart it away from sexual interest. If one lets up, kundalini will resume its normal behavior which is full time sexual interest.

Unfortunately, there is no cure all. It has to be worked out painstakingly by the individual. It is something that is complex which involves relationships from many past lives.

It would be much easier to find a cure for the most dangerous disease than it would be to find a solution to sexual susceptibility. In the final analysis however, each person must manoever his/her exit in a gradual way over a period of time.

There is no quick fix. Kundalini *shakti* grafted itself into the psyche of the individual, and lives with the coreSelf like a good wife or husband. It is near impossible to get a divorce from it.

Keep striving. One of these days, perhaps in another universe, some trillions of creative cycles down the road, it may be achieved. In the meantime, be sure to support and endorse righteous lifestyle and complete sexual responsibilities if they present themselves.

At first kundalini is in the father's body. There it is wants to survive. It finds however that it is restricted in the father's form. It moves into the mother's form for further development for a more sophisticated means of survival.

Listen to this carefully because one needs to understand this. So much of existence is sublimal and subconscious as well as unconscious and as yogis we need to know this, because if one goes for surgery one should know that one's objectivity will be wiped out during the time. One will lose control.

At first kundalini is in the father's body. There it wants to survive. At first its desire and urges are to survive. It finds however that survival is the only feature it is allowed in the father's form. In his form there is no potential to do anything else. It feels undone because it cannot develop further. It senses that it should go elsewhere so that it can do more than just survive. It moves into the mother's form for further development for a more sophisticated means of survival, to do other things besides just survive.

Kundalini *Up the Front* Rise

Kundalini *up the front* movement all by itself without arousal in the spine through the spinal chakras is a rare way for kundalini to rise. It does occur spontaneously when doing kundalini yoga. Or it may happen spontaneous even when not practicing.

This experience is denoted by a bliss energy moving from the groin area through the front part of the subtle body but usually it stops at the neck and does not reach into the head.

The value of this practice is that it reveals to the yogi, the frontal *nadi* passages. It clears away impurities and dark energies which are lodged in the front trunk area of the subtle body.

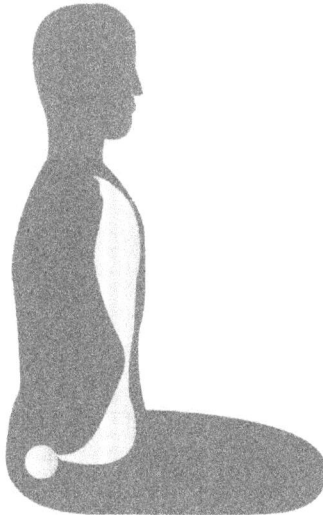

Kundalini is Motive

Kundalini can be awakened without motive. In fact, on its own kundalini operates the physical body anyway. It does many functions without our input or willpower being applied. But kundalini is motivated basically by an instinct for survival.

Motivation is there as urge in the psyche, both as conscious and subconscious urge. For instance, an infant develops until it reaches puberty, then there is the sexual urge.

That may not seem to be a motivation but it is. It is a motivation to reproduce but a person may argue that it was not deliberate. That is the correct argument which shows that motivation can be indeliberate.

Kundalini is about motivation. It is motivation.

In kundalini yoga, one makes a deliberate effort to raise kundalini daily as contrasted to it rising spontaneously. It is like breathing. Usually we breathe involuntarily. We take the benefits of that by staying alive in the physical system. But an athlete may do extra breathing exercises to derive particular benefits beyond the regular means.

In kundalini yoga we take hold of kundalini and direct it. During the exercises, kundalini is raised and controlled. It is directed through subtle passages and zones.

This does not stop its spontaneous arousals. This is in addition to those experiences.

Motivation is present in kundalini. In the kundalini yoga, one tries to get a handle on that so that kundalini loses interest in mere survival and other interest of the lower chakras. It gains a perspective in the higher dimensions through its infusion into the higher chakras.

For direct evidence that kundalini affects the vibrational modality of the consciousness get some high proof alcohol. Take a small glass of it. Alternately take a mind-altering drug. These substances affect the vibrational consistency of kundalini and one will immediately notice the effect on the mind and emotions.

Using air in *pranayama* practice to infuse kundalini is another way of noticing what can be done to it by infusing it with energy. Liquor is chemical. Air is also chemical.

Sex Energy - Kundalini Rise

Swami Atmananda sent a message, stating that I should give this information. This concerns occasions when the sex energy refused to take passage through the base chakra and it acts on its own to create an upward rush of energy.

When this happens, kundalini shadows or follows the sex energy upward. They meet in the head in a blast of bliss.

A question arises as to why the sex energy avoids the standard kundalini path on these occasions. The answer is that when the sex energy of an advanced yogi is attracted to sexual intercourse, it may fail to complete that sexual involvement. It may go upwards instead. This happens to those yogins who effectively sealed the passage of sex energy from sexual intercourse. Since the system is sealed any effort of the energy to go through the sex chakra results in an upward movement instead. This is great for the yogi.

Yoga and Yawning

In terms of yoga, yawning will hardly happen if one takes the proper rest and has a steady breath infusion practice. Infrequent practice is not steady practice. Some events with infrequent practice have nothing to do with yoga but is the body's way of alerting the person of other problems.

My guess is that if one gets insufficient rest and one is in buildings where there is little fresh air, where the ventilation is machine regulated and the filters and apparatus are inefficient, then when one does breath infusion, the kundalini realizes that it is oxygen starved. It yawns to alert about that.

Yawning and stretching just after awaking like the cats do, is done by kundalini for its own purposes. Stretching is done by kundalini to open nadis and let energy flow unrestrictedly to certain areas. Yawning is its way of saying that it is fresh air starved or that the muscles of the body are achy and need rest.

Rest is not meditation. Rest is not yoga practice but it is necessary for the kundalini to rejuvenate the cells which it has to service from moment to moment. Yoga practice is not a substitute for rest. Yoga practice can enhance rest by giving kundalini much energy to use for rejuvenation during rest.

Let me stress that the exercise session will not replace rest. One requires a certain quota of rest or the physical and psychological systems will suffer, with or without yoga.

Raise Kundalini from a Sex Place

In yogic lore, there is a *kanda* mentioned which is in the lower part of the body and from which kundalini may raise. This is in contrast to the spinal passage which is known as the *sushumna nadi*.

Sexual energy in the *kanda* becomes a nuisance when the energy in it accumulates and causes sexual agitation. To get its charge dissipated one may do rapid breathing, *bhastrika*. By directing the charge to the *kanda*, one may ignite it and cause it to attract kundalini from the base of the spine to go upward through a central passage in the body, not even using the *sushumna nadi* spinal passage.

Yogeshwarananda's Kriya: July 7, 2010
Kundalini Swipe-Back to Crown Chakra

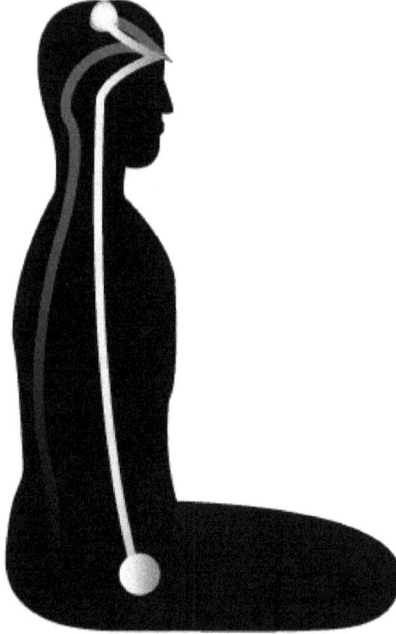

Practice:
Do bhastrika rapid breathing for at least 50 counts.
Raise Kundalini from sexual energy kanda in the subtle body.
Do not raise it from the base chakra to brow chakra.
Hold energy at brow chakra while drawing it back to crown.
Energy will try to disappate at brow chakra.
Mentally prevent it from doing so.
Be sure to hold the coreSelf in naad sound while this takes place.
Naad is the anchor zone.

Yogeshwarananda's Kriya: June26, 2010
Kundalini Swipe-Back to Crown Chakra

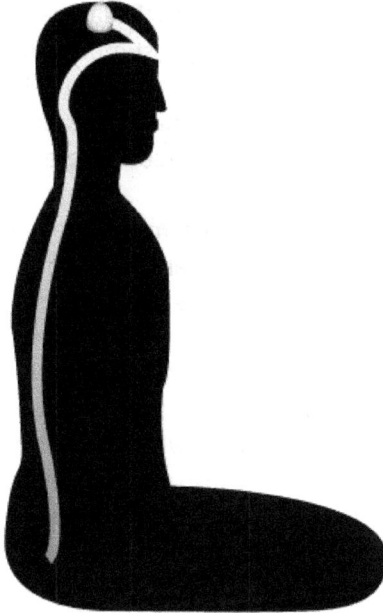

Practice:
Raise Kundalini to brow chakra.
Do bhastrika rapid breathing for at least 50 counts.
Hold energy at brow chakra while drawing it back to crown.
Energy will try to disappate at brow chakra.
Mentally prevent it from doing so.
Be sure to hold the coreSelf in naad sound while this takes place.
Naad is the anchor zone.

Special Note:

This works if the yogi first raises kundalini to brow chakra. Kundalini has to be active and pliable to do this. Kundalini will try to leave through the forehead and dissipate itself there but the yogi can contain it and pull it back to crown.

If one is lucky one will find a bell-shaped chamber there with the self in the centre of it. Remain there while keeping the coreSelf anchored to naad sound. Do not lose contact with naad.

Raising Kundalini

Few people realize that recreational drug use is a method of raising kundalini. It is one of the easiest methods of doing so. Another common method is sexual indulgence. Addiction to any of these methods means an addiction not to the method itself but to the particular way in which kundalini arises when it is prompted by the substance or stimulation.

Many people who begin with alcohol and then shift to marijuana, sometimes return to alcohol when they make the comparison of how kundalini is stimulated by each drug. Some persons prefer the kind of altered state they get from alcohol.

One common opinion of those who use marijuana is that alcohol is an inferior recreational drug, but what that amounts to is saying that the movement of kundalini under the influence of ganja is preferred by that person as compared to kundalini movement under the influence of alcohol.

Why not abandon recreational drug use for kundalini yoga?

The answer to that is simple, kundalini yoga practice takes time and effort. It is flawed in one important aspect which is that it does not totally remove one's sense of responsibility or sense of duty. Smoking a reefer takes no effort and it immediately causes all those bothersome responsibilities and duties to disappear. In fact, they disappear and leave behind a mental and emotional state of humor which is very much desired by the self in this dismal world of imposed social norms.

The fact that responsibility is an undesirable is demonstrated by the widespread use of contraceptive medications and devices. Nearly every human being who can reproduce considers the negative aspects of responsibility.

The desired feature is sexual pleasure not responsibility for progeny.

Kundalini yoga does raise kundalini but its downside is that it makes one more aware of responsibility. Which begs the question: Why were we deposited in this world of responsibility?

Looking Down into the Body (July 15, 2013)

In doing breath infusion, the student should develop a sense of the quantity of air required to saturate the physical system and the astral body with new energy, displacing the used lingering energy which was consumed already by physical cells and by subtle energy areas. Initially it is a stress on breathing out *(kapalabhati),* doing the breath infusion rapidly with great force on the outbreath.

Later when one becomes proficient in this, it shifts. One develops a sense that one should have a certain quantity of fresh energizing energy. One actually feels the need for it and feels the system filling more and more as one proceeds with a session of the breathing practice.

Looking down in the body is necessary. One should train the mind to do that. By nature, the visual sense is eager for information about the external environment because the idea for being here is to exploit the environment any which way any time. However, the yogi performs a *pratyahar* sensual energy withdrawal practice by looking down into the subtle body while infusing the breath.

This is advantageous. If the yogi becomes proficient at this looking down into the body, over time the visual sense will release its hold on the external environment which is outside of the physical and subtle bodies. Instead, it will be attentive to what happens within those forms.

Sex Pleasure (July 15, 2013)

The sex organs are special and sacred because it is through that faculty that one takes an embryo. As nature would have it, in most mammals, the organs are allied to urination and are situated close to defecation.

Is this a hint?

Did nature put those facilities together to reduce interest in the organs?

The problem with pleasure addiction is memory. If one removes memory, if there is no recall of a pleasure incidence, there would hardly be a special interest in it. It would be engaged only in the normal course of its natural functions.

Defecation is something that people usually forget. Or they postpone it to the extent of causing the solid waste to dehydrate in the colon which in turn causes health issues. Urination is not forgotten because usually nature causes an inconvenient feeling when the bladders are filled. Otherwise we would also forget that or postpose it for as long as possible. By design the colon can dehydrate solid waste but the bladder cannot evaporate urine.

But sex, no one forgets that.

Why?

What is the difference?

Obviously, it is the pleasure yield but that is reinforced by memory. Remove its memory and one would have no interest in it except when nature induces one into it the way animals are induced in a mating season. They do not have the capacity to remember sex. They are not concerned with it until nature forces the need of it in their minds.

They experience the pleasure but there is no recall after an incidence.

Because the sex organs render the valuable service of providing embryos, they are very special indeed. That one function elevates them but because of the pleasure yield, their mode of operation is passion. For begetting the embryo this passionate mood is useful and is supportive of responsibility.

There is a certain degree of abstraction in sexual pleasure, so much so that it is a feat for anyone to get their objective consciousness around it. Usually the objective consciousness is undermined by the pleasure feature of it.

The indulger cannot understand the pleasure, as to its components, outcomes and motivations. In this way, sex pleasure confuses the psyche.

Lower Body Infusion

As one advances in breath infusion practice, a student should make the effort to cause energy infusion in the lower part of the body. First one should target the groin, then the base chakra, then the thighs, then the legs and feet.

Overtime this can be accomplished. The first process of breath infusion for which a student may be certified is the pushing down of breath energy through the navel area into the groin, where there is a mix between the breath energy and the sex hormones. This combination will jump to the base chakra and cause kundalini to move up the spine. Though this is a big event for any student, it is preliminary in siddha yoga practice.

Algebra is a big event for high school students but it is the ABC for postgraduate mathematicians. Similarly, what is so grand in the world of yoga on the earthly planet, is elementary to the siddhas.

As soon as one accomplished the routing of kundalini through the spine into the brain, as soon as one is confidence that one can do that daily using breath infusion, one should seriously consider talking to a siddha about the higher course of yoga.

Some student gets disappointed. They complain like this:
- I thought this was it.
- I thought this was liberation.
- Why do you rate this as preliminary?
- The impression I got is that this raising of kundalini would make me a siddha for the least. Now you say something else.
- I do not like this depressing information.

It may well be, but even in the course of striving for liberation, facts are present. When a student is confident of his ability to raise kundalini into the brain, when he knows for sure that he can do that on a daily basis without fail, then consider sending infusion energy down through the bottom of the body, to the lower extremities. What about having kundalini rise in the thighs, knees, legs, feet or big toe, for instance.

Can that be achieved?

Will it only be the head which has insight consciousness?

Paradox

Where I grew up in Guyana, there were instances where someone would do his/her very best, and would get an unpleasant result anyway. In resignation to the fate, the person would then say:

I cannot win for losing.

This means that no matter what one does, no matter if one does one's best, still in the end one will lose everything.

In a way, this is painful. It is an unwanted reality but all the same it is humorous. It is a cause of inconceivable happiness.

If something is reality, how can it be unwanted?

This is a paradox, like if something exists but it should not exist, like if something is real but it should be unreal.

The very nature which promotes the development of this world is itself hard at work tearing everything apart. Why is this? This freaked Gautama Buddha.

Think of paradox in this way:

Suppose a secondary branch on a tree does not trust the primary branch to which it is attached, then what?

That is called an absurdity. It should not be and yet it is pronounced. It speaks for itself as being an upset reality. Such is this world.

On one hand nature produced the social identity which each human being currently uses. On the other hand, nature does everything it can to demolish that psychological construction. Why?

Kriya Yoga / The Long Wait

There is what is termed as the long wait in kriya practice, where the student waits and waits, day after day in meditation, for the insight perception consciousness. This is the linking into the chit akash sky of consciousness and the perpetual sure access to that dimension.

Can the student raise kundalini on a daily basis without fail?

Can the student reach the chit akash at least once per day?

How long will a student have to practice to achieve that?

Can the student hold out?

Will the student become frustrated not attaining that goal after months or years of practice?

What of the method?

Is a competent guru available?

An astral guru said this:

No amount of human endeavor will alter the dimensional layout. Whatever it is, it is. If you cannot control the weather, how do you propose to gain access to what is beyond the physical?

Grabbing the chit akash will not happen. The grabbing action may happen but the actually taking possession of that supernatural place, will not occur.

As always work with what you have. Take wood and make fire which is so lacking in weight that it goes upwards, a habit which is contrary to the action of the wood involved in fire production.

Darkness is light. And from that light will dawn the chit akash. But you must wait in meditation.

Siddhas and Siddhis (June 18,2013)

The question arose in an astral conversation last night, as to why a siddha would be with a woman. Why conversely, would an accomplished yogini be with a male partner? If sexual intercourse is the bane of yoga, then why would any of the perfected or near-perfected entities who are masters and mistresses of yoga, be sexually connected or related with anyone else?

First of all, a siddha is a perfected male yogi. A siddhi is a perfected female yogi.

Much of what happens to anyone has to do with fate. Fate is a serious aspect. It can demolish anyone's yoga practice. There are many stories in the Puranas of yogis who reached near perfection and who were intercepted by fate, which caused their salvation to be forestalled.

Vishwamitra gave up his position as king after he defeated by a mere cow whom he wanted to put in the service of the state. Just as we exploit the earth and the governments tax us accordingly, Vishvamitra wanted to exploit a magical cow for the benefit of the country. We mine mineral or extracts crude petroleum for human industry. Vishvamitra thought it was a good idea to get unlimited supplies of money for himself and country.

The cow did not like the idea. It resisted. There was some tugging and pulling as human beings usually do with domestic animals. There were threats. Vishvamitra considered arresting or killing Vashishtha, the yogi who owned the cow.

In response the cow urinated, farted and pooped as animals which are scared sometimes do. Out of that waste warriors appeared and destroyed Vishvamitra's army.

After this Vishvamitra considered that a yogi acquires special supernatural powers which over-ride any other proficiency. He became determined to be a yogi.

On the way to siddha perfection, Vishvamitra was targeted by the Indra supervisor of certain astral paradise worlds. There was an angelic woman by the name of *Menaka* (Main-kaa or Mai-nuh-kaa). Indra instructed her to seduce Vishvamitra. At the time Vishvamitra did not have sufficient insight to understand the ruse. When Menaka showed up, Vishvamitra was out of his wits about her but she was aware of her mission.

They had a daughter, an attractive girl named *Shakuntala*.

It took some time for Vishvamitra to realize that his trysts with *Menaka* were preplanned by the Indra supernatural being. It was not the yogi's original idea. It popped into his mind while he was under an influence.

But suppose Vishvamitra had the insight to see the motive of Menaka when she first arrived? Would that insight prevail to stop him from accepting the woman?

A man saw an approaching train and yet it killed him. What will be the statement of inquest?

Would it state that he saw the train and it was too late for him to jump out of its way?

Or would it state that he saw the train and had sufficient time to get out of its way?

Again, why would a siddha accept a female companion?

Willpower and Rebirth

Inquiry:

Is a child able to gain a body as effectively as an adult in the astral world? Are they conscious of how to do this?

MiBeloved's Reply:

One does not have to know how to get a body to get one. The getting-body business is more like the sleeping business, where even if you do not understand what happens to cause it, you will fall asleep anyway.

An aunt of mine once explained that she had no idea of sexual intercourse and never even considered doing it, until my uncle got her into a room and introduced the act to her.

She got pregnant and did not comprehend the event, even though her stomach was distended and people noticed. At first, she considered the distension as body fat.

There are so many things which we do not have to be aware of or even know of their formation. Yet, these events occur. Death is one such incidence. Birth is another.

Suppose also, that my uncle did not understand what he did when he got the young lady pregnant. Suppose he explained away his action by saying that he was inspired from within his mind and emotions even though he had no objective understanding of a sex act. Would it still produce the pregnancy?

Neither disembodied infants nor those disembodied elderly people need understand the process of transmigration, because if they have the information or if they do not have it, if there is a tendency in the subtle body to reincarnate as a physical form, the transit to another womb will undoubtedly take place.

It is not the desire in the conscious observing mind which causes one to take another body but all the same if there is such a desire, then one is likely to think that it was the cause of the new body. Such is the confusion where we fail to distinguish a primal urge of nature and the willpower.

Four Noble Truths

I read the *Knowing and Seeing* book of the Venerable Sayadaw, a recent Buddhist master who stuck to the original methods given by Gautama Buddha. It is a very painful thing, as a spiritual son of Gautama Buddha, to hear people misrepresent him and give distortions and totally crazy ideas about the way of enlightenment he pioneered.

There is much distortion, and to make matters worse, these increase day by day. The problem is that it dismantles what Gautama Buddha tried to give humanity. It setbacks the very persons who formulate the misrepresentations.

Venerable Sayadaw, in keeping with the original Pali text, dished out the Four Noble Truths as

- Truth of Suffering
- Origin of suffering
- Truth of cessation of Suffering
- Path leading to the Cessation of Suffering.

In modern American English, I translate this again as follows:

Four Essential Insights

- reality of trauma
- origin of trauma
- realization that trauma can cease
- application of an effective method for terminating trauma

Reality of Trauma

First of all, one cannot be a Buddhist if one does not reach the first essential insight. One cannot reach that insight if one is not completely detached from sense enjoyment. Buddhism is not for persons who are essentially attached in their regular lifestyle. This is because like Buddha one has to come to certain realizations and be moved by these to take renunciation.

Who is the example of this?

The answer is of course, Buddha himself. He saw some traumatic incidences of human existence and reacted drastically. He left the convenience of royal social life and never resumed it. If you are not willing to do this, if you feel that this is not necessary because Buddha himself developed a Middle path after doing gruesome austerities, then Buddhism as Buddha delivered it is not for you.

This does not mean that you may not benefit from a study of Buddha's life and teaching, but it means that your adjustments and adaptations will block full access to what Buddha stood for and did.

If you feel that Buddha's Middle Way is what you want to do, then at least realize that this middle way did not include a resumption of social life, because Buddha never went back to the life of a prince. He never resumed political task as the son of a King or chieftain. Therefore, the Middle Way cannot be defined as anything other than a monk's life style in the forest moving from place to place as Buddha did.

The first noble truth or essential insight is the reality of trauma. We have heard this repeatedly as being the truth of the suffering or the realization that essentially, we are cornered on all sides by the threat of suffering.

Why is this?

In fact, is this truth?

Can one be a Buddhist without this negative outlook?

One can be but one should not claim to be following exactly like Buddha unless one can keep this perception about trauma in mind.

The first thing to realize is that there is no way around the trauma of material existence because this reality comprises an energy which is lined with trauma every step of the way. There is no escaping it, either by having money, by having a beautiful body, by having a youthful form, by having high pedigree, by becoming famous, by being enterprising, by conquering territories, by making others into slaves, or by seeking and enjoying pleasures. There is no escape from it.

The realization of this is what stirred Buddha into action. There is promise in fighting an enemy so long as there is some hope that one may overcome the opponent but if one realizes that victory is not possible, one should abandon the fight.

Gautama Buddha, the old father, realized that he was boxed in by trauma. He decided to review the situation to see if there was any way he could escape. To do so he left family and royal responsibilities and never looked back.

If trauma is on all sides, if one cannot find a way out, it means that one should either become resigned to one's lot like a condemned man who waits in the execution chamber or one should become a genius overnight and discover a way out.

Supposedly, and people believe this, where there is a will there is a way. Or stated non-poetically, if you are determined to do something, there is a high probability that nature will afford you an opportunity. It may not be exactly what you conceive of but if you are flexible, you could negotiate to the best of your ability whatever chance nature affords.

Origin of Trauma

What is the origin of trauma? To effectively deal with something, especially something which has such a large and varied lay out as material nature, one should know about the origin and development of that subject. From one angle it should be easy to figure the origin of trauma, especially if it is universal. If something is everywhere, we should easily recognize and penetrate it.

But in this case, that reasoning fails.

Despite its all-pervasive aspect, trauma is not easy to figure as to its roots or origin. This is because the trace back to the origin has many misleading starts and stops. As nature developed, it split itself into multi facets, so much so that from our position, a backtrack leads nowhere.

In this case we should take help from a genius of psychology who is Buddha. He gave hints on what to trace and what to ignore, on what is a good lead and what will cause frustration.

If I cannot find the origin of trauma I am stuck and cannot be a Buddhist.

Realizing that Trauma can cease

I must somehow get some realization to know if trauma can be terminated. At the surface level trauma cannot be ended because it is integrated into material nature. Unless I am assured that it can be terminated, I will not have the require confidence to take the path set by Buddha.

In Buddha's case he heard about monks going into the forest to realize the end of trauma but when he took up the methods available in the area of India where he resided, none of these systems brought about the end of trauma. He therefore pioneered a new method.

People think that Buddha did not find a method in India and there was no method but the only thing I know for sure is that there was no method available in the area where Buddha did austerities. In that area there were no teachers of any method which was fully effective in removing the individual from the realm of trauma.

After Buddha and because we believe that he did do the austerities and did achieve the termination of trauma for himself, we have confidence that it is possible. Here, there is no alternative but to have faith because we have not realized in fact that trauma can be terminated. Even us, the faithful followers of Buddha, his spiritual sons, must exhibit faith in this regard, at least until we can gain the experience of a state of consciousness or realm of existence where trauma is completely absent.

Application of an Effective Method for Terminating Trauma

Once we have faith that trauma can be terminated, even if we fail to evolve that faith into personal realization and direct insight, we may began applying the effective method. This again could be done on the basis of faith in Buddha. It is interesting that in a path which does not give credence to a Supreme Being, which advocates personal endeavor and personal capacity for liberation, we utilize faith in someone. We find faith to be useful even on this path which advocates autonomy for the individual seeking liberation.

Buddha is unique because he got the insight that trauma could be terminated. He developed an effective method for attaining that. In our case, we do not have the insight. We have not seen the realm or level of consciousness where trauma is conspicuous by its absence. Yet we attempt to use the effective method for terminating trauma. This happens by the grace of the life of Buddha. If for any other reason, his life has this value to us, that gift of faith in the fact, that there is a state of consciousness which is devoid of trauma and there is a method for attaining that level.

Part 5

Chit Akash Secret

After working for over forty years steadily day after day, to consistently make contact with the chit akash sky of consciousness, my conclusion now is that the process of reaching it, is easy. All the same it is difficult and hard to reach indeed.

Recently with some assistance rendered by one of the old fathers, Lahiri Mahasaya, I reached chit akash by a method he showed which is so easy as to be humorous.

It has five parts to it:

- breath infusion into the lower reaches of the subtle body
- absorption in naad sound
- blink perception contact of transcendental glow light in naad sound
- the short or long wait
- the lack of anxiety when chit akash light appears

The problem with this list is that it is not easy to complete. Even though it is listed in clear terms and I can vouch that it worked for me, still that does not make it easy for anyone else. It may however give one some increased confidence if one practices Patanjali meditation.

The first item in the list is the most important. It is beyond raising kundalini on a daily basis. It has to do with taking away the authority of kundalini and allowing the coreSelf to regulate the psyche energy which is in the trunk of the subtle body.

The aspect of it which is really hard to get under control is the feature where we are trained in material nature to focus through the senses. To do this one has to use the route of the sensual energies through the intellect. This means an addiction to the intellect or to the functions of the intellect which is thinking and visualization. This addiction like sexual addiction is hard to abandon.

We have two psychic adjuncts working against us. One is in the head of the subtle body. One is in the trunk of it. The one in the head is called the intellect. This keeps the coreSelf spell bound, hypnotize as it is. In the trunk of the subtle body we have the kundalini psychic mechanism, it has tremendous power and can strike at any time, immobilizing or suspending the command power of the core.

Kundalini does have varied interest in the trunk of the subtle body but as nature would have it, its primary concern there is in sexual pleasure. Due to this, its ally which is the intellect, developed an interest in sexual intercourse, and by that, it is forced to descend into the basement of the subtle body for the purpose of getting the much-desired sex pleasure.

For its part, the kundalini lifeForce stays close to the sexual function like a heavily armed security guard protecting a bank vault. Since it needs information for procuring energy to run the sexual pleasure complex operation, it must take information from the intellect orb and from the senses. For this it sends energy into the head of the subtle body.

This sending of energy caused the coreSelf to become dependent on the passage of psychic power through the spine of the subtle body, which in turn makes kundalini yoga a necessity.

By the grace of several teachers who assisted me on the astral planes, I completed the kundalini yoga practice. Of note in this respect is Yogi Bhajan who introduced me to the practice. Others assisted with it but he was the first person to give the method of breath infusion, as *kapalabhati* or *bhastrika pranayama*.

Kundalini yoga as he taught it is not the complete package but it is about 75 % of the course, so much so that if one completes that to proficiency, one may get help either from him or from another yoga guru for completion.

What is that completion?

It is the infusion of energy into the trunk of the subtle body with expression of that energy into the thighs, legs and feet without respect to spinal kundalini. It is infusion in such a way that the kundalini is no longer in charge of the lifeForce which runs the subtle body.

This is not a difficult thing to do once you gain proficiency in raising kundalini at least once per day. Eventually if you do that correctly, kundalini will from time to time jump into the brain abandoning its haunt at the *muladhara* base chakra. It will do this. Then it will resume its lower hideout. Eventually if the student persists, kundalini will permanently abandon its lower residence and take a position in the lower back of the brain.

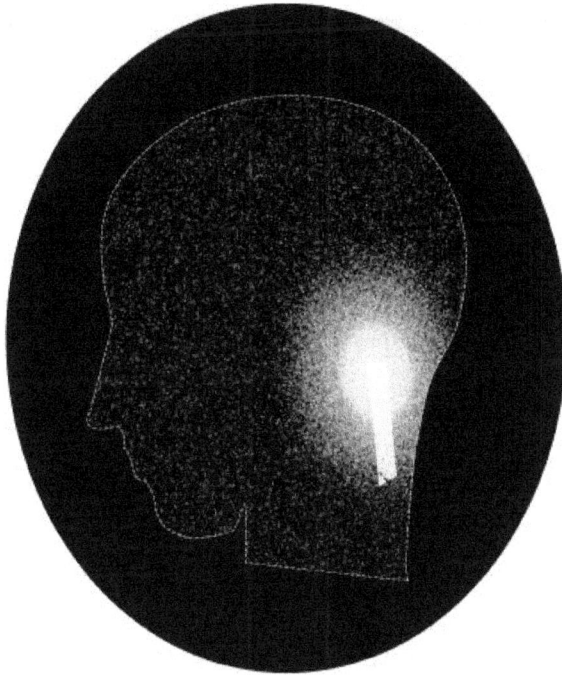

This is when the coreSelf will begin doing infusion without involving kundalini. This is when the student can really penetrate through the subtle body, attaining the first requirement of **breath infusion into the lower reaches of the subtle body**.

Absorption in naad sound has to be done for weeks, months or years, until the coreSelf finds itself in a relationship which is comparable to an infant sucking the breast of its mother peacefully and with full satisfaction.

Once there is this stability in naad sound, the student finds that the coreSelf is automatically embedded in naad anytime he/she sits to meditate. From time to time, these will be a **glow light in naad**. This will happen spontaneously where when one is in naad, one hears naad and then sees this glow. For me it was a white-gold color. This light is similar to the first throw of light in the early morning before dawn.

After remaining in that repeatedly in naad meditation, the student has to indulge in the **short or long wait**. This is the wait for the arrival of the chit akash sky of consciousness.

The chit akash light will first appear only momentarily, for seconds for the most, but when it does, the student will find that he/she enters a state of anxiety and tries to pursue and focus on it. This is a mistake but it is an inevitable response which the student must eventually control in time. This anxiety causes the rapid disappearance of chit akash contact. When this is understood, the student deletes this tendency from his/her consciousness.

Reaching Brahma's Celestial Place

This morning during the meditation session, I was shown a method used by siddha yogis to reach the Brahma deity. A question as to why one would desire to reach that deity may be entertained.

Siddha yogis who want to go higher cannot do so unless something from a higher astral domain or someone from a divine domain requests their presence. In that sense the *siddhaloka* attainment is a terminal place, a last stop on the travel route from here upwards.

Some hints about higher places come to the siddhas in the *siddhaloka* places. Based on those hints, the yogi aspires to go to those other places. Where do these hints come from? These hints are derived either from a yoga guru who knows about the higher places, in fact, or by a deity of those higher places, or by a recruiting agent of the deity.

The yogi is advised on what to do to become compatible with the deity of that higher domain. Say what you like, there is always that lingering doubt in the mind of yogi as to if a deity desires to see him.

One may be a devotee of a famous deity. One may be an atheist. You may believe in energy. Irrespective, if one is unwanted in a higher domain, one will not go there. On this planet there are devotees, there are energy believers who do not want to live in poverty or in an undeveloped country. They want to live affluently.

In our experience on earth, we sometimes find that wealthy people, whom everyone considers to be gracious, forgiving and compassionate, are in fact vicious personalities. Still these persons live in high-class communities which are barricaded from the poor people.

Sometime a person who has nothing, who is dirt poor, who is of a lower unwanted racial stock, who has an ugly body, who has no skill to get a decent job, is found to exhibit saintly behavior.

How does one qualify to be called by a deity?

This procedure which I was shown which is used by some siddha yogis who want to see the Brahma deity, is one where the kundalini energy which courses through the spine is removed. Then the yogi continues with breath infusion energy exchange. After a time, a streak of energy like a thin laser beam shoots from the body of the yogi. This comes from the lower center of the trunk of the subtle body. It passes through the body, through the head and goes upward until it reaches the plane of the Brahma deity. Then the yogi does this repeatedly and waits.

Will he get a reply from the deity?

He may or may not get a reply. The deity is under no obligation to respond. The yogi should therefore be open-minded knowing that the deity may never respond.

We read in the *Bhagavata Purana (Srimad Bhagavatam)* that *Hiranyakashipu*, even though he was a criminal turned yogi, got the Brahma deity to visit and give boons. Brahma did not allow *Hiranyakashipu* to go to *Brahmaloka*, but Brahma left that place and went to speak very favorably with the sorcerer.

The woman *Amba* who held resentment towards *Bhishma* performed austerities. Even though she did not reach Shiva in his domain, the deity came to her and granted boons. *Dhruva* did not go to the *Vaikuntha* realm of Krishna, but Krishna came to *Dhruva* and granted boons. People think that it is not possible for a badly-motivated yogi to see a deity like Shiva or Krishna but the history of Puranas contradicts that view.

Sometimes devotees of Krishna are struck with wonder and ask the question as to why Brahma went to see such a criminal as Hiranyakashipu who was not a devotee and who did no service to Krishna as devotees do. In this way, people who worship Krishna question Krishna's activities and harbor doubts about his decision-making ability. Others, to satisfy their egos, explain that Hiranyakashipu was a devotee in a past life and that Krishna wanted to retrieve him. In that way we fall every which way on rationalizations which suit our fancy.

If I work hard for God, to please God, if I am a devotee, why should God neglect me and take care of someone else who has no service history like me?

Going the Brahma's place may be a real non-fulfilling situation, because once you get there you may not like the status which you must assume in that situation.

- How will you fit in?
- Will you be a leader?
- Will you be a nobody?
- Are the people who reside there much greater than you?
- Do they have better bodies?
- Are they more skilled than you?
- Will you be Brahma's shoeshine boy?
- Will you be the girl who picks celestial fruits which he looks at and does not eat?
- Will your body in that place be devoid of sexual pleasure?
- Will you marry the man or woman of your dreams?

It may be that life on earth is the best place for you!

Music/Videos and Yogis

Earlier today a friend invited me to see a TV show. He said it would be very interesting. Lucky for me the show was at the time when I would do the afternoon breath infusion.

I did not attend it. I will explain why I avoid videos and music. These media continually wreck yoga practice. Say for instance, I make a few months progress in meditation, then I become absorbed in a film, I find that this wrecks my practice where I find myself struggling with images and impressions which I absorbed from the film.

Somebody said that it was simple to deal with, which was to be detached, but that does not work for me. If I see images in a video, these are replayed later in the mind. Some simply refuse to leave my mind. They prevent me from going to deeper levels of insight.

Music is the same, even devotional music which plays back in the mind during meditation.

Is this happening to everyone? I do not know. I do not care. Let other yogis who have no problem with videos and music use those to help their meditation. I can only speak for myself.

After I worked say for six months day after day and made certain progress in gaining deep insight during meditation, I would be a fool to allow a video or a music rendition to bash that in and hurl me back to struggling with music pieces playing in my mind when I do not want them there, and scenes from videos popping like a wild brush fire, which I have to run here and run there in the mind to extinguish.

Only a foolish yogi will sabotage his progress.

Breath Infusion Details

Many meditators are into watching and/or counting breaths or counting the relative duration between inhale-pause-exhale-pause. People make a big deal out of this. In the Americanized system of vipassana Buddhist meditation, this breath observation is taught.

I want to give those who are doing breath infusion using rapid breathing, some hints about how to go about keeping track of breath.

First of all, do not keep track of breath during meditation. During meditation keep track only of the components in the psyche, the psychic adjuncts. Do not be involved in the breath. Let it be on its regular automatic operation. In other words, forget about breath. Let it take care of itself.

However, this is because you should pay attention to it before meditation, when you do breath infusion. There is a time for paying attention to breath in the system which I teach. It is not while meditating. It is during the breath infusion practice.

Here is a list of the way a student should keep track of breath, in the order of advancement proficiency:

- Track the outbreath by pushing it out with as much force as you can muster and with a rate of as much as you can muster in the specific posture you are in.
- When you feel that the system is almost filled with air, then as the breathing takes place rapidly and automatically, keep track of the compression of the air and its distribution into the hard-to-reach somewhat inaccessible places in the psyche. Mentally help the infused energy to go to those places.
- At this point when you feel that the system is filled with air and will take no more of it, switch focus to the in-breaths. *Kapalabhati* means focus on the out-breaths. Thus, this new recommendation for in-breath focus is the reverse *kapalabhati*, where, as the breathing takes place, the student pulls hard on the in-breaths and lets the out-breaths take place automatically. This is different to what is stressed for a beginner. A beginner should stick to focusing on the outbreaths for at least three years or more of daily practice because he/she will gain very little, if any, from focusing on the in-breaths. In the advanced stage however, there is benefit from this reverse *kapalabhati* practice. Some student should try to do *bhastrika pranayama* which is the full *pranayama* but those who do so should notice that the breathing rate may slow and the compression aspect may be reduced which means that they should abandon *bhastrika* (dual in/out breath focus) and stick with *kapalabhati* (out-breath focus only) which will give them the maximum desired infusion

Neck Twitch Twist Kriya

This is something that some siddhas do in the effort to permanently de-exist from the subtle material world and transfer to the chit akash sky of consciousness.

Getting to *siddhaloka* is an achievement but one can easily get stalled there, meditating repeatedly for days or years even, entering specific *samadhis* and being absent from universal events in that way.

Ultimately, as a self, one needs an environment. People who speak of oneness, and void state, have yet to realize this but we experience that teenagers also have no sense of responsibility and think that life will be one enjoyment after the other, one excitement after the other without accountability or cost at any time.

In this kriya the siddha yogi, reaches a state where there is just a head for the subtle body and a bubble chamber below it. There are no limbs protruding. This makes it easy to keep only high-grade subtle energy in the psyche. If there are hands and feet, there arises a need to keep those extremities filled with fresh subtle energizing energy. Some siddha yogis successful change the configuration of the subtle body so that it has no thighs, legs, feet, genitals, arms, forearms nor hands.

At a certain stage suddenly, these siddha yogis get a feeling to do a twitch twist of the neck. This stops the passage of energy through the neck into the head of the subtle body. Then they infuse fresh energy into the bubble form which the trunk assumed and check it closely to be sure that not even a speck of de-energizing energy is in it.

This happens after the yogi was alerted by a teacher, that the reason for a stall in *siddhaloka*, the cause of failure to transfer fully into the sky of consciousness, is that some lower subtle energy is still in the psyche.

Samadhis, even though they are much desirable, and are considered to be legendary, can become an impediment when one reaches the *siddhaloka* places. There, no disturbances will reach the student except for his/her inner flaws.

There is no materialistic civilization there, no employment, no relatives, no objections from anyone for practice. One may go into a *samadhi* there which may pass for days, weeks, years or even ages. Then one may come out of such a state and realize that a time cycle transpired.

A yogi who goes into *samadhi* there, may be transferred during the trance. Later after waking up, he may find himself alone, with not a soul around other than himself.

He wanted to be alone. He felt that the world was imperfect, that the God of the world was a myth. He thought that there was a flaw in everyone but himself. He felt that if anything he was God and that he could make it on his own because he was the complete reality. Then he entered into a meditative state, and after several million years passed, he became objectively conscious again, but only to find himself all alone and blue. He began to wonder,

"Where is everyone else? I prefer to be with others."

Sometimes when a siddha awakens from a *samadhi* session, he/she has no idea of what happened. Then the student will ask about his/her guru. That guru may have left and gone into the dispersed spatial spiritual energy, the brahman, or gone somewhere like Brahma's planet, or to the spiritual places, like where Shiva or Krishna or Narayana is, or descended into material existence for one reason or the other.

The student will ask other siddhas about the guru and be informed of what happened. Some gurus disappear from the *siddhaloka* place without informing their disciples. Why they do this no one knows?

How can a mother who has infants, pack her bags and leave them to fend for themselves?

Chit Akash Location

One yoga guru who does not want his name mentioned because he does not want to be in contact with anyone said to me this morning that the location of the chit akash is determined by going to *brahmaloka*. He said that just outside of the *brahmaloka* place there is the chit akash energy. That is where it begins.

Even though a successful yogi makes contact with that and others make contact with it haphazardly, still it is located just outside the *brahmaloka* place.

What is the relevance of this information?

For those who are interested in how they can reach the *chit akash* sky of consciousness from our location in the physical world, using the astral body and going through environments which are outside of the astral form, they can do so by journeying to the *brahmaloka* place.

Yogis are not supposed to pursue that course but should reach the chit akash by shifting vibrations within the psyche with no dependence on astral travel.

Agnisara Subtle Body

The agnisara practice is well known even to flaky yogis who do not know what they are doing or who think that yoga is for making a slim waist. The belly pumps are amazing especially to person whose stomach is distended.

Because of the tongue's tyranny, the stomach, intestines and colon suffer day after day from being overworked processing a bad diet. In this world, as soon as one is expelled from the womb, one cries saying the rudimentary sounds nature permits.

One expresses feelings:

"Mother, come here. Mother, do not leave. Mother, where are your breasts?" Then the tongue spoke up because it wanted to declare its supremacy. It said to the rest of the body,

"Now hear this! I am your king. I am your queen. You were born to serve me."

The other parts of the body were quite surprised to hear this declaration. Still, they remained silent because they were afraid of repercussions if the tongue decided not to taste anything. They grumbled in the background. They said:

"This tongue is arrogant. Who appointed it to rule us? Since we do not know our status, let us be silent for the time being. We must get nourishment somehow. If the tongue refuses to taste what will happen to us?

"When we were in there, (pointing to the mother's passage), we had no need for a tongue. We were nourished. Now the tongue arrogantly subordinates us. Now even to get something from the breast, we are blackmailed by this tongue. We were unhappy in there. We are unhappy out here just the same."

The second stage of agnisara practice has nothing to do with belly pumps. It has everything to do with breath infusion, so that the breath alone does whatever should be done. This stage concerns breath infusion into the arteries and veins. It concerns movement of fresh energy in the subtle body, beginning with the areas of the intestines.

Externally nothing is seen as contrasted to belly pumps where the lift and release action of belly is clearly noticed.

Bones and Siddhas

Breath infusion this morning was focused on bones in the thigh and leg. These bones can make it or break it in the attempt to develop a *siddhaloka* body.

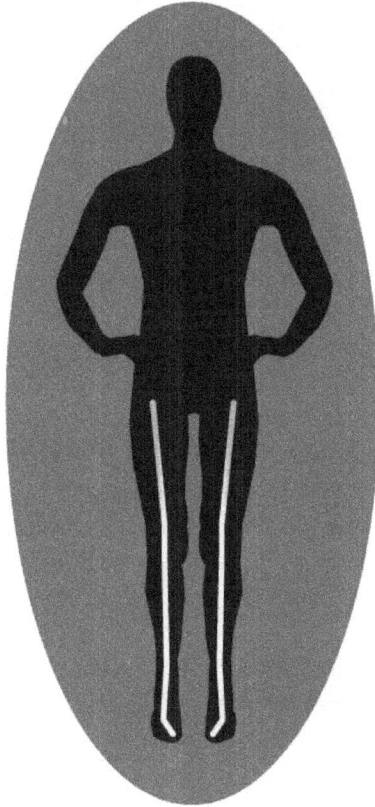

It is not so much what happens in the head but what takes place in the extremities. The head space is the easiest to energize and regulate. Still, getting the head space under control is a hassle. Once the student achieves that, he/she can target the *hard to reach* places. Then the *nadis* in those areas are cleared, where polluted energy is removed, being replaced continually by energizing subtle energy.

There is a connection between naad meditation and this. There is also a connection between this and the perception of the *chit akash* sky of consciousness. If every part of the subtle body is energized with infused energy to the point of full saturation, the reach into the *chit akash* can take place consistently instead of in a flash followed by resuming the dark cloud of mental energy which surrounds the coreSelf.

Chit Akash Momentary Contact

I practice an instruction given by Lahiri Baba last month. This according to him, should produce results in six months. I do not know that I will follow this to the letter, but I will do my best. That six months may be six years or six hundred years at the current pace. There is always time and circumstances which we term as fate or destiny which affects whether we succeed or fail.

During the meditation session, I had some improvement in this process for its ability to bring about contact with *chit akash* during the meditation session which follows a thorough breath infusion.

Naad was evident when I sat to meditate. It was contained in the back part of the head, taking up the full space from top to bottom back. coreSelf was lodged into it like a tick which was attached into a dog's ear.

Focusing on the coreSelf by itself is one practice which is part of the pratyahar sensual energy withdrawal. However, the coreSelf's reliance on naad is another stage. coreSelf unto itself has very little meaning because there is no such thing, no such circumstance, as a totally isolated self. It is not possible. This begs the question as to what is the appropriate reliance of the core. Naad is the first reliance, the first non-harmful energy dependence.

Once you realize that you are a relative being, the next thing is to find a reliance which provides for your wellbeing. Where do you begin that investigation?

As soon as the coreSelf found itself adhering in naad sound, it viewed light, a glow of light. According to Lahiri, the student should focus in that but in a way to imbibe it, to feed on it. The yogi feeds on naad sound. Then he feeds on naad light.

Naad light?

Yes, naad is described primarily as a sound vibration but there is also a naad light expression. When that is in the frontal part of the head it is like there is no intellect there, like it never existed. No thoughts are generated. The yogi is not terrified by an uncontrolled mind creating this and that sound and image. There is a glow light. That is all. In the back there is naad sound only and no lights, but in the front, there is the glow light.

Then patiently feeding on that naad sound and especially on the naad light, the yogi waits and waits but not in anticipation, not with anxiety and nervousness but as like when a child took half of the milk from the mother's breast. Feeding on naad sound initially is like when the child was hungry and then began taking milk but the milk was nourishing and still it did not have a specific taste that caused craving in the infant.

But then feeding on naad light is like when the child extracted the milk from one breast. The child is neither hungry nor full. The child is neither grabbing the breast nor releasing it. The child's hand is on the breast. It is neither completely relaxed nor completely tense. The mother looks at the infant. She thinks, "Hurry up, child. What is the matter with this infant?"

Then waiting in naad light in that state of not being totally satisfied and not being greedy either, there happens to appear two very bright lights near to each other, so near that they touch. These are very bright lights. The yogi sees them and knows that is the *chit akash*. The wonder of it! But it does not last for long. It is definite beyond any doubt but it only lasts for three or four seconds.

After about three minutes, there is a flash of light from the cosmic intellect, a brilliant flash, coming from the *chit akash.* That ray strikes the intellect.

The idea behind this practice however is consistent steady contact with *chit akash,* not this momentary stuff which after all is progression but is not sufficient for success.

Hanging out on the Causal Plane

This morning I was shown a passage from here to the *brahmaloka* plane of existence and another from there to the causal place which is just outside the *brahmaloka* place. This method does not use the subtle body itself but rather the energy which is inside the high energy infused subtle body. This is not an astral projection method but a psyche energy projection method where the astral body stays put, while some energy within it is projected through various planes of existence.

Just by doing breath infusion thoroughly, a yogi, from this earthly location or even from the astral world which is adjacent to this physical place, can transit directly to the causal plane. Once he transits there, it is like no existence.

Even though the causal plane is rich with the energy from which this material world emerged, still it is like a no-place no-activity consciousness location. The big value for a yogi, is that he/she may become immune to the idea of mandatory expression in the physical world.

Once there is an itch, it becomes necessary to scratch.

Once there is sexual urge, it follows that there should be a climax to the experience.

Once an idea lodges in the mind, it follows that one should enact it physically. That is how we are conditioned and supported psychologically in the physical world.

To bump against this, one should go the causal plane.

I will answer one question, which is this:

How can someone reside in a no-place no-activity consciousness-location?

Think of it in a way of going back through time to the time when you were grafted into the mother's uterus. You went there, an excited living little something, a tiny fish which swam in body secretions. You lodged into the surface of whatever it was. To you, what was it, but an irresistibly attractive surface, a place which you were attracted to? You began to feed there somehow or the other, even though the experience was not objective.

The causal plane is similar in that one has no objective idea of himself/herself or anything else, except for a faint, very faint, sense of

- I do exist.
- I am incredibly tiny.
- I am near to nothingness.

Surrounding me is this vast region of potency from which the worlds are produced. There is value here. There is sustenance here. There is desire in compressed form here. There is compressed energy for motivation here. Everything is here unexpressed. This is the ultimate concentrate of whatever was done, whatever is being done and whatever will be done.

Feeding on this will free me from having to fulfill myself in the physical existence. One drop of this energy is itself the equivalent of trillions of universes with their potential displays and involvements. My need for being in the physical world can be dismissed if I could feed here and fully appreciate this.

When kundalini is expended in the subtle body, when the yogi can infuse energy all the way through the subtle body in every nook and cranny of it, through to the extremities, then he/she may reach the causal plane by the squirting of an energy out of the surcharged subtle body, through the top of the head.

This energy came from the toes and rose through the subtle body out through the subtle head. For this to happen, every part of the subtle body must be infused with breath energy. There is no special spinal column with *sushumna nadi,* no special kundalini anywhere, no special sex organ bliss energy, all parts of the subtle body are equally infused with energy.

Naad Pratyahar / Chit Akash

The yogi should do a thorough breath infusion. He should feel that he did enough and that the subtle body is filled with fresh subtle energy, having the used low-grade energy removed from the form.

Instead of raising kundalini through the spine, there is no kundalini at the *muladhara* base chakra, instead the infused energy mixed with the energy in some part of the trunk of the subtle body or in the thighs. When it was infused sufficiently, it fired, exploded, at that place within the subtle body. The yogi compressed the explosion inward itself. The compression caused a second more powerful explosion which he directed into the thighs, legs and feet. This burst in all directions but was focused mostly in the thighs, legs and feet. Some residual energy from that final explosion rose through the thigh and spread through the trunk of the subtle body like shrapnel from a big bomb. The yogi sees those chunks of energy floating, turning and turning but glowing with energy force, glowing white-yellow, white-blue, white-orange.

After this he sits to meditate. As soon as he sits, his tongue is folded up and back so that the tip of it touches the soft palate. He hears naad sound in the top back of the head. He realizes that the coreSelf, the iSelf, is lodged into naad sound spontaneously.

He settles down with naad like an infant in the arms of its mother.

He is with naad. He is happy even though it is not a sensational happiness. It does not have excitement.

It is naad and the yogi. He is aware that the tip of the tongue touches the soft palate but he notices that with that, he feels as if the energy in the trunk of the subtle body is pulled forcibly to the point where the tongue touches the soft palate. Every bit of energy from the trunk travels to the tongue tip.

With that pulling force beneath him, he becomes aware of naad light but it is not where the naad sound is located. Naad light is in the front part of the subtle head.

What is naad light similar to?

It is like gold nuggets shining dimly in dimly lit room giving off a gold glow of light.

After a while, after an exhibition of patience, he finds that there is penetration into the gold glow of *chit akash* level of existence.

Saturation of Subtle Body

This morning I reached the level where Lahiri Baba resides. He explained an important verse of the Yoga Sutras:

जात्यन्तयनश्रयणाभ् प्रकृत्यानूयात्॥२॥
jātyantara pariṇāmaḥ prakṛtyāpūrāt

jātyantara = jāti – category + antara – other, another; pariṇāmaḥ – transformation; prakṛti – subtle material nature; āpūrāt – due to filling up or saturation.

The transformation from one category to another is by the saturation of the subtle material nature.(*Yoga Sutras* 4.2)

Recently a student asked the question of how to do this. Here is the answer, given by Lahiri.

He explained that essentially there are three methods of transiting into other dimensions. These are:

- astral projection into that other environment
- energy projection out of the astral body which enters that other place
- pulling energy from that other place into the astral body

The last method is the one which is Patanjali's saturation process.

The first method is the most unreliable one, that is the one which uses astral projection or the movement of the subtle body into other environments by transiting the entire subtle body as one moving force. This is similar to the modern feature of jet travel, where a metal container passes through the atmosphere.

The second feature is where the yogi projects energy from within the psyche into the desired dimension and makes contact with it in that way. This is like when telephone messaging was first introduced, where a signal which carried an impression of a person's voice, was transmitted from one place to another.

The third feature is where the yogi pulls energy from the desired environment so that the psyche becomes filled with that energy, as suggested by Patanjali. To do this, the yogi must have access to the desired environment and must have the technique of pulling some energy from that place into his/her psyche.

What sort of Body?

Students should know how to make even a bad meditation session productive, so that every session has benefit. There is something that I learned from butchers when I grew up in Guyana, which is how they make a profit from every part of the animal killed.

As a boy, on some Saturdays, I was sent to the abattoir. This is the official place for butchering animals in a British colonial territory. This body which I used was derived from a mainly African descent family which ate flesh. In some tribal societies in Africa cows are maintained not for milk but for blood. Their blood is extracted through a sharp straw from a main vein and used in cooking or even for drinking raw.

I was sent to the slaughter house to buy parts of a butchered cow. There were two motives for doing this. There was hardly any refrigeration which meant that people wanted to have fresh meat. There was the factor of not being able to afford it. The slaughter house was the lowest price place to acquire flesh but it was stationed a little distance from the main population. Respectable women would not go there to buy meat. Some male member of the family was sent, even the boys.

Most people got meat from butchers in the market but there you did not get the blood of the animal and special body parts like the heart or liver. There you got only the carcass which was the trunk with limbs attached, which a butcher cut apart in public at the market.

Those carcasses were hung on large meat hooks for all to see. It did not dawn on anyone that such carcasses were similar to human bodies. Looking at those carcasses everyone saw something to eat but there were Hindus who did not go to that part of the market but most of these were self-righteous people, who felt that they were too dignified to even see such carcasses hanging because to their view no one should kill a cow. They consented to killing a sheep or goat but not a cow.

Their tradition was that cows were sacred, a divine animal, a pet of God and the gods. Their opinion was that only black people, lower caste Hindus and terrible white masters of civilization ate beef.

In any case in many of my previous lives, I used Indian brahmin bodies. I did not eat beef I was into the same superstition about cows being sacred. In many of those births as a yogi, I broke out of that superstition and saw that there was no difference between butchering a hog, cow or human being.

It has nothing to do with the religious ideas about cows being sacred. That is not it. It has to do with understanding that a body is a body. If you can eat one animal you certainly can eat some other.

The body itself has a desire, so that if a brahmin yogi who did not eat animal bodies, takes a body from a family line which does that, then that same brahmin yogi will find himself/herself desiring to eat animal carcasses.

He/she will have to fight his/her way out of the habit. If the habit of the genes is strong, one may lose the fight.

As a child, I went to the abattoir. Sometimes I would go into the slaughter room. The guy doing the job would not object. He would look on me as if I was a son and would do it in a way to show how it was done. I would be barefooted in a short pants with a torn old shirt. We were a poor family.

One man would tie the horns of the animal so that its head was on the ground so that the throat was exposed in a certain way. The legs of the animal would be tied tightly so that the animal could not move. Then another man would come in with a special wide nozzle gun. He would put a slug through the center of the eyebrows. The animal would begin twitching this way and that way as much as it could.

Then a butcher would come with a sharp knife, slit the throat and before the blood would gush out, he would have a large bucket set under the throat which would hold the blood.

It was interesting to see the detachment of these men. As a boy I would look on in wonder at how detached they were. I would pretend to myself that I was an adult and was detached as well. This caused a psychological shift from being concern to being neutral to the reactions of the cow's awful sounds and movements.

After this to keep the hot blood from gelling in the bucket, this man would put his hand into the bucket of blood and briskly stir it. Then he would take the blood out to the abattoir fence and sell it to women who made a food called black pudding which was a much-desired delicacy among some people of African descent.

I watched how this food was prepared on Saturday nights by ladies who sold it from their homes. They would have partially cooked rice, salt and herbs and would mix in this blood. The mixture would be stuffed through a funnel into the intestines of a cow or pig. It was forced through the throat of the funnel using a round wooden stick. After this each end of the intestines would be tied. This would be placed in a large pot and boiled for hours. Then it would be cut up and sold.

This is similar to sausage.

People would line up to buy just a slice or two of this and would feel like they were in heaven eating this. Actually, it has to do with the body. I had such a body so I know how it felt and how heavenly was the feeling of tasting the boiled cow's blood using the tongue of that specific human body. What has it got to do with religion?

After seeing this killing business, I would see how the dead animal would be pull up in the air using meat hooks which were punched through behind its Achilles tendons. Then another man would come with another type of knife and gut the animal. It was interesting to see the entire middle portion of the trunk fall out of the body of the animal as this person expertly gutted the animal. Every part would be sold. Every part was worth money. The testes would be sold to someone at a high price.

The heart would be sold. Sometimes I bought a heart and took it home to the delight of relatives. I was just doing what I was supposed to do in that family tradition.

A man would come and skin the animal. That was valuable to those persons who were leather tanners. Some person bought skin, boiled it and ate it. It has much protein in it if you are into that. Someone would buy the eyes, cook that and eat that. Some considered the ears to be a delicacy. From female cows, the ovaries were a specialty. Everything was edible.

What did I learn from this?

That one should make use of every experience in spiritual practice, even those bad meditation sessions, even that time when one lost the battle with the mind. In every respect one should learn from everything. Even the cow dung which came out of the animal's bowels was sold as manure.

This morning the session of meditation was not so good but the breath infusion was great with Yogi Bhajan being present. Up above where I exercised, there were two yogis in minute form on a branch of an astral tree. They spoke to Yogi Bhajan who stood beside me. They said that he was in a ruling family and that if it was about 200 years prior to his birth, he would be known as a Sikh guru like Guru Gobind Singh.

Yogi Bhajan commented on the current stage of my practice, saying that even though I got some techniques from other yogis, still what I do is part of the natural progression of an attentive practice using breath infusion

When I sat to meditate, at first everything was agreeable. The coreSelf adhered to naad sound. Then I saw naad light. Energies in the trunk of the subtle body came up to where the tongue pushed on the soft palate. Then there was a very trivial thought which took my attention. When I looked at it, it was nothing important. I turned away from it. Then another one came. Then I decided that something was amiss. I checked to see what happened. I immediately became glued in naad and immediately saw naad light.

Part 6

Khecari Mudra

This morning I got a message from Lahiri Baba about *khecari mudra* practice. He said that the purpose of it was to draw up the nutritional urges in the subtle body.

What are these urges?

These concern more than just the tasting sense. From the onset as soon as a living entity leaves the causal plane, initially, there arises this need for nourishment. At once a sense grows out of the self which begins to grasp on whatever exists which would provide nutrients for the subtle body. Over time this develops into an organism which seeks fulfillments in whatever environment it happens to find itself.

Naad meditation is the center of this practice. First, naad meditation is a sound current detection and absorption process; then naad meditation with light is established. Then there is the pushing of the tongue back to the soft palate. Then meditation on this, on the three actions of hearing naad, seeing naad light, and making sense contact of the tongue tip to the soft palate.

This last action has within it the tasting sense, the touching sense and the smelling sense, which means that all five senses are capture with the hearing sense captured in naad, and the visual sense capture by naad light in the front of the subtle head, and the other three senses captured at the focal point where the tip of the tongue contacts the soft palate.

If one does a thorough breath infusion beforehand, right before the meditation session, and if the energies of the psyche are uniform throughout, this tongue press back action will result in the causal nutrition sense being arrested which will cause any wayward sensual energies which are outside the grasp of the coreSelf, to be retracted. This is the full arrest of the system which qualifies the student to begin Patanjali's higher yoga process of *samyama*.

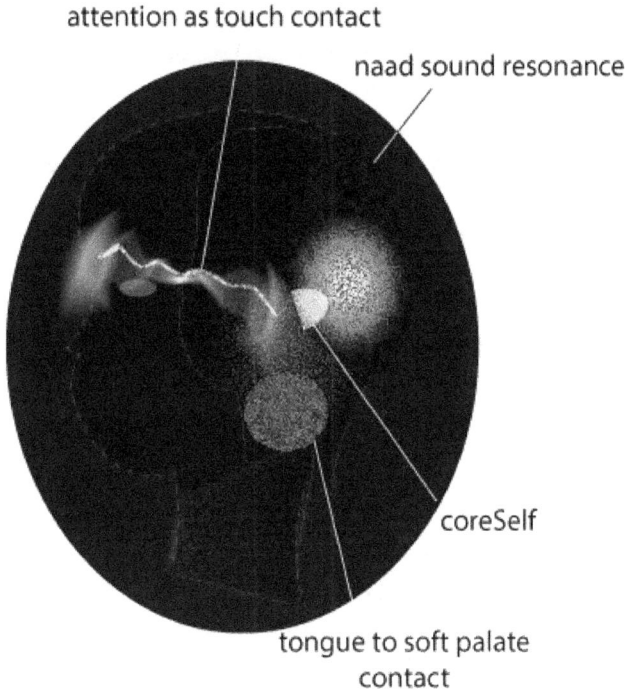

attention as touch contact

naad sound resonance

coreSelf

tongue to soft palate contact

The student keeps this meditation going until *chit akash* sky of consciousness dawns.

Yoga Injuries

Over the years, I was approached by students who got injured doing postures and/or breath infusion. People have this strange notion that there should be no injuries while doing yoga. Their view is that yoga is perfect and should give wellbeing.

However, yoga as in any other bodily and mental exercise may cause injuries at any time, even in the advanced stages. Today I pulled a muscle in the neck while doing a posture I did for many years. This happens.

Yoga is capable of causing both physical and mental if not emotional injury. It is just like everything else we do in this world, where even if you awakened as such and such a person day after day for years, still a time will come when you will awaken no longer. Then what will you say? Who will you blame for the death of your body, especially if it dies from natural causes?

Note the injury. Take steps in the next practice session, if there is another one, to take care so as not to repeat or aggravate it. Some exercises which cause injury can be resumed after the injury heals but some other exercises should not be repeated. You should judge for yourself which exercises you can continue doing after healing and which you should prohibit yourself from performing.

Causal Plane Energy

Lahiri Mahasaya sent another message today about the contact with the causal plane. This place is just outside of the *brahmaloka* situation, which is also known as *satyaloka*.

Instead of waiting for the *chit akash* sky of consciousness to dawn in one's consciousness one can push to accelerate the process of making contact with it by taking energy from the causal plane of existence. This is not the *chit akash* but it is closer to the *chit akash* than any other of the subtle material planes of existence.

What is the kriya?

It concerns first clearing the subtle body so that one can reach at least the *brahmaloka* level of existence. Once one reaches there, one can then do some more breath infusion. That may cause one to reach the causal level of existence. But instead of going out of the subtle body to that causal plane, as some great yogins do, one should remain in the subtle body and pull energy into it from the causal plane.

Sometimes it becomes necessary either through desire or through necessity for a great yogi to leave his subtle body somewhere in some dimension, exit from it and go to the causal plane. The yogi then stays in the causal plane for a time and then comes out again and resumes the subtle form. He appears in this existence again but on a high subtle level.

A yogi is not allowed to remain forever on the causal level but stays there for as long as his previous austerities permit in terms of how long the subtle body can remain in a trance state. It is similar to when a yogi goes into *samadhi* from the perspective of his physical body and then awakens as it suddenly, like when a polar bear wakes after a hibernation phase. Some of it is controlled just by the laws of psychic nature. Some is regulated according to the degree of austerity of the yogi.

This technique is used so that the yogi does not have to go outside of his subtle body to reach the causal plane. In fact, this student yogi as instructed, has no authority to enter the causal level and may not even leave the subtle body to do that. He may bring energy into the subtle body from the causal level. This causes such changes in the subtle body, that the *chit akash* becomes manifested more definitely in meditation practice.

The immediate benefit of having energy from the causal plane in the subtle body is that it loses interest for heavenly life in the celestial world. The substance energy from the causal plane is desire concentrate. When one is in touch with it, one is not attracted to desires in the subtle or physical world.

This does not mean that such a yogi will have no desires but it means that internally he/she has no interest in it even though he may on occasion participate in physical history. This is called manifested attachment with full detachment as its inner force.

A person who lived like this and used a material body was *Vyadha* (vi-ad-huh) a butcher in the *Mahabharata*. Even though he was involved in a vicious most despicable lifestyle, he remained as a liberated soul and was more advanced than *Kaushika*, a brahmin, who followed pure principles and had approved lifestyle.

Gift of Naad Sound and Light

Getting naad sound and naad light are two of the greatest gifts for a student yogi. If one has the perception of these, it does not matter if the universal has a light-out which is when all the suns and stars are no more shining, when the system of galaxies collapsed, when nuclear energy fizzed.

But this is possible only for those who no longer have the need for physical existence. If one enjoys benefit in physical existence, the yield of naad sound and naad light will not have as much value.

It is about value and where that is placed. It is not only the value of an item but the placement of worth in the item by the person.

Take faith for instance. In some cases when people request assistance, I cannot render a worthwhile service because their confidence was invested somewhere else. Still, they may insist on being assisted. They define what that assistance should be. Still, if there is no confidence, they cannot be assisted.

There was a man who needed gold coins. He asked another man how he could acquire the money. The other man told him about a place where he could get paper currency which could be converted into gold coins by bank exchange. It was a faraway place but due to the desire to have the gold coins, the needy person went there.

He spoke to someone who give him a wad of paper currency which was sufficient for the gold exchange but on the way to the bank, the needy man began to think like this.

"Why should I carry this wad of paper? It has no value. This is paper. This is not gold. Who would believe me if I said that I could convert this into coins?"

After thinking like this, he threw the wad of paper currency in a river. He returned to his city. He was satisfied that he did the right thing because he had no faith in paper currency.

Yogis and yoginis, if you have naad sound and naad light, that special combination, you do not need anything else. You can dump unhappiness and trauma. The lights of the universe can go out. There could be darkness in every direction. You will be free of anxiety and satisfied.

The prospect for reaching into the *chit akash* sky of consciousness would be bright. The future would be contained in the palm of your hands. The room in the existential luxury hotel of *chit akash* would be prepared for you.

Time Acceleration/Deceleration

Have you ever noticed that on some days, time seems to go slowly; then on other days it seems to be at the normal rate; while on some others it slips in a hurry?

Do you feel this is only relative to your mind?

Have you read books or heard lectures which describe that everything that happens is in the mind and is dependent on one's mental and emotional configuration; that one can control reality; and that no one or nothing can affect one?

Here is my view:

There are personal factors of psychology which affect how an individual is related to the passage of time. Time is independent of the limited self. It has its own existence which is negligibly affected by the tiny unit person entity. Even though it adds up, still the incremental selves make no big impact and are in fact conveyed in the current of time, the way dust particles are carried in the flow of a tornado. One particle is for sure a part of that flow and contributes to the power of it, but all the same it is not a determinant factor. It is rather a subordinate energy which has irrelevant impact on the total movement.

Besides the minute unit person, there is the colossal time factor which is represented by the celestial bodies like the sun and moon. These influences bear down upon and massively take control of the minute unit persons, dictating to them through circumstance what they can or cannot do, providing and deleting opportunities.

It seems that these heavenly bodies may target one individual so that on a certain day, he has excess time to accomplish his plans; while another individual is frustrated every step of the way despite having expertise and resources.

The individual can cause an increase in accomplishments if he reacts with proficiency when time affords an opportunity. Or he may when time objects to his ideas, relax and not let it invoke a negative attitude. Either way, if he maneuvers effectively or not, time has its way. When it restricts him, he will not have the power to restrain it.

The final say of time is the death of an individual's body in a particular dimension. It is then that there is the closure of direct participation of a limited unit entity in that specific environment. We observed however that some individuals wield influence from other dimensions. They influence the course of history in dimensions in which they lost the privilege of having a material body. They achieve this by influencing the minds of those who have bodies in the dimension to which direct access was denied.

Summary Statement:

Supernatural influences manufacture an ongoing inscrutable time factor in which the limited beings are transported like twigs in a rapid river. Sometimes for a reason which is outside of our scope of understanding, the river slows. Sometimes it seems to stop flowing and remains placid like a lake. Something it moves so fast that we cannot observe what transpires. We become preoccupied being mere sub-particles.

When time facilitates, I am everything or so it seems.

When time opposes, I am just as if I were nothing, or so it feels.

I can observe how time treats others, or that is a perspective I am afforded from time to time.

Time, I conclude, is *supreme*.

Naad Light Distinguished

Psychic Correspondence:

Is there a difference between the speckled darkness seen behind closed eyes in meditation, and the naad light which you frequently describe?

MiBeloved's Response:

There is a difference. Naad light is not the usually speckled darkness seen behind closed eyes. It is not the usual whatever one sees behind closed eyes. Naad light only becomes possible, first of all, when the vision energy is first withdrawn so that whatever is seen behind closed eyes is no longer seen.

To see naad light certain accomplishments are required:

Adherence of naad sound by turning about in the head of the subtle body and facing the back part of it. This must be done for as long as it is necessary so that it becomes a spontaneous practice and so that there is no spring back effect, where as soon as it is done the coreSelf returns to its default position. It must abandon its default position willingly and remain in naad sound.

After this is accomplished the next stage is to retreat to naad sound while facing forward. One must do this and adhere to naad just as if you were glued with superglue some fifty feet up on the outside of skyscraper. You remain glued there and make no exertion to do so. The glue is the adhesive.

It keeps you there. No effort is made to remain there. You cannot move from there. This is why I use the terms *adhere to naad*.

Once this is attained one must be there with introspective eyelids closed. One sees nothing. The vision interest energy is inoperative. One can feel it as when a person feels that the eyelids are closed. One looks forward but sees nothing. One can feel the eyelids, the usual speckled darkness or whatever is there. It can be there if one desires by opening that vision interest energy.

One can hear naad. That is the only perception. There are no chakras except for nodes of naad. There is no sound except for naad. There is no other perception except the vibrational consistency of naad.

Quietly you look forward but you do so with the vision energy closed. There is nothing ahead. Suddenly within the small space between the coreSelf and the covering membrane of the vision energy a light comes. It is a glow light. That is naad light. It begins from where you are in the back of the subtle head, glued into naad. It moves forward slowly. If you allow it, it will spread forward but only behind the vision energy membrane. Outside of the membrane there is the usual speckled darkness or whatever one usually sees.

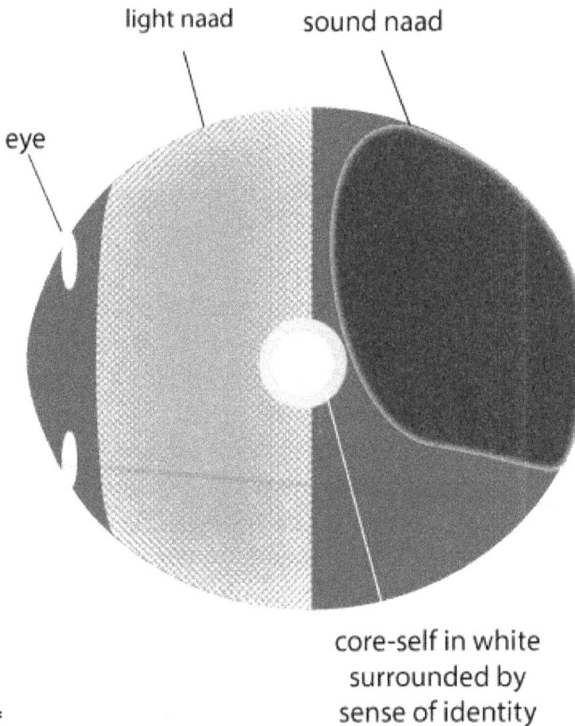

light naad   sound naad

eye

core-self in white
surrounded by
sense of identity

*

You can test this. If you open the vision interest energy to see forward, you will again see the usual speckled darkness or whatever you usually see. You will know that it is different to naad.

Special Note:

I do not recommend that students imitate what I experience. One should work at one's level. The example to follow is to do the practice daily and report what happened in the session. The example is not to imagine my experiences.

Obviously, I am practice on a different level. I have a different history of practice. Even though from time to time the experiences will seem to be similar, one cannot expect that one will have the same experiences. Do not imagine for a second that one has the same senses which I have. There are different species of subtle bodies just as there are different species of bodies in the physical world. Even in the human species there is difference within the species itself. I may have senses that you do not have and cannot develop at this time or for all times. It is unreasonable to surmise that you have every one of my experiences

The repetition of what I do is that I do the practice. I meditate. I report. That is it.

Even if you have the same experiences that does not tell us anything about your insight level and how you can put the experiences to use. Develop yourself along the lines of your individual progression. That is the example to follow.

High-End *Pratyahar* Sensual Energy Withdrawal

Preliminary *pratyahar* means withdrawing the energy which pours out the face of the subtle body in search of fulfillments in the subtle and physical worlds. This energy appears to pour from the coreSelf directly.

Initially one should act within as if one pulls energy back into the coreSelf. However, it is not possible to do this, because the subtle material energy cannot make direct contact with the core no more than a white-hot piece of metal can be grasp by the bare hand of a human being.

That simply cannot occur because the heat of the metal will prohibit the material of the human hand from directly making contact with the metal.

Initially one must act as if the sensual energy pours directly out of the core. This practice does work to stop much sensual energy from pouring out of the face into the subtle and physical worlds, but that is only the beginning stage. And yet for a student that is a major achievement.

What should one do after this initial practice?

The next stage is to settle down and be the coreSelf as one experiences the most inner composite of the psyche. One has to meditate like this for weeks, months or years and reach a place where components of consciousness begin to be segregated. It is one thing to sit in the driver's seat in a car, and drive it here and there. It is another matter to realize that the machine comprises not one something but a composite something of parts.

Is your body beautiful?

Is it ugly?

Is it a cheap product of nature?

Is it precision-manufactured?

Did nature insult you by giving a dumpy looking body, with a big nose, awfully shaped teeth and crude hairy limbs?

Or did nature live up to your expectations by giving a handsome frame which is irresistible and causes other humans to rave about your beauty?

What are the parts of a body?

What are the components of a mind?

What happens when the one you are discovered to be, is a set of parts put together in a haphazard and dysfunctional way?

Pratyahar, the 5th stage of yoga has a place in this practice, where the student perceives the various components of consciousness.

Is that frightening? To discover that you are a set of parts? That what you thought you were and what you were accepted to be functionally, was a composite of various energies and special components?

This morning by the grace of one yoga-guru, I was introduced to another aspect of *pratyahar* practice which is done during the last stages of emptying the used energy of the subtle body and then emptying all energy and replacing that with energy from the highest astral planes and beyond.

This is the technique.

To feed the greedy needs of the face of the subtle body, the entire psyche has to contribute energy which is used to scan the material world for desired objects of sensual consumption. It is not the coreSelf alone which is involved in this contribution of energy. All parts of the psyche are involved, and since the other parts have an existence all by themselves, efforts must be made by the yogi to retract and then reinstall the energy which was continually being confiscated from those parts.

This cannot be done on the lower levels of consciousness because it is not perceptible there. It did not occur there initially. Initially when one was a subtle something in this existence, there were no physical materials. Thus, one has to reach that level of awareness before one can perceive the flow of energy out of the various parts of the psyche into the face of it for sensual exploitation of the world.

When the energy is retracted it will revert to the matching part from which it emanated in the first place. This may be a place in a toe of the form or in the finger and not in the coreSelf, or not even in the kundalini, or not even in the intellect. Wherever the energy originated, that is where it will be retracted to automatically when one reaches that advance stage of practice.

One way to know when one does this practice, is that the energy retracted will cause a narrow spiral of energy to go from the location to which it was retracted through the top of the head into outer space.

Spiritual Senses / Territory of the Real

At present we have no idea of spiritual senses. Our concept of it, the reality of it behind our concept, is the senses of the physical body. For some of us with a little mystic insight, it is the senses of the subtle form.

What are spiritual senses?

- How do they operate?
- Do we have such senses?
- If we do, can we use them?
- If we have spiritual senses, how is it that we are limited to physical and subtle sense perception?

Presently under the tutorship of Lahiri Baba who long passed on from this physical world and whose reputation is legendary in the kriya lineage, I practice an advanced *pratyahar*. If this is not the final practice, then it must be very near to the final situation. It is an abstract process. It has no use for concepts and visualization. This is in the *territory of the real*.

First of all, the student must be anchored in naad sound. Failing to do that for whatever reason, the student must be in the back of the subtle head away from the jurisdiction of the frontal part where the thinking and imaging takes place.

Once established in the back spontaneously, the coreSelf should wait silently for naad light to manifest. This comes either suddenly, like when a switch is thrown to turn on a light, or gradually like when there is a gradual glow of light at dawm. This light remains as a glow, a dim glow. It may come on gradually until it reaches its brightest illumination or it may begin suddenly with its brightest illumination. In either case that brightest illumination is dim light. It is not a blare light. It is not a stunning light which illuminates anything clearly. It is a glow like when the first crack of dawn appears and one can barely distinguish one thing from another.

Once this light dawns, the student should check to be sure that this is not the usual speckled darkness which is seen in the subtle head or in the physical head behind closed eyes in the frontal part of the head. If the student notices that it is the usual situation, he/she should conclude that it is not naad light and it should be abandoned. One should close the vision energy from that usual situation and remain with naad sound vibration only.

If the student verified that naad light is there, the student should remain in naad light while listening to naad sound and remaining stuck fact in naad vibration in the back part of the head.

After this practice is done for some time, weeks, months or years, and the student finds this to be a spontaneous condition just after sitting to meditate, he/she should take up the practice of *khecari mudra* without doing any extreme measures like cutting tissues under the tongue. The only requirement is that at first, one should be in naad sound, then be in naad light, then check to be sure that naad light is not any other light or lights and is naad. The student should roll the tongue up and back to the soft palate.

This action will cause the nutritional-need energy to manifest and with it will come the taste sense, the smell sense and the touch sense. Being that the hearing sense and the vision sense are involved in naad, those other three senses will need to be captured by *khecari mudra*.

Once this pull of the senses occur, where they are pulled to naad and parked there like vehicles in locked garages, the yogi can then study his/her original manifestation into material nature.

How did the manifestation of my individuality occur in the first place? As there is supposed to be a background radiation from the initial time explosion which began this universe, there is energy in the psyche which can give insight into our original condition when first manifested in material nature.

What sort of subtle or supernatural body did I have then?

Did I have limbs and senses like a human body?

If I did how is it that some life forms do not have limbs and pronounced senses.

Did I lose these at some stage?

Did I develop these under the evolutionary pressure which is applied by material nature?

In this respect there is a *pratyahar* celibacy practice that has nothing to do with sex impulse or gender designation. This is the pratyahar practice which restores the even distribution of self energy through the psyche with no stress on any given sense at any time.

It is a total restraint of the survival tendency, rather than of the sexual function.

What happened initially to divest the energies so that there were specific senses and specific pleasure yielding organs like the genitals?

Is the eye pulling energy from the toes and from other parts of the body, so that the eye may see and may range in the subtle or physical environment?

If the eye does this, is it possible to reverse this so as to restore that energy into the toes and other parts and cause the eye to lose its authority over the psyche? Is it possible to have an eye which is not involved in the *hunt capture kill* system of survival?

Naad as Breasts of a Mother

Today's meditation was highlighted by a loving feeling in the arms of naad sound while seeing naad light and also reaching *chit akash* on its very edge.

I realized that I had not adhered to naad as usual. I was curled like a premature baby who the nurse placed near its mother's breast, hoping that the mother would have sufficient interest to feed it, and knowing that such feeding would cause the baby to gain weight quickly.

Am I starved of a mother's breast milk?

As I was there in naad as that infant, naad assumed the feelings in the milk-laden breasts of a loving mother. I reflected on how milk-starved I was. If somehow, a yogi gets some grace from naad or from a deity or yoga-guru, the yogi should take that and use it to make progress and to develop confidence and a sense of security.

If nobody loves me, I am stuck but still as a yogi, I must push ahead. But then if someone, a deity or a divine energy loves me, that is all the better to pull me in the direction of the spiritual atmosphere and release me from the terror of physical existence.

Naad held me in its arms and fed me its breast milk. I was relieved, because here in the physical world, I invest energy to get this practice on the move and to assist others.

Here it is like serving in an orphanage with many neglected infants on all sides. As soon as the nurse pushes a bottle into the mouth of one infant, another one cries:

"Feed me! Feed me! I am hungry. Feed only me. The others are greedy. I am the only one who deserves nourishment. I am the best baby."

In the physical world, there are those who are sympathetic to others. They feel that yogis need a mother.

Really!

Maybe, but from where will this mother come?

From which side of existence?

The first mother which comes from the other side is naad. Why?

Because the yogi is not a phony. He does not have imagined female deities to assist him. He does not have contact with the spouses of the divine lords. They do not live on this side of existence. He does not know if he is directly connected to one of them. Can he even perceive them?

He has naad contact, or stated more precisely, if he has naad contact, naad will be his first divine mother in whose tender loving arms he will curl with the breast energy of naad like the softest most milk-smelling pillow under his little head.

Kundalini Yoga Certification

This is to clarify what kundalini yoga certification is, and how to get it from me or from someone who was trained and is certified by me.

First of all, kundalini yoga concerns the subtle body. It is for targeting and adjusting energy in the subtle body. The physical system is used in this process, but the objective is to affect the subtle form.

You do not have to master the postures to be certified. This process is mostly a breath infusion process on the physical end. It is not so much about postures. Even if a person was expert in postures, say if a person was a gymnast for instance or a contortionist, still that is not kundalini yoga.

You may be strapped down in a wheel chair and I may certify you even though you cannot move the physical body into postures, but that is provided that you can operate your diaphragm to do breath infusion.

The question is:

Why do I teach the use of postures while doing the breath infusion?

The answer is that in the advanced stages of the practice, it is necessary to target specific *hard to reach* areas of the subtle body. To do so one must assume various postures which allow for the infused energy to penetrate those areas.

For the initial certification one does not need to target those parts. It is sufficient to just raise kundalini up the spine into the brain. Therefore no one should feel that the lack of assumption of many postures will disqualify one from certification.

Where the Past is the Present

During the night I had an astral encounter with a lady whom I knew when this body was about 10 years of age in Guyana. I had not seen this lady since around 1965. Right now, she is deceased and was so for many years because her astral body was restructured like when a person is deceased and has become a permanent residence of the astral dimension which is near to this physical existence.

She was all smiles when she saw me, like when one saw a long-lost friend. This lady used a body which was around 50 years of age when my present body was about 10 years of age. She was an elder to me but was not a relative.

In the astral encounter, I found myself as my astral body standing on a street which was about two blocks away from the cottage in which I lived. There, I walked towards a metal gate. The lady came to that gate and walked through the wire without opening the gate. Her astral body ignored the gate as if it did not exist but I knew mentally that she was aware that the gate was there and just found it unnecessary to open it.

She was all smiles. She embraced me and kissed on my cheek, the way the elderly people would greet children affectionately. I was to say something to her when she silenced me and expressed feelings of great satisfaction of seeing me again.

She was happy that I made it through this life and was now on the verge of leaving my body but with accomplishments achieved. After this when she felt satisfied, her astral body and the whole astral dimension which she resides in, disappeared.

There in that place there is no electricity, no mechanical contrivances. There are no automobiles. I saw no animals. I saw nno one else but I could feel other persons there even though they were not visible. There were dirt roads which were smooth. There were vegetation and housing but it was based only on the mental concepts of the persons concerned. There was light like sunlight but there was no sun present. There were clouds and a sky.

Except for the lack of electricity and mechanical contrivances, everything was there as before, as like when I was ten years of age. It was, that the past suddenly become the present, the now, the history reality. In that place it seems that time froze so that the lady lived in a world which was a repeat of what it was like when I was ten years of age. She wanted me to come back to that time and live there as we did as if the past was present time perpetually.

Chit Akash Access

During breath infusion this morning Yogeshwarananda was present. I have no idea about where he is staying in the astral existence or how to contact him there. His energy is such that it seems that he has no particular residence.

He reviewed the condition of my subtle body, and noticed that the kundalini was absent, in the spine. This development was due to some years of effort in that regard.

During the meditation session which followed, he was in the head of my subtle body but his presence there was like a diffused something instead of a miniature form. He said this,

"Everything is here. Break out from here. Pioneer these methods. Leave a trace."

He explained how I should develop a way of reaching the *chit akash* merely from within the psyche and without anyone infusing energy into my psyche from outside.

He showed a procedure which was to be situated in naad, then pulling the nutrition need-energy to the place where the tongue is curled back and touches the soft palate in the back of the throat, and then to be in naad light but to keep the whole experience under wraps in the innermost part of the psyche where the coreSelf is housed. It is like being within that last layer in the very core of an onion and breaking out from there to whatever is outside all other layers.

Gender

If liberation means being without a physical body and the troubles that entrails, then astral existence is liberation but the traditional meaning of liberation is different.

Liberation became a famous word in India because of the efforts of Adi Shankara. As far as I know he spoke of liberation from both the subtle and physical existence, not just from the physical level of it.

Death of the physical body does not mean the end of the problems of the individual limited entity. In the astral existence all the problems we have on the psychological level, like stress and distraught emotions will continue unless we find a way to change the nature and operations of energies in the subtle body. Therefore, death of the physical body will not put an end to the *klesha* mento-emotional afflictions and trauma which attack us from time to time.

The situation of gender does not go away by losing a physical body. In the astral world there is gender. In some astral places there is more sexual intercourse than we can imagine in the physical existence. When one is deprived of a physical body either by self action, suicide, or by being killed by another, or by being killed by a disease, one is still left with gender.

A limited being does not have the power to remove his/her gender, even though there may be alterations in gender and distortions of it or dysfunctionality of it. Gender is like life, in the sense that in a living body you cannot remove the life of it even though you may act in a suicidal way or contact a disease which may threaten the life of the body. So long as the body is alive the life of it is present. Gender is there in some way as a primal basic format irrespective of what we wish to do about it.

It is totally false to propose that with the death of the physical body, the gender of the person will end. I have seen more gender and sex in the astral world, then I ever will see in the physical plane of existence.

Time the Regulator

Whatever one has must be relinquished in time as demanded by time. Time is reliable in that way.

With the support of time, we may achieve something. But all the same, time will see to it that the achievement is demolished.

Who is satisfied with this attitude of time?

Limitations of Sensual Pleasure

This is from the *Knowing and Seeing* by Master Sayadaw:

Questions & Answers 4 (page 140-141)

Question 4.1: Is a bodhisatta, including Arimetteyya bodhisatta, a worldling (puthujjana)? If Arimetteyya bodhisatta is a worldling like us, then at the time for him to come down to become Metteyya Buddha, what is the difference between the conditions for him to become a Buddha and for us?

Answer 4.1: the difference is that his pàramãs have matured, like for our Sakyamuni Buddha as the bodhisatta Prince Siddhattha. Such bodhisattas will for many live have been fulfilling their pàramãs, such as the pàramãs of generosity (dàna-pàramã), virtue (sãla-pàramã), lovingkindness (mettà-pàramã), and wisdom (paꞩꞩà-pàramã). Although they enjoy sensual pleasures, their matured pàramãs push them on to renounce the world. In the last life of every bodhisatta, he marries and has a son; this is a law of nature. I forget the names of Metteyya bodhisatta's wife and son. According to the Theravàda Tipiñaka, no arahant including the Buddha is reborn after his Parinibbàna. Parinibbàna is the end of his round of rebirths. They will not be reborn anywhere.

Take our Sakyamuni bodhisatta: in his last life, before his enlightenment, he was a worldling. How? When he was sixteen years old, he became prince Siddhattha and married princess Yasodharà. They had a son. He enjoyed sensual pleasures for more than thirteen years. He did not have five hundred 140 female deities on his left, and five hundred female deities on his right, but was surrounded by twenty thousand princesses. This is kàmasukhallikanuyogo: enjoyment of sensual pleasures, or indulgence in sensual pleasures.

After he had renounced those sensual pleasures, he practised self-mortifications in the Uruvela forest. After six years of this futile practice, he abandoned it, practised the middle way, and before long, attained enlightenment. After his enlightenment, in his first sermon, the Dhammacakkapavattana Sutta (Turning the Wheel of Dhamma), he proclaimed:

'...kàmesu kàmasukhallikanuyogo hãno, gammo, puthujjaniko, anariyo, anatthasaÿhito.': 'this enjoyment of sensual pleasures is inferior (hãno), the practice of villagers (gammo), the practice of worldlings (puthujjaniko); it is not the practice of the enlightened ones (anariyo); this practice cannot produce any benefit such as Path, Fruition, and Nibbàna (anatthasaÿhito).'

So, in his first sermon the Buddha proclaimed that anyone who enjoys sensual pleasures is a worldling. When he was still a bodhisatta, he too had enjoyed sensual pleasures, that is, with Yasodharà in the palace. At that time, he too was a worldling, because enjoyment of sensual pleasures is the practice of a worldling.

This is not only for our bodhisatta, but for every bodhisatta. There may be many bodhisattas here among the present audience. You should consider this carefully: are these bodhisattas here worldlings or noble ones (ariya)? I think you may know the answer.

MiBeloved's Comment:

This gives insight into the real Buddhist process as compared to what we are told about Buddhism by others. This is directly from the Pali canons and by a teacher who has no motivation to see something cheap as the Buddhist process.

It begs the question as to why the sensual pleasures which are highlighted by sexual pleasure, cannot be serviceable for liberation. Also notice that the term *anariyo* was used also by Krishna when he condemned Arjuna as not acting as an elevated human being *(arya)*.

Eliminating the Need for Physical Bodies

Lord Buddha showed me two balls of energy which he said needs to be shattered in order to eliminate the samsaric need in the psyche. Samsara is the feature of the subtle body through which it has the inborn desire to develop and use physical forms.

This is not an inherently bad feature of the subtle body. In fact it is a good feature but all the same for those who will be siddhas in the near future, this feature should be eliminated. So long as it is in the subtle body, the student yogi has no hope of becoming a siddha, because the subtle body will undermine his/her efforts.

Who is your enemy?

It is certainly not me.

Who is my enemy?

It is certainly not you.

The enemy is housed in the psyche along with the coreSelf. It is present as the coreSelf's inability to control its adjuncts

Bhagavad Gita is about external social behavior and internal order of the coreSelf and its adjuncts but kriya yoga is only about the internal order. In chapter one of the *Bhagavad Gita,* Arjuna was concerned about the external social order. Then we read that Krishna smashed Arjuna's arguments and explained the *buddhi* yoga process in chapter two of *Bhagavad Gita*. Then Krishna explained how to apply the psychological maturity one derived from buddhi yoga to the social order of the human interaction. That process is karma yoga.

Krishna said that he was the only person who could teach karma yoga, because it requires the kind of insight only God has. Moral people who chalk up what is right and wrong, cannot do it. It is complicated. It involves past lives, future lives and the relationship one has with the Universal Form of Krishna. No limited being can successfully figure it. Bhishma who was a supernatural ruler, and Drona who was a leading brahmin and mahayogi could not figure it.

Kriya yoga is not karma yoga. It has no concern with external social order. For the purpose of kriya yoga, one is required to turn one's back on the social order and to lose concern with the standards of behavior which involve that. Kriya yoga cannot begin in earnest unless one turns one's back on the social order and faces the internals head on.

Buddha showed me a ball of energy which is in the lower belly, just above the pubic area. This is a ball of non-sexual energy. It is nutritional energy. This ball is about four inches in diameter. During breath infusion this is like a ball of translucent colored granite.

There is another ball, a small one which is about half inch in diameter. That is at the base chakra at the end of the spinal column. Both balls should be infused with energy until they glow and fracture apart in an explosion where there are billions of bits of it, shattered like pieces of granite, moving outwards in an explosion.

The successful shattering of these balls through breath infusion will in time cause the need for a physical body to be removed. With the absence of that need, the yogi can rest assure that he/she will attain a yoga siddha form.

Resentment and the Yogi

It is important to avoid being with people who are habituated to holding resentment energies in their psyches. If a yogi fails to do this, his spiritual progress will be nil because the resentment energy he absorbs from others will consume his practice potency, the way a dry sponge uses liquids or the way a herd of elephants draw water from a shallow pond.

Even some student yogis are resentful of others, especially of others who are more proficient and others who are well-to-do and who are not yogis but who hold positions of authority in society. These types of students should be regarded as superficial friends only. Their actual interest is to find something to resent and compare in their friends.

I took a day nap today in which I made contact with the subtle bodies of four persons who live in Guyana. These persons were awake on the physical side but thoughts about me flashed through their minds. They thought that I had something to do with some causes of irritation and frustration in their lives. It is not that they considered me to be the cause of the frustration but they felt that I had the power to relieve some of it but I did not do so.

This view is incorrect. I do not have the power. Nevertheless, their mistaken notions about me does nothing to stop the resentment energies and registry in their minds of my association in relation to it.

As soon as I was near these persons astrally, their subtle bodies began to release out a toxic subtle energy which was the pent-up resentments. It was so dangerous that I began to smile and give them some relief energy so as to cause them to relax as the toxic energy was released. Some of the energy entered my psyche. Some of it was released in the atmosphere because that part of the energy was directed to others, some of whom are deceased and some of whom still use physical bodies.

Even though I did this, my advice to student yogis, is that they should not do this. If you can avoid such persons and make no contact with their toxic energies, it is in your interest to do so.

When at last you leave this body one more time, for good, and cannot get back into it even if you feel you should, be sure to avoid contact with such persons in the astral domains.

Yoga Results

Yoga pays off even if one follows the wrong method but this is provided that one is consistent and loyal to whatever practice one uses. It may be that one follows the incorrect method or the correct one in the wrong way with the wrong motivation but even then, if one is consistent one will reach an impasse where one will say to oneself that it is not working because of this or that defect.

If one is sincere, sooner or later a proficient teacher will come with a valid method. Then because one is serious one will adjust without complaint. One will apply oneself in earnest. But then again it will happen that one made a mistake. Then again one will do that for some time. Then again, a proficient teacher will render advice. This will go on for a time, until one reaches a stage where one is on course and nothing can stop the progress.

There is a lesson to learn from wealthy people who are obsessed with finances day and night. They always think of amassing more and more money. Even if they make millions of dollars and get into a leverage position, still they are never satisfied. After the first million, they act as if that amount is irrelevant. They create more business methods to cheat more unfortunate human beings.

One should keep on with the objective of yoga no matter what, no matter the failure, the wrong methods, the incompetent gurus, whatever, the aches, the pains and restrictions involved. Keep on keeping on with the practice come what may, just as the money-hungry persons do in the quest for more wealth.

Thighs in Kriya Yoga Practice

In a way the sexual facilities of the body are the most open, most emphatic part of the psyche but in another way these areas are completely sealed and are non-observable. In higher yoga the sealed non-observable aspect is revealed.

How so?

Unless one breaks open the sealed and very abstract operations which are behind the sex facility, one cannot reach the chit akash. This little secret was explained by Lahiri in terms of so much misleading information which is found in the yoga discourses.

To get to the thighs one must break open and keep open the sexual area sealed configuration which keeps one out of interest about what happens in the thighs of the subtle body. Most students are concerned with meditation in the head of the subtle body. Some are concerned with meditation in the chest of the form.

What do they know about meditation in the thighs of the form?

The sexual facility is like a prison, a maximum security one, which keeps the thighs off limits to the entity who uses the body. Keep the thighs, the way an army keeps its food supply. The sexual facilities live by taking energy from the thighs. It has no intentions of allowing the coreSelf to penetrate. No army unless it is careless and inexperienced, will allow its enemy to access its food supply.

Thus, if the yogi can successfully bash apart the sexual facilities, he/she may then get into the thighs and raid the food supply of the enemy. Eventually a firm occupation can take place where what was the main stay of the enemy becomes the mainstay of the coreSelf.

Religion in the Astral Regions

Last night astrally, suddenly, I found myself as the astral body, floating down from the sky to a place in Guyana, where a man sponsored a religious ceremony. I became aware of myself as the astral body floating down to a astral dirt roadway, as I was about to walk to a house where a religious function was held. My astral body knew where the house was.

As my astral body touched the astral ground, I saw four Guyanese women whom I knew. They chatted and laughed but were in a hurry as if they were late for the function. Two of the women glanced my way and smiled.

They wanted to say something but they were pressed for time and had that, "We will see you later," look on their faces.

By this time, they were at the back part of the house where the assistant family members go to assist with cooking and serving.

Realizing that the function already started because I could see people sitting under the house for it, I hurried but I realized that my shirt was not buttoned sufficiently. My pants were not fixed as they should be. This was a Vedic ceremony which is called a *hawan*, meaning that in this ceremony there would be ghee, grains and herbs, offered to a fire which was sanctified with Vedic mantras.

There was a sound from a loud speaker even though there was no loud speaker, no electricity in that astral place, nothing. It was the mental desire being manifested for a loud sound. The man who sponsored the function called out, "Where is Michael? We need Michael. He should come to the fireplace."

Then another voice sounded loudly, saying, "There will be no start for this until he arrives. Let me go and see if I can locate him."

Then from the area where the fire was to be lit, the sponsor walked towards me. At the same time, the other person who was among the people sitting on the floor, got up and walked towards me. Seeing them I hurriedly fixed my clothing.

Then instantly the three of us were transported back under the building where the other people sat. I offered the customary greeting of bowing down on the ground to the two persons as was fitting for those who are elderly. The two men are both deceased and were brothers in the most recent life.

The one who sponsored the function was younger. The elder was a man who did many religious functions as a priest and teacher of Vedic information. He had a school in Guyana where he taught Hindi and the singing of the *Ramacharita Manas* chowtals.

He was an alcoholic. It is a hell of a thing, and in fact it is admirable, how a person can be stone drunk at a religious function, then be asked to speak and speak perfectly about a religious topic despite being blasted out of his mind.

Before this experience, I was at another astral location in Guyana with my deceased father. He was a teacher at a school, which portends in a way, that in his next life he will not be a sailor. He taught some students at an astral school but he wanted to discuss with me the factor of the percentage of homosexual males in society today. His view is that proportionately there was a large increase in the number of homosexuals to say before 1962.

I did not make a remark. He did not request my opinion. He wanted to state his observations. He wondered of what percentage of the boys he taught would declare themselves with homosexual preference.

Love in Yoga

Love in yoga is about the process of yoga and the teachers who show us how to apply the process. For instance, there are instructions in Patanjali *Yoga Sutras* about clamping down on and completely ridding the self of the *chitta vritti* mento-emotional operations. The statement is there but still one may need to get firsthand information from someone who is proficient doing this.

To make a nuclear bomb may seem to be simple if you read about it in a science journal, and still it is not as simple as the instructions given there. One will need to have a practical physicist on hand to give pointers.

Even for those persons who are advaita vedantis, even for the nihilistic Buddhists, there is the necessary step that they must take help from other persons. On one hand they advocate and are convinced that persons are illusion. They are not persons, they say, *anatta (anatma)*. And still they go to persons to get information about how to remove illusion. Can you imagine how essential persons are, that even though on one hand I may be convinced that there are no persons and that all individuality is illusion, and that there is only oneness without differentiation, still I should go to some person for information about a process for the realization of my conviction?

In the systems, in those where there is a conviction that there is a personGod, and in those where there is the idea that there is no such person, there is necessity to relate to a teacher and the process taught.

Love in yoga means that sincere relationship with the process and the teacher.

Brahmarandra Meditation Permission

Yogeshwarananda came this morning. He gave permission for a meditation in the bell housing of the *brahmarandra* chakra.

Why is his permission necessary?

Anyone can meditate on *brahmarandra chakra* if that person knows where it is located, or if that person can perceive it in one way or the other. Even persons who cannot perceive it and who merely visualize it based on information they get from others or from a book, can make the attempt to meditate on it.

Guidance from a yoga guru however should not be underestimated. A guru if he/she is proficient, can pilot the student for rapid success.

Yogeshwarananda wanted a relocation of the coreSelf into the bell housing of the *brahmarandra top of the head* chakra with naad sound adhering to the coreSelf. As soon as I did this, I noticed a glow light from brahmarandra which is brighter than the naad sound light. I will do that meditation for a time, until other instructions are provided.

Brahmarandra Kriya

In meditation this morning I returned to the kriya which concerns the coreSelf floating into the *brahmarandra* bulb which is on the inside top of the subtle head.

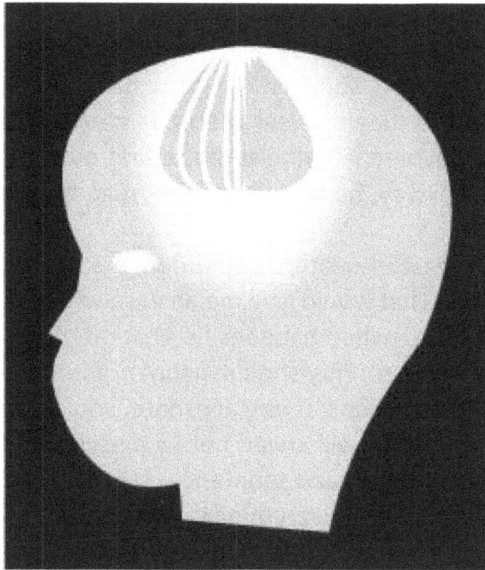

First the student must secure the coreSelf in naad sound. The breath infusion practice should be done just before this and there should be effects so that there is no chatter in the mind.

Once the student stops the infusion and sits to meditate, there should be an automatic adhering to naad sound. If this is not so, one should not do this practice but should instead become resolved to adhere to naad by doing more naad absorption.

Whatever an advanced student does is practical for him/her. That is not useful for the novice except in the future. A student should take note of what the advanced yogi does so that in the future the student can apply that process but in the immediate sense what the advance person does has value only as a notation.

Suppose I am dead tomorrow, as people would normally say, which really means that I become absent from the social history of the earth, then how will a novice reach me for instructions?

That will be possible only for those students who have keen mystic perception. All others must rely on what I wrote about the advanced practice. I am not the only yogi who practice advanced kriya, but it may be that I am one of the few who take the time to jot down the methods. In anticipation of the need for advanced kriyas, I took the precaution to jot down my practice sessions and give details.

All the same wherever I would be I do not want to have afterthoughts about what I did not do to leave notations. No one should think,

"He was a yogi. We heard of him. Who knows where he is? Concerning all the bad things he did, it could be hell. It could be heaven, considering that he did some good. Maybe God will wait to punish him. Maybe he became nothing or merged into the universal energy as nothing. We had the feeling that he was a fake devotee, an atheist of the first order. Who knows where he is located? But anyway, he was decent because he left the information. God bless his soul."

In this way at least in death, I could derive some good energy, some goodwill from others. That would give me an ease wherever I may be.

In the meditation, what happens is that at first, there should be adherence to naad sound. This should happen without effort. You sit to meditate. You find that as soon as you are there, you are in naad, being kept there by some force, not by willpower, not by a psychological action of your own. The coreSelf is there in naad spontaneously.

Then you make sure that everything is in order.

You are in naad, you look around and you realize, "I made it. It is just like he said, just me and naad. This works. No thoughts, the nuisance mind stopped. This is it. I am a yogi"

Once there in naad the coreSelf should attempt to move into the top of the head. This means either a jump action or a gradual shift to that location. Once there, the core should stay put.

At first it is just the location which is of interest, like when you move from one place to another, from one building to another. Then once you are there, you check to see if you can stay there. Is the coreSelf feeling that it has to go somewhere else?

If it does, you should hold on there and resist that feeling?

Or should you return to the back of the head in naad?

To settle this one should speak to the yoga guru or just make a decision on one's own and execute it.

Once you can stay at the top of the head with the naad sound in tow, the next stage is to be fully there. What does this mean?

It means to adhere there just as you did in the naad practice before, where you were in naad sound and there was nothing besides that.

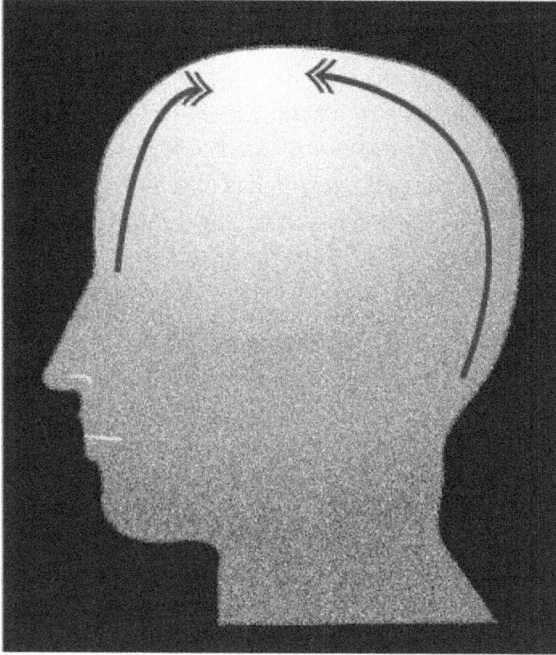

Shivananda on Astral Heavens Transit

During practice this afternoon, Shivananda appeared, floating in the sky in a very colorful astral body, which had pastel colors. He was in a jovial mood but wanted to confront me about people thinking that he was an impersonalist.

He said,

"Why not defend me when people suggest that I am an impersonalist?"

I replied,

"What is the use of defense if someone read your books and got the idea from there, or if someone goes to your ashram and gets the idea from there. A defense would appear pretentious."

He then said,

"If anyone asks you, at least you should state that I am not an atheist. Krishna is my prime deity. I wrote favorably about Krishna, who is dear to me."

I replied, "Yes, Guruji. I know your position, if someone asks, I will explain that the Swami status from Shankara's lineage required certain philosophical positions but that does not mean that Swami is an atheist."

Shivananda then changed the subject, even though I know that he felt that I should forcefully denounce anyone who feels that he is an impersonalist and that he is not fully convinced of Krishna in the *Bhagavad Gita*.

He began talking about how to shift from Indra's heavenly world *(Indraloka)* to the *Maharloka* place, which is the lowest of the higher heavenly worlds. There is above *Indraloka*, *Maharloka* and then *Janaloka* and then *Tapaloka* and then *Satyaloka* which is also called *Brahmaloka*, meaning the residence of the Brahma deity (not the brahman world nor brahman effulgence).

This what he said about jumping from *Indraloka* to *Tapaloka*:

A yogi must be proficient in the complete pull-up test and must transcend the opposite gender of his/her body. Generally speaking, a male yogi has to cause the success of at least one female disciple, because that shows that he knows what he is doing through and through.

The female psyche has different motivations for doing yoga. Even though for males, motive is important, for females usually it has little, if any, significance. For them it is the ability to listen. It is not a matter of motive or reason for them. It hinges on the ability to listen to someone who can give them the techniques which would elevate them beyond Indra's world.

Males may think their way out of Swarga but females must feel their way from there.

MiBeloved's Comments:

If a yogi goes to the Swarga angelic world after death, his chances of going higher are just about nil.

Why?

Because the situation there pilots the yogi to exploiting pleasure energies in all shapes and forms.

A few yogis however do go higher. They go to the first of the highest astral planes which is called Maharloka. When such a yogi gets that transit, he smiles and considers that the Swarga angelic world is comparable to a ghetto. Then he considers what an animal he was to be enthralled by such a place.

A dark damp dingy mold infested cupboard is heaven to a cockroach.

There are some paragraphs from Buddhist Master Sayadaw book, *Knowing and Seeing*, page 148, which are relevant to this discussion:

He wrote this about a Buddhist yogi, based on stories from Lord Buddha's life.

If he does not get the chance to listen to the Dhamma from Dhamma-teaching devas, he may get the chance to meet friends who were fellow meditators in his past human life in a dispensation. Those fellow meditators may say, for example: 'Oh friend, please remember this and that Dhamma which we practiced as bhikkhus in the human world.' He may then remember the Dhamma, and if he practices Vipassanà, he can attain Nibbàna very quickly

But a paragraph which is in the printed version, is missing from the online pdf of this book, it reads this:

An example of a lesser Steam-Enterer who was reborn in the deva realm, and who attained Nibbàna very quickly afterwards, is the Venerable Samana-Devaputta. He was a bhikkhu who practiced samatha-vipassana earnestly. He died when practicing, and was reborn in the deva realm. He did not know he had died, and continued meditating in his mansion in the deva realm. When the female devas in his mansion saw him, they realized he must have been a bhikkhu in his previous life, so they put a mirror in front of him and made a noise. He opened his eyes, and saw his image in the mirror. He was very disappointed, because he did not want to be a deva; he wanted only Nibbàna.

This statement is very important. Can you understand it and put it into perspective in terms of your present yoga practice?

There is no statement in the book that this ascetic attained the Swarga angelic world. It only says the deva world. I am saying that it is the Swarga world because of the situation of how the female residents of that place approached him. For one thing he did not know that he was transferred into that world and that his physical body passed on because he left that body in a samadhi before it was deceased.

After leaving that body, his astral form grafted into the dimensional existence which is known as the *swarga* world. There he automatically got a palatial residence and consorts of the angelic type. Note that he did not realize that his astral body was transformed. The angelic women realized that he was deceased from physical existence but knew that he was unaware of the transit of his astral form into their world. They knew how to shift him from *samadhi* into that world.

So as to not confuse him they put an astral mirror before him so that he would know that he was now an astral body and was no longer a yogi ascetic in rags doing austerities as recommended by Buddha.

By making a certain sound, they disturbed the *samadhi* and jolted him so that his focal consciousness was synchronized into the *deva* world of Indra. These females were to be his consort there but when he opened the eyes of that body and saw the reflection of his appearance there, he was shocked and disappointed. He immediately realized that he failed to reach the territories of the Buddhas, the *Tushita* heavens.

This is unusual because normally after death, a yogi would be happy to be in the *swarga* heavenly world where he would be awarded several consorts who are angelic women of incredible beauty.

Because this yogi was highly indoctrinated in the philosophy of Buddha, he could not regard the *swarga* place as being fit for habitation. He was frightened that he transited to that place. His physical body died before he could attain the higher place which he aspired for. His subtle body was only energized to the level of the *swarga* angelic world.

Shivananda made a joke by asking me which or how many females I could elevate beyond the Indra world. It is both a joke and a serious consideration. A yogi must know however that first he should secure his release. Then he may consider others. A yogi is not a bodhisattva who feels that he must release others before he can gain release for himself.

First you save yourself. Then if you are commissioned you may assist others.

Self or CoreSelf

Email correspondence:

Is the self and the coreSelf the same?

MiBeloved's Response:

It depends on how self and coreSelf are defined. In normal usage they are not the same. In normal usage self is the psyche of the coreSelf. Or stated differently self is the coreSelf + adjuncts+ a psychic container (subtle body).

Normally in New Age philosophy, the self is not the self but is the container + the coreSelf + its adjuncts. However, one may not realize that there is a unit spiritual self plus psychic adjuncts and that the subtle body is a container for these.

When one meditates on the self and realizes the inside of the so-called self, what/who is within the self?

Usually when someone claims to meditate by going into the self, this is a misnomer in the sense that what the person really does, is focus within the subtle body (the container for the coreSelf and its adjuncts). Because this coreSelf is naturally fused and synchronized with adjuncts, it does not realize the fusion. It feels that it is the container or subtle body with the contents.

Thus, when someone says he/she goes into the self, the real meaning is he/she focuses within the subtle body, not within the coreSelf.

Consider me. Consider my house. Suppose when I go into my house, lock the doors and shutter the windows, I declare that I entered me. What would that mean? Did I really enter into my body the way a virus would? Or did I merely enter my house and felt that this was a meEntry (me-entry). When one meditates and restricts one's focus within the subtle body, within one's feelings and emotions, this may not be entry into the coreSelf but entry into the container which houses the core and its adjuncts.

What happens to that individual after losing the astral body?

If the astral body is destroyed and the individual is not released to a divine world, a spiritual world, that coreSelf spirit which used that astral form enters into what is called the bodiless state.

This is not really a bodiless state but it is described as such because we speak in reference to having a subtle body with pronounced limbs and senses. There is a verse in the *Yoga Sutras* which mentions that state.

बहिरकल्पिता वृत्तिर्महाविदेहा ततः प्रकाशावरणक्षयः ॥ ४४ ॥
bahiḥ akalpitā vṛttiḥ mahāvidehā tataḥ
prakāśa āvaraṇakṣayaḥ

bahiḥ – outside, external; akalpitā – not manufactured, not artificial, not formed; vṛttiḥ – operation; mahā – great; videhā – bodiless state; tataḥ – thence, from that, resulting from that; prakāśa – light; āvaraṇa – covering, mental darkens; kṣayaḥ – dissipation, removal.

By the complete restraint of the mento-emotional energy which is external, which is not formed, a yogi achieves the great bodiless state. From that the great mental darkness which veils the light, is dissipated. (Yoga Sutras 3.44)

Even though this is great for these yogis, it means existing as nothingness in nothingness. For others who do not have the degree of insight perception of the great yogis, they remain in this state by force of cosmic destiny. When a universe begins again, they discover themselves as subtle bodies. They begin the history of actions again *(samsara)*.

Transfer of Instinctive Confidence

Confidence, faith, trust are real aspects of nature. These cannot be abolished merely by stating that one is independent of everything or that one is connected *(samyoga)* with everything.

Reliance is one thing which we will never eliminate. So long as there is a you and there is a me, reliance will be engaged.

In teaching yoga, one should be careful not to interfere with the instinctive confidence of others, even those who come as students but who cannot possibly transfer confidence from other aspects of belief to the yoga. If a teacher adjusts the trust energy of a student before the student evolves sufficiently, there will be a backlash from nature as it enforces the old application of faith.

It is experienced, that some students come. They express faith in the yoga process as it was delivered by Patanjali or as it was explained by Krishna. Then these students go away and resume old habits which are counterproductive. This happens because they did not evolve sufficiently from the old applications of faith.

Nature is not concerned to protect anyone from folly. In fact, it may encourage foolishness and impracticality. It does this by reinforcing a person's confidence/trust energy even when it is being applied to something which will frustrate the individual.

Why does nature give this support even to impractical ideas, which it knows it will not honor?

Perhaps nature *(prakriti swarupa)* itself should speak the answer.

Naad Stabilization

Suppose that suddenly there was confusion within the physical body, where the heart decided that it would operate like the liver and the spleen decided that it should abandon its duties. What chaos would that be?

In the field of medical science, physicians struggle with the chaotic activity which occurs in the bodies of patients. But the same thing occurs within the mind, where the energy configuration may be obstructive to higher meditation.

Is a healthy body and mind, your God-given or nature-assigned right?

Were you supposed to go through your life without a hitch, with everything in order at all times?

Why do some persons fall apart even with a little stress while others welcome more anxiety with open arms?

Breath infusion practice this morning was as usual, very interesting. The thing some students do not get is that you have to make the practice interesting by plowing your mind into it, by investing your interest in it. Doing the practice, because you are told to, is not enough. You may begin practicing with that instruction from a teacher but at some stage, you must have an interest in the practice. If a deep interest does not come naturally you may have to push your interest into it.

During the practice, Lahiri beamed himself into my psyche using a supernatural shadow form. He said this:

> There is another method, which is to reach there by going downward. If the yogi penetrates through all nadis, even those in hard to reach places, that will cause him to contact the causal plane and beyond.

After the infusion session, I sat to meditate. At first, I was with naad sound at the back of the head. After feeling stabilized there, I transferred to the top back center of the head. Then I moved to the *brahmarandra* area. All the while I checked to be sure that naad was by my side.

When I first entered the crown chakra, I pulled back and closed the visual interest energy. This causes a glow light to appear. It is better to say that I transited to another plane where a glow light is evidenced.

Part 7

Which Self?

The practice of pratyahar, if completed successfully, gives the student the insight into how the energy is generated and how it is sent out of the psyche into the external world to hunt for procurements which can be enjoyed. Keen observation of how this occurs, gives the student some insight into the psychic components. He/she realizes that there are psychic components and the coreSelf links to these and synchronizes with these or are linked to these and is forcibly synchronized with these to create a composite self or person, a social utility.

To understand what happens when one realizes the self in this way, study the teachings of Ramana Maharshi and those of Visarga Datta. These individuals explained that the bare self has nothing to do with the psychic adjuncts like kundalini, memory and intellect. In this usage kundalini is the sensual energies of the subtle and physical body combination (psychological stuffs essentially).

What is the self?

If the person, the social person, is a composite reality, then in that configuration what is the self *(atma)*?

You sit to meditate which according to Patanjali is *samyama* or the three higher states of yoga in one sequential development, but have you mastered pratyahar sensual energy withdrawal. If you did not, then we may question the validity of Patanjali. If the 5th stage of yoga is unnecessary, why did he not declare that?

If one is successful to reach a *samadhi* state, one will have separated from the social memory from this life. Therefore, when one comes out of the *samadhi* one will need to again reconnect with that social memory. In some persons this reconnection occurs instantly. In others it will not happen in that way. For a time, those persons are spaced-out. Then over time they again feel like the normal social self with the skills developed as that person in this life.

Let us consider what may happen in a dream. I dreamt that I met a beautiful woman but when I resumed my physical self, I could not recall meeting her in the physical world.

When I met this beautiful woman in the dream, I forgot my life here on earth, where I am married and have a family with several children. There is no way that on earth, I could have a love affair with a beautiful woman other than my wife because it would ruin my prestige and destroy my sense of honor. And yet in the dream I went into a bedroom and was sexually involved with the beautiful woman. When I was in that dream, I did not know myself as I know myself in this physical existence. I had no wife there, no children, nothing. It was just me, a person who was fully absorbed by the beautiful astral woman.

When I first came back to being myself as the physical body, I did not remember my wife here or my children. It took about three minutes before I got my bearings and knew who I was. Then inside the mind, I was shocked to compare the loving feelings I had for the astral woman because those feelings were more intense than the feeling I have for my spouse in this world.

Question is:

Where was my composite earth self when I was with the astral woman? I know it was not destroyed, otherwise I could not resume it after three minutes when it again came into focus and I acted as I normally do in this world.

What was the process through which I again became that composite person with the skills and status which I earned?

In the astral dream where did I get the identity to be the lover of the beautiful woman? Over there in the astral dimension, the woman acted as if she knew me all along even though she just met me. How did I become the composite personality who was the lover of that astral being?

Samadhi?

It is legendary. Every half-baked yogi, craves it.

There is such a thing as stupor *samadhi (jada samadhi),* where a person enters into a trance and comes back into ordinary consciousness without insight.

If I enter *samadhi* and become disconnected from my composite person parts, then if I lose memory or when I return to physical centering, I would be out of it for a time, until nature (or whatever psychic agency) reconnects me to the earth memory and skills.

But at least the stupor *samadhi* can help us to realize that the *atma* (coreSelf) is different to the social additives which make for the present earthly identity. The person that I am known as presently is a composite. The *atma*, the bare coreSelf, the inmost layer of identity, is a reality unto itself. But others say there is no core. Regardless, we know that there must be a core in this case, because two distinct person composites operated, one in the dream and the other when the dream was over and I was back as the physical person.

Twittering Shingles Kundalini

This morning during breath infusion, there was a twittering shingles of white light with a camphor colored hue emitting bliss cramps in the forearms and elbows.

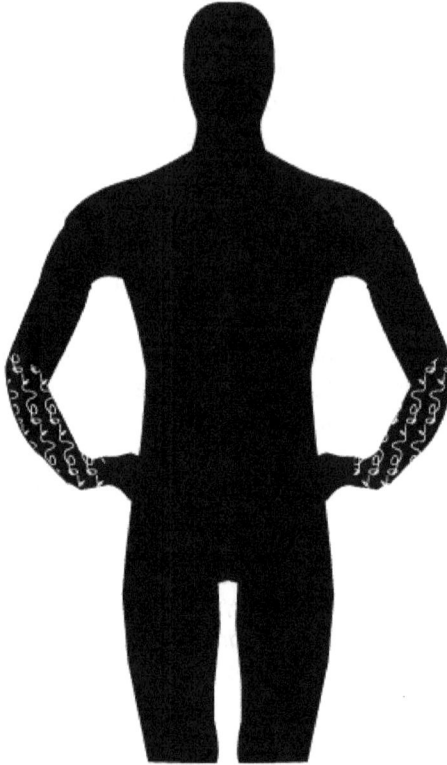

This was due to breath infusion into those parts of the body, even though I did not direct the energy there. In some instance, the energy goes here or there but when it reaches *hard to reach* areas, into unknown or unrealized *nadis* this is much appreciated by the yogi, because this means that the entire subtle body is filled with light, not just the head and spine regions of it.

That is a big deal because it means reorientation to a subtle form which has bliss potential in every part. That frees the yogi from the conditioning to sexual and other specific types of pleasure orientation.

Apsara Angelic Being

During breath infusion practice, on the subtle side, I was approached by an *apsara* (up-suh-raa) angelic lady who is currently using a physical body. This person came to learn the breath infusion.

This is expected for a yogi who is proficient in yoga practice. In fact, at the time of death of the body, there may be hundreds of such angelic beings approaching but mostly these will be persons who are permanent residents of the *swarga* angelic heavenly astral places.

There are various classes of angelic beings and the *apsara* are one class. Some of these take birth as human beings for a time, hoping to gain access to yoga practice, so that they can elevate themselves to higher worlds which are beyond the *Indraloka* place.

This particular person who approach was not seen by me physically for over thirty years. She followed a religious path from India but it panned out. Realizing that she was not progressing and seeing others fail who followed it, she had doubts. This inspired her to see me astrally about a year ago.

I was not interested in convincing her about the breath infusion process because anyone, whom I convince of it, may be a responsibility, which may well if I fail at it, become a dead weight around my neck.

There is uncertainty for every swimmer who is out there in the middle of the Pacific. Thinking that as such a swimmer one can save others is sheer folly. Every added person is another weight around the yogi's neck and that sure decreases his chances of survival out there floating in the middle of nowhere. It does not matter how good a boat one is in nor how good a swimmer one may be. If a storm is manifested, and if it is powerful enough no boat will survive it, what to speak of loading it with many passengers.

I did notice in the psyche of this person an energy of delay and reliance, which means that her subtle body has an energy to remain in the astral world in delay just in case she leaves her physical body before I leave mine. She does not want to use her pious credits to go to *swargaloka* heavenly places. Somehow, she generated a delay energy so that she could meet me after I leave my body if I leave after her.

If perchance I should leave my physical form before she leaves, she has an identity energy in his subtle form which will cause her to appear to me no matter where I may be. In that statement where means somewhere in the astral domain.

In her mind, she hoped that I would not qualify to enter the *chit akash* sky of consciousness because that would be inaccessible to her. That illustrates a problem with disciples where they may wish bad things for the teacher, just so that they can access him/her.

Samadhi Adjustment

For efficiency, a person who leaves a *samadhi* state, should do so with full consciousness focus over into whatever. In some cases, there will be a delay as the lifeForce in the body takes time to reconnect the coreSelf with the appropriated psychic perception equipment which is necessary for functioning in the dimension the person finds himself/herself to be in.

If the lifeForce fails to connect the coreSelf to the equipment, the person will be lost for a time. This may be considered to be due to a lack of mastership of kundalini yoga or the cultivation of an efficient relationship with the kundalini which controls the sleep-wake cycle of the physical body and the synchronization and resynchronization of the subtle body into the physical.

This problem would be solved by mastery of kundalini yoga. Gorakshnath taught *hatha* yoga as kundalini yoga where the kundalini is subdued and transformed so that it does not put the self or the psychic equipment into a lull.

There is a story from the life of Buddha which may give insight into advanced *sattva guna samadhi*. This is told by Master Sayadaw on page 148 of his book, *Knowing and Seeing*. On the basis of the Pali cannon literature about Buddha, Sayadaw wrote:

> *An example of a lesser Steam-Enterer who was reborn in the deva realm, and who attained Nibbàna very quickly afterwards, is the Venerable Samana-Devaputta. He was a bhikkhu who practiced samatha-vipassana earnestly. He died when practicing, and was reborn in the deva realm. He did not know he had died, and continued meditating in his mansion in the deva realm. When the female devas in his mansion saw him, they realized he must have been a bhikkhu in his previous life, so they put a mirror in front of him and made a noise. He opened his eyes, and saw his image in the mirror. He was very disappointed, because he did not want to be a deva; he wanted only Nibbàna.*

Here we read of a person who was in *samadhi* and who was unaware that his physical body died in this world. He became consciousness in the *Swargaloka* heavenly place to which his subtle body was transferred. But as soon as he became conscious there, he knew what was what and what he should do which was to complete the austerities to attain liberation. He did not space out for a moment and had his faculties with him.

If a yogi does not master kundalini yoga, then his sitting to meditate may not yield the insight consciousness which is required for prompt assumption of purpose and duties after a *samadhi* state.

Incidentally *vipassana* really means *vi-pashyana* which is insight. *Pashya* is from the Sanskrit for seeing and *vi* qualifies the perception as supernatural vision.

Pleasure Starved

Currently we are spell bound by a few pleasures. We do everything in our power to procure these, on the individual, familial, national and global levels. What are these sensual pursuits which keep us attached?

At birth of the body, it begins with the quest for air, the subtle and very abstract quest to devour the atmosphere.

Soon after this, once the air is procured, we focus on food, as a liquid drawn out of the mother's breast or the artificial nipple of a bottle.

Then we crave to have the company of the mother, the touch of her skin.

Then we aspire to play and make demands on the world in which we found ourselves to be conscious.

This is how it began, this quest for pleasure.

When will it end?

At the death of the body, will another phase of this begin?

Practicality of Patanjali's Method

Patanjali, though long departed is one of our yoga gurus, so much so that even though he existed years prior, still his instruction is effective in our lives just as if he was physically present. That is the potency which we feel from his *Yoga Sutras*.

It is not necessary to become Patanjali to derive benefit from his method. Someone else who is not Patanjali but who is attuned to his instructions can make progress just the same and advance along the guides and syllabus established by him.

In regards to kundalini yoga, the mastery of it is attained over time by any sincere student who has a capable teacher or who does not have a teacher but who has the required psychic sensitivity to study the movements of kundalini in the psyche and then put checking influences on it.

Mastery can be attained even if one is not as powerful as the opponent. This is done by careful study and implementation of a method which will eventually cause one to overpower the opponent.

In the *Srimad Bhagavatam (Bhagavata Purana*, Canto 4), we hear that when Narada describe kundalini to King Prachinabarhi, Narada said that Puranjan, a great king, was occupied enjoying the features of the human body but did not pay attention to the five hooded serpent which was the maintenance agent in the city of *Bhogavatee*.

From that we learnt that if we were attentive to the kundalini, we would in time take control of its territory, the psyche, and then over time we would control it properly.

First you must somehow procure an able teacher, who mastered kundalini and then get a method from that person. This teacher could be long dead and gone like Patanjali, or he/she may be using a physical body. It does not matter if the teacher is dead or alive, because in every case, of being deceased or of using a physical body, the entity is spiritual existent and can be reached for advisories.

Hell Visits Heaven

I am presently at a house where there are indoor dogs and cats. It is very interesting to see how these animals live, in a physical heaven, where they have no jobs, very little responsibilities and where they enjoy air conditioning and as much foods as they can gobble.

Why did this happen to these animals, when millions of human beings long for these privileges? If human beings are so important why it is that nature did not afford everyone these basic luxuries. The animals have no jobs, earn no income, sleep when they desire, get affection from their owners and enjoy lying on soft couches. They do not have to clean what they excrete or soil. They live like aristocrats who have servants.

Are these animals the ancestors of these owners, but in animal bodies?

But there is another more interesting part to this, where one of the animals spends more than half of its waking hours biting and scratching its skin. I spoke to the owner about it. He was aware of the condition and once gave the animal a medication which seems to relieve the dog for twenty hours, after which it promptly began the biting scratching engagement again. It has to contort itself to get to some itchy areas. It could not reach because its limbs do not allow it to access those places.

That reminded me that no matter what, whatever irritation, whatever trauma, one is due to have, it will come to one even in heaven. One cannot escape. Nature plays its game with precision, where if you are to be in a heaven in the maximum comfort, if it feels that you should suffer some anyway, it will make sure that in your heaven you see some hell.

Imagine what it would be like to be in the position of this itchy-skin dog, where you are in luxury and have every comfort and all the food your little heart desires, and still you have some other irritable condition which absorbs your attention so that the luxury cannot be enjoyed fully.

Is that the life?

Will my desires for the best, always be spliced with some of the worse?

Spiritual Body Orientation

Yesterday I continued a breath infusion procedure which I cultivated for some time. This is where the yogi takes control of the psyche from the kundalini. By this act, he gets rid of the chakra system which novices are so proud of.

The chakra system is against the spiritual body realization. Yet novice yogis are very pleased to operate it.

Kundalini is depicted in the tantras as a beautiful goddess. It is that from a certain perspective.

Which is better to be enslaved by a pretty woman or to be dominated by a not-so pretty one?

Someone would agree that it is best to be under subjugation of a pretty lady, because then one will have something pleasant and appealing to adore. Perception of beauty may provide some relief when one is in a bad way.

A cool breeze is a worthy distraction during a term in hell.

A yogi must break away from kundalini by first getting it confined and then infusing it with subtle energy from the higher astral regions. After that is established, one should see if one can get rid of kundalini.

Being that kundalini has this tendency to take physical bodies, the only way to handle that is to get rid of kundalini. The melting away of kundalini occurs by the burning of it in the subtle body. This is done by breath infusion, *pranayama*. It is no whimsy that before *pratyahar* sensual energy withdrawal, there is the stage of *pranayama* in the *ashtanga* yoga system.

Pratyahar means shutting down the kundalini sensual spread of influence, the constant hunting for enjoyments in the physical and subtle material worlds. This is the disbanding of the obsession with pleasure. The word ***pleasure*** is related to the word, ***please***.

Who or what is pleased?

Is it the coreSelf?

Is it the sense of identity which is fused around the core?

Is it the analytical powers used by the core?

Is it the kundalini psychic lifeForce?

If I drive a vehicle, who or what is pleased directly when gas is burnt in the engine?

The cultivation of the spiritual body for the coreSelf has to do with understanding the operation of pleasure and pain. Pain is also a form of pleasure, even though we deny this at every opportunity.

Since pleasure is our obsession, we should stop and review how we access, process, sense it and are motivated to procure it?

In a spiritual body, there is evenly distributed pleasure potency. To understand this, to get some insight, the only regular experience which comes close to it, is the sexual pleasure experience. There is another method which is the use of drugs but I do not recommend that due to the risks involved.

Sex is also risky and yet we may use it. It is endorsed, supported and pushed by nature on everyone. It is in the body itself and the person does not have to harvest, and smoke it or create it in a chemical lab and then ingest it.

The spiritual body is such that it may be compared to having a material body and having sex pleasure spread from any sensual contacts which it makes. In other words, the ultimate omni-sensual fetish. Imagine a body in which if you look at your lover, you experience a full sexual pleasure experience.

- Then again if you speak to your lover, you again experience that.
- Then again if you touch your lover with just the tip of your finger you experience that.
- Then again if you hear the voice of your lover, you experience that.
- Then again if you speak to your lover you experience that.
- Then again if you sit to eat with your lover you experience that.
- Then again if you smell the odor from your lover's body, you experience that.
- Then again if you lick the skin of your lover you experience that.
- Then again if you think of your lover you cannot complete the thought because you are overpowered by that sexual pleasure.

What an existence that would be?

What would you accomplish in a body like that where there would be pleasure at every contact? Even the slightest psychic contact, would serve as a trigger for sexual pleasure in its fullest expression. In a way that would be a condemned existence. But that is how it is in the spiritual body.

How will you prepare yourself for being a body like that?

Right now, I am involved in moving into a body like that, into being that. Using some help from some mahayogins and by the grace of the *Blue Divine Boy Krishna*, I make headway to assuming myself as such a body.

While the natural kundalini system involved focus on the sexual organ, this system causes first a de-focus of that and an in-focus on every subtle cell of the astral body.

In this system the individual cells of the astral body are infused with breath energy. Each of these cells fires its own kundalini, so that there is no massive spinal kundalini operating and giving dictates to the individual cells. In this practice when kundalini fires it is not spinal kundalini. It is cellular kundalini. Think of it!

Existential Condition

The reports I make on practice, come in a series of articles from 1969, when I first started to record what was experienced. If you examined my notes over the years, you will see a progression of incidences but still sometimes when I write a report there is negative blow back from others who feel that the report is motivated or that it is influenced or that it was meant for this or that purpose, or that it was to benefit someone specifially, or that it was to insult or motivate someone.

Some people object to these reports. Or they feel something negative or develop a cynical attitude. They attack in one way or the other about these reports.

Yesterday Yogeshwarananda complained about this. He said that someone took an advancement I made after getting much help from several yoga gurus including himself, to be something else and expressed negative thinking energy about it.

Why does this happen, that someone reads a report I file and then goes through the numbers and expresses negative feelings, when in fact the writing had nothing to with that person or even with that person's advancement or anyone else's? It was a progression of my practice from years of effort on my own and also from years of efforts and grace contributions from my yoga gurus.

This morning the Brahma deity entered my psyche. This was quite unusual. He checked the condition of my subtle body, as to the nature of the energy within it, and as to if it really had some permanent changes. He gave remarks. I saw him looking every which way. He did say something however like this,

"People fall from the higher levels because of internal qualities, not because of being cursed or dismissed by a deity. It is the existential condition of the person which causes the fall. Inform people of this."

Guru Connect

Guru connect is about being in touch with a yoga guru in relation to following the instructions for breath infusion and meditation. Connection to the instructions is itself connection with the guru but the execution of the instructions is the key connection point.

Initially a student should have confidence in this *connection by practice* method of association.

Does this mean that the guru has to be a woman if the student is a man and that the guru has to be a man if the student is a woman?

Is it easier if the guru is of the opposite sex and there is an attraction between the two?

The first yoga couple we hear about who were sexually connected was Lord Shiva and Goddess Durga. Except that when Shiva taught yoga to the goddess, she was inattentive and did not listen to a word of what he said. It was on that occasion that the fish who later became known as Matsyendranath heard of the technique of kriya yoga.

This shows that sexual attraction between a spiritual master and a student does not necessarily facilitate learning of yoga, even in the case of the supernatural rulers who are more intelligent than mere human beings.

In the many years using this body when I took instruction from invisible gurus, I had instructions for a total of twelve days in all of those years with a female guru. And still I made progress. In those twelve days there was no sexual relationship with the female guru. It was a purely student disciple relationship and nothing else, with the female guru being an authority and not a lover or beloved.

Thus, the idea that a spiritual relationship is accelerated when there is sexual love between the yoga guru and the student does not hold up in most cases. Love between the gopis and Krishna was there but there is little evidence in the Bhagavata Purana then the gopis were spiritually accelerated because of it. Later, people said that there was an acceleration based on paramour affection (girlfriend-boyfriend unmarried conjugal love) between the gopis and Krishna, but we hear that when the gopis were visited by Uddhava who was to instruct them about Krishna, those gopis were insubmissive to Uddhava and had something to say to him about the faults of Krishna's attraction to them.

Uddhava's mission as their guru was stymied because of the love resentments they had for Krishna.

The point is that the instruction from a yoga-guru for practice is accelerated by the instruction-connect only and nothing else. If the student has the connection there will be progress.

It has nothing or very little to do with sexual love. It did not have it for the Goddess Durga so we do not see how it will have it for others. It did not serve the purpose for the gopis. In fact, it made them hostile to getting spiritual realization from Krishna, so we do not see how it can be proven otherwise.

Thus, there is no excuse especially for male students of male yoga guru not to make progress. The males should make the most progress, by the very reason of the lack of sexual attraction.

When Krishna instructed Uddhava in the Uddhava Gita, Uddhava resisted Krishna every step of the way but still near the end of the discourse,

Uddhava yielded and listened. He complied with the instruction. But the gopis never yielded. Their conjugal love for Krishna actually retarded their ability to absorb spiritual methods of practice from Krishna.

Mantras and Deities

Saying Vedic mantras is a technical affair. If one does it whimsically one may incur a fault but one will for sure not get the desired result.

It came down recently in some lineages from India, that it does not matter how one says the prayers, that one will get a result regardless of if the prayers are said carelessly or not. This idea has scriptural support in each of the Puranas.

Yet for the practice of inSelf Yoga™ (Patanjali's *samyama*), mantras which are said carelessly and without permission will cause the student to retrogress.

There is always that big question of the source of a mantra. Who shared it to me? Did I draw it out of thin air? Was it inspired into my mind with no personal source discernible?

Do I have a relationship with the deity who is to be addressed in the mantra? Did I see that deity?

In the case of *Yajnavalka* when his guru who was *Vaishampayana* gave him some mantras, which were acquired traditionally from Srila Vyasadeva, an empowered literary agent of Krishna, *Yajnavalka* got into a quarrel with his guru so that *Vaishampayana* immediately told the student to cough up whatever he got from the teacher.

Yajnavalka complied and then left silently. He proceeded to do yoga austerities. Later the sunGod came to *Yajnavalka* and gave mantras, specifically the mantra known today as the *gayatri* mantra.

In that case the deity gave the mantra of himself to the student directly. This may be compared to an ordinary citizen who thinks constantly of the President of a country, and who finds that one day the President comes to his house to meet him and give him a phone line with direct access to the presidential mansion.

What about the citizens who would like to meet the President as well and who are constantly thinking of him and even making daily phone calls to the presidential office but never getting an opportunity to speak even one word into the ear of the president?

What about them?

I guess they should keep doing that and those who have a vivid imagination should imagine that they are in fact talking to the president because someone said that if you think of the president and if you shout his name, he will hear you and respond anyway.

In the process of inSelf Yoga™ there is no possibility of calling the president directly unless you actually have that relationship with him. What should you do with these holy names which you were already introduced to?

Well the question comes back again as to:

Who gave the mantra?

If that person did not meet the deity, then the process may be imaginary.

If swami gave me the mantra, and if swami did see the deity, I may use it on that basis of having seen the swami not on the basis of having seen the deity. When I use the mantra, I need to use it with that understanding. If the Swami did not see the deity, obviously his gift of the mantra to me is connected with some dishonesty even though it may not be contrived.

The sunGod came to *Yajnavalka* but will the deity come to me?

Be truthful to yourself, so that if you have not met the deity, use the mantra as advised but on the basis of the relationship with the advisor and not thinking that you reached the deity.

Knowing someone who saw a picture of the President, is not the same as knowing the President directly. Stop fooling yourself!

Psychic After Shocks

During the night I was in some astral lands where the people were mostly Hindus in their previous lives. These were deceased people. There were no asphalt roads only dirt tracts which were slightly dusty, very dry. There was no sign of rain or water and yet it did not feel as if it was a dessert.

These persons pulled my astral body to that place because of knowing that I am a yogi and that I am familiar with the rituals of their religion.

There was only one book in that place. It was an astral energy of their information from the past life from what they followed as Hindus. The book did not exist there unless one person, the main priest there, wanted it, otherwise it de-existed immediately.

He wanted me to check the book to be sure that it was correct but as soon as he provided it, he was fearful that I would find something in it which was incorrect. He desisted and changed the subject immediately.

A lady who was not deceased came there astrally. Since she was used a physical form, her astral body could not register there. Instead when she came, she was there as an invisible astral form while everyone else there registered visibly.

Even though I still use a physical body, because of my special existential situation, my astral body registered there but I could see the lady's invisible astral form. She smiled because somehow, she perceived me. She got some satisfaction from my being there, because she influenced the priest, asking him to have me check his procedures.

After a short time, the priest complained about the astral weather. He said this,

"Even here we are affected by what they do. They should stop polluting the earth. Where will this lead, except to disaster, here in the astral realms and there in the physical existence."

He expressed hopelessness in this regard.

Realizing that there was nothing I could do about. I explained that to him and told him not to worry but to see if he could find some scriptural reference about going to a higher astral place where he would not be affected by the psychic aftershocks of what happened on earth.

Brahmachari in Yoga Sutras

The term brahmachari is misunderstood and distorted.

It is a touchy topic where some persons want to stick to it as meaning celibacy. Others say that it does not mean celibacy, especially persons who feel that celibacy is impractical in their personal lives.

If one reads Patanjali, the term there meant something specific but generally no one is concerned with that. Generally, we write or interpret our meanings and pretend that we know what Patanjali meant.

Take into consideration the cultural medium in which Patanjali lived with its caste structured Vedic society and with its division of lifestyle which was ideally divided into four or two parts namely:

- brahmachari single student (ages 1-25)
- grhasta married life (ages 25-50)
- vanaprashtha retiree (ages 50-75)
- sannyasi full social detachment (ages 75-)

Or two parts of:

- brahmachari single student (ages 1-25)
- sannyasi full social detachment (ages 25-)

In that cultural medium because of the restrictions, single student life means no sexual contact in the first phase of the life when the person was in a gurukula ashram situation. There is no way around this.

Nowadays we do not have such a cultural environment. Sexual activities are encouraged during the student life. It is different.

Me as a Last Emperor

For our convenience, there is a kundalini energy which regulates the formation, living condition and death of the physical body. As well as the proneness of the subtle body to transmigrations in various physical forms at various times and in places.

Question is:

How can one ever become liberated if one is not freed from the influence of this kundalini?

If this energy has as its innate urge, survival, how can one change this, being that innate means 'essentially the nature of.'

Such a manager of the psyche, as kundalini, should be discarded. But how is one to do so?

In addition, if one does so, how will one manage?

The last Emperor of China?

- He could not button his shirt.
- He could neither put on his shoes nor tie the laces
- He could not scrub his teeth.

Was it his fault?

From birth he was served every which way. Doing something for himself was superfluous, and in some cases, downright prohibited. Neither the senior members of the royal family nor the menial servants under them would allow him to serve himself.

But you say:

"That is him. He was a fool. He should have figured it. I am different. I learned to do things for myself. Do you think that I am stupid?"

That is not the point.

I too am a last emperor. I am the person who cannot digest my food. I cannot process my food waste into stools. I cannot strain my blood to extract urine. I am the person who cannot keep track of my breathing. I cannot always operate the blinking of my eyelids. I am the person who cannot operate the heartbeat. I rarely can operate my breathing. I do not know some organs in my body. I never saw my rib bones. I do not know how my emotions are produced. I am ignorant of the components of my psyche.

I am a helpless emperor. Can you assist so that I can learn to serve, so that I can for myself dismiss the physical and psychic servants (services), many of whom I never met or saw?

Teaching Kundalini Yoga

The likelihood is that in a short time, say within a few years, someone could become a kundalini yoga teacher, but that is only if he/she persists in the practice, day after day for a time. A yogi reaches the potential because of his observational powers and the demands he places on himself. To be qualified as a teacher one must see not only one's kundalini but that of the student. This is why this process is taught one on one.

Suppose I teach fifty students in a large park, how will I keep track of those kundalinis. Even if I do, how will I communicate with each student as to what to do if kundalini rises suddenly in say twenty of them at the same time and in a different way with a different intensity, going in a different direction somewhere in the psyche.

From this one should get the importance of individual practice and *one on one* teacher to student training. Of course, if I have forty-seven advanced students who are trained to watch their kundalini energy, then I may have fifty students, because only three will need the close supervision.

Yogi Bhajan use to hold kundalini sessions with hundreds of students on occasion but then again, he was empowered to keep track of this. Others should not imitate him.

There is also the method of diluting the process so one can teach many students simultaneously but, in a way, where kundalini does not rise fully but only rises just a little, enough so that students cannot lose control of their bodies if they are not trained in how to overpower the aroused kundalini.

My Astral Job

Have you considered writing your astral résumé? Do you think of your status in the astral world hereafter? I have friends who will not think of that. They assumed the *now* perspective, where they do not worry about the future. They face the situation as it is now, even though now is moving target because of shifting time.

These friends are persons with at least one degree from a university. Some of them have master degrees. Still, these people convinced themselves and intend to convince me that they are into the Now.

They were not in the *now* as infants when they were forced into classrooms. They were not in the now when we were in college. Then they were into the big *then*, the big future time when they would get the highest jobs making the biggest salaries and living in the *well to do* places.

Are you ready for that big *then* in the astral after leaving the body? Or will you fool us with the big *now* of when you live the good life on earth, at least until they cart you off one last time to the Intensive Care Unit of the most prestigious hospital in the country, all by virtue of your *then* considerations while we were in college.

Lucky for me I do not have a degree, not a house nor home. I cannot afford to be in the Big Now of a status life with good income. I think of the big *THEN* in the astral hereafter. Last night I was offered an astral job.

My epitaph:
- Poor in Life
- Poor in Death
- Never had anything of worth
- Always stuck in the THEN
- Never enjoyed a NOW

In the astral last night, I realized myself as the astral body in an adjacent parallel world, where a friend of mine who is presently using a physical body, owned a store. His astral body looked different to his physical form but he greeted me in the usual jovial way. He did not recognize me as he would if we met physically but he was friendly as his psyche had in it a friendly predisposition towards me.

There was no electricity in the place, no asphalt roads; only dirt roads which were dry and a little dusty. Everything in the store was lit even though there was no sunlight or electricity. As soon as I entered the store, he came to me. He offered a job. He said, "What are you doing? Please come back tomorrow. You could work for me."

I replied, "How do you know if I need a job? What would be the pay for employment?"

He did not answer. He smiled and again asked what I did. I explained that I had some employment at a church where I worked on earth some ten years ago. I also told him that under the present economy, things were not bright and I may be interested in taking the job.

He then said that I should meet him there on the next day to begin the employment. After this my astral body left that place and assumed itself as part of my physical body on earth but with full memory of the incidence.

There was no indication of currency in that place but the people there have the currency idea in their minds on the basis of life in the physical world, where currency is mandatory for product exchange. This is because the astral body there carries with it the social energy reference from this level and uses that as its psychological basis for reference in transactions.

Does this mean that since I am a nobody on earth in this life, I will be a nobody in the astral world hereafter? Really, if that is the case, then I had better learn some lessons from my educated friends and get to understand how to practice the NOW consciousness. It may come in handy hereafter when again I am a common laborer.

Spiritual Body Potential

In relation to the spiritual body, one other way to know about that is to consider if the entire human body was all of brain matter and it was capable of the intense pleasure of sexual fulfillment in every part of it.

If the entire subtle body becomes capable of what happens in the head and spine of that form, then one would get some idea of what a spiritual body would be like.

If between now and the time of death one does not experience such a subtle body, there is the likelihood that the spiritual environment will be off limits, completely outside of one's scope, after death.

Transiting from here to the spiritual place, may be compared to the possibility of the development of eyes in eyeless salamanders which live in totally dark caves. What idea can such a reptile have of sunlight? How does it move from having no eyes to developing vision?

I Remember First Thoughts

Today, September 7, 2013, I remember some incidences which occurred when I was first aware of this body outside of the mother's form. Initially I could not see anyone, but within the form there was the thought energy of

- What is this?
- Who is there?
- What noise is this?
- What was that movement?
- Where am I?
- How did I get here?
- What was the transit?

At first in spiritual life, we hear that the big question is:
Who am I?

Some great yogis made a name for themselves asking visitors about this. However initially that was not the case when I first found myself to be this physical body outside the mother's form. It was more about what was not me. The inquiry was:

- Who is that?
- What is that?
- Why the disturbance, the pushing and stretching?
- Why was I pulled out?

(I was pushed out but from the perspective of the embryo, I was pulled out.)

Then after a time, when my mother began to breast feed, it was always the question of,

- "Where is my mother?"
- "Are you sure you are the one?"
- "Are you the same lady who fed me yesterday?"

Then after a time when I began to see objects in this world, I developed a *for sure* confidence because I knew the looks of my mother. Then there was no doubt about it, that I breast fed from that lady.

But when other women were present, there arose the idea of:

- Who are they?
- What species are they?
- Why are they speaking?
- Why do they laugh?
- Why are they anxious about what may happen?

When men would be there, thoughts would arise like this:

- They seem to be like me
- They do not have the same humor as the ladies.
- They do not become anxious over the same events
- Despite their similarity, they have no way to care for me

Protect the Senses

What do I do when I am in an environment in which my senses are subjected to features of existence which are counterproductive to meditation?

When I am in an environment where there are sensual features which may cause the next meditation session to be on a lower plane of existence, what do I do to minimize the assault on my senses?

This morning I was in a dental office, where there were two sensual assaults which were counterproductive to meditation practice. The first was a radio which produced popular music. The second was a worldly conversation between the dentist and his assistant.

The problem with music is that after it is heard, the mind usually replays the songs at random, and especially during meditation. This means that if one allows the mind to become inlaid with music, later one should expect that the mind will replay those tracks even during meditation. One may or may not be powerful enough to stop the replay, which means that for the time it replays one will be distracted from the objective of the meditation.

The problem with hearing a conversation between a dentist and his assistant, their small talk, is that even though such discussions concern what Is trivial, the mind will indulge in analysis and value assessment of features of the conversation. Later during meditation, it may recall those stories and rehash the incidence and even project outcomes about the incidence or imagine conclusions about why the incidence formed in the first place.

If I meditate, for say thirty minutes, how much time would the mind use for rehashing the radio songs and the trivial conversation between the dental technicians?

Someone suggested that I should enter meditation, focus on my objective and let the mind re-hash as it desires. But I say that such advice does not apply to what I aim for in meditation. My aim is a clean mind chamber not a contaminated one in which I sit and focus on my objective.

What did I do when I was under those undesirable sensual influences?

I instructed the hearing sensual interest not to absorb the radio songs, telling it that those songs were not a desired commodity. This worked on this occasion even though I must admit that this is not always effective, especially when the particular sense involved is hungry for whatever is in the environment, even if that is counterproductive to meditation.

As soon as I released the instruction to the hearing sense, it lost its enthusiasm and was like when tires of a car are suddenly deflated on a highway, and the car loses acceleration. The hearing sense lost its enthusiasm for the radio songs. It was like they were on the other side of a thick glass wall

Soon after I achieved this, the dental assistant came in. This person had an obese body. As soon as the visual sense saw that, it reported that to my intellect faithfully. Noticing this, I instructed the intellect not to consider it. I told it, that the situation of obesity was none of its concern. Lucky for me, the intellect took note of this instruction and desisted from considering the obese condition. The eyes for their part, after noticing the lack of interest of the intellect, ceased its interest as well.

The dentist came in and gave instructions to his assistant. Soon after this, the dentist was busy doing this and that in my mouth. A conversation began in which the assistant shared with the dentist some incidences from the previous evening.

Due to the noise made in my mouth by the dental implements, the ear could not clearly hear everything that was said but it was interested and did its best to collect bits and pieces of the conversation. Noticing this, I instructed the hearing sense not to make those collections and to discard whatever it accumulated so far from the conversation. Lucky for me, it dutifully did that. Thus, in the meditation session, I will not have to deal with replays of these incidences. That is all the better for the practice.

Eating Flesh

From another angle, it is not about the animal eaten. It is about the eater of the animal, about being really selfish for yourself, concerned about yourself, where you feel that you do not desire to continue as a predatory profile.

Forget the animal eaten. Think about yourself as the predator. Is that your idea or ideal for yourself?

If you are religious about it, if your God permits and supports it, then where does that permission end?

Is your God involved in animal slaughter for edibles in his kingdom? How are the angels using animal foods there? Do they have a well-organized slaughter operation as we do on earth?

If they do not, will your predatory instincts suddenly end when your physical body dies. Otherwise, living in heaven will be a hell without flesh foods.

Yogi and the Angelic Woman

This morning during breath infusion there was a slight split off between an angelic female being and one of my yoga gurus. This is a normal development in the course of becoming a siddha where one reaches a stage where one attracts both diversions and grace assistance.

When doing breath infusion proficiently, there is the likelihood that one will attract angelic beings. If one's subtle body becomes energized sufficiently, they become aware of one's existence on their level of life. During the practice there may exude from one's psyche a nectar energy which is craved by some angelic beings. This will attract them to the location where the yogi practices the technical aspects.

Sometimes when one of these angelic beings arrives, a yoga guru will simultaneously arrive. The yoga gurus also perceive the practice efforts of students who are on the earth. When the practice intensifies the yoga guru may come to render advice.

This morning a female who uses a physical body and whom I have not seen in at least twenty-five years came while I did practice at about 4am. This person even though using a human body at this time, is from the *swarga* angelic paradise world. This is an astral place. She left that place in the hope of using a human physical body to earn her way to a spiritual world. So far her efforts failed. This is because of an underestimation of what it would take to attain a spiritual world and her buying into a fantasy method created by authorities in India.

There is this belief that if one leaves the *swarga* paradise world and takes a human body, one has the likelihood of going to a place which is higher than the heavenly paradise world. Some angelic beings buy into this idea. When they take the human body, they become stranded as earthlings and neither return to the paradise world nor go to a spiritual world. This happens because of following the counsel of fantasy gurus who may or may not be devotees of valid deities.

Suppose you are in a helicopter some two thousand feet above the ground. Going for the ride are two gentlemen. One is a theist and one is an avowed atheist. The theist says that if you jump to the ground, you will land safely especially if you do not have a parachute. The atheist objects and begins to argue saying that no one has ever survived a two thousand-foot jump without deploying a parachute and that the theist was a liar of the first order and should not be trusted.

Then the atheist makes a convincing argument, where he says that the only way, he would accept what the theist said is if you attach your parachute but do not use it after you jump. His idea is that faith in God is nonsense and that the parachute is the real thing and that the jumper can do it if the jumper has the parachute along even without deploying it, provided the jumper has confidence in science.

What do you think will happen if you jump with the chute or without it?

Recently the angelic woman could find no evidence of anyone in her belief system who transited to a spiritual world. She harbored doubts even though she felt that maybe the system would work if people followed it sincerely.

Some years ago, she became aware of the method which I used and which is mentioned in their scriptures. Now that her body ages, she scrambles to find a method that works because at least intellectually she keeps telling herself that she does not want to take rebirth.

Her attraction to me however is disadvantageous even though it may be in her interest. To make matters worse her subtle body locates mine by natural intuition that for her works every time she gets an idea that she should see me, but all the same she is unwilling to do the austerities. This morning she reflected on when she first heard about breath infusion. She said:

"I could have joined with Yogi Bhajan in the 1960's. Somehow, I did not. If I had done so I would be one of the leading persons in his organization. But there was a disadvantage in that I would not have heard about Krishna as much as I did from Bhaktivedanta. On one hand with Yogi Bhajan, there would be no mention of Krishna and on the other hand with Bhaktivedanta, there was no mention of breath infusion. In either case I lack one aspect. O well! It is too late to change that now."

"Maybe I should stay with you. what do you think?"

I made no response to this dangerous remark. I continue the practice keeping track of the infused energy and the kundalini bursts which occurred in my psyche. Observing that I did not response, which to her indicated pure intolerable indifference. She suddenly lost her clothing and became nude. In the astral world it is easy to do this. One does not have to remove clothing as we would have physically. By a thought one's clothing can either vanish or be changed completely.

Once she stood there nude, she began to rub her right breast over my face. I kept doing my practice. This is all a normal part of the course of those who would be siddhas in the near future.

The real secret of this behavior is the energy which exudes from someone who is proficient in practice, where angelic beings (fallen ones or ones still in the paradise worlds) become attracted to the subtle energy which secretes and which is like a nectar cream. They rub this on their bodies or rub their bodies on the body of the ascetic to get this cream on their forms. When this cream makes contact with their forms, they feel an intense pleasure which makes their hairs stand on end. It is very similar to a sexual pleasure except that no genital participation is involved.

While this happened, Lahiri Mahasaya gave instructions in my subtle head about what I should do to continue on the course to reach the siddhas. When he first arrived and the angelic person arrived simultaneously, he pretended not to notice her but the look on his face said this:

"Why is she here? These people always appear when a student becomes serious. When will that existence disappear? This is the edge of nowhere. You can cross it and that will be no more. Keep practicing regardless."

Nutrition Orb

Lahiri within the past two weeks gave directions about destroying the nutrition orb.

You may hear of celibacy. That is a big deal for yogis. It is known to be part of the brahmacharya spiritually-supportive behavior in student yogis. Sometimes people assume that because a yogi is single, a bachelor, he has a good chance of becoming liberated. They feel that if a yogi is sexually involved, he is doomed.

Broadly speaking this may be true. The lack of celibacy may be a big factor in the reason why many ascetics fail. Still the technicalities of how a specific person will become liberated is not all theory. It is not as simple as being celibate. Celibacy can be a cause of not being liberated. There are obligations which an ascetic may be required to fulfill before permission for liberation is granted. Some of these obligations may involve abandoning celibacy on occasion.

The *Mahabharata* opens with the story of *Jaratkaru* a wondering celibate ascetic who had to abandon his celibate stance at one time in his life.

Even though sex desire is big on the list of yoga failures, it is nothing in comparison to the need for nutrition. In fact, initially when the living entity got in touch with the material energy, sex was nowhere in sight and had nothing to do with it. Sex desire developed much later. The initial urge was the nutrition urge.

Once a yogi gets sex desire dissolved out of the psyche, then he/she will see the other more important problem which is the need for nutrition. There is what is called a *kanda* or small bulb of sexual energy which is in the central groin area of the subtle body. This may be dissolved by doing aggressive *pranayama* practice.

Once that is achieved, the nutrition orb comes into vision. This is a slim oval shaped subtle object which rotates in the lower belly area.

This is required to be dissolved. When that is achieved one finds its origin point which is where the tongue touches the soft palate when the tongue is rolled up and back in the mouth *(kechari mudra)*.

There is a connection energy between that nutrition orb in the palate and the naad sound which is heard at the back of the head. A yogi has to loop the three contacts, which are the slim oval nutritional orb in the lower abdomen, the sliver shaped nutritional orb in the back of the tongue and the glimmer-point of naad resonance in the back of the head where the brain has its lowest back point.

Assistance as Interference

Sometimes we find someone in the subtle world without this or without that part of the subtle body. Sometimes there are violent acts towards a subtle body by another subtle body. Those violent acts may cause dismembering a limb, but the limb reforms as quickly as it was amputated.

To understand how this works, we may go to a pool of water and slice a knife through it. It cannot be said that the knife had no effect but even though it did, it does not remain apparent except for a split second. It seems that the water which was separate by the passage of the knife blade, immediately reconnected. The subtle body may be hurt in the same way and then it will be instantly reconnected.

A subtle body can be bruised by resentment energy from another person. That may last for a second or for years even, all depending on the subtle impact of the offensive energy.

In the *Bhagavad Gita,* an astonished warrior, Arjuna, saw some people being bitten and chewed by a deity but this happened on a supernatural plane of consciousness.

People who find themselves being punished in an astral hellish place, are sometimes repeatedly hurt and then immediately after they find themselves in an unhurt condition, and then again, they are hurt again afresh. Imagine if I was a serial killer. I killed ten people, say. I am arrested and charged with these crimes. Evidence is provided sufficiently to condemn me, then it is decided that I should be killed in various gruesome ways which correspond to the methods I used to murder the victims.

On earth it would not be possible for this to take place because here the justice department can only kill a body once. However, in an astral prison condition, the authorities can kill my astral body and then it will again reform itself in a wholesome way. Then they can again kill it in another way and on and on. I will feel all of these violences afresh as being real damage being done to me.

There are also circumstances, psychological ones, where some entities are missing certain psychic components and have defective ones. Think of a person who lacks recall of events as some elderly person displayed in Alzheimer conditions or dementia. In the astral bodies, one may find that the intellect is defective or that the memory compartments are damaged or that some part in the head of the subtle body is missing.

Take me for instance. I did three commentaries on *Bhagavad Gita*. Even if these are filled with error, still it is an achievement. Anyone can conclude that my intellect functioned. Still later in the life of this body, I may reach a stage where I cannot even tell you the sum of 1+1 as 2. People will say, "He made three commentaries on *Bhagavad Gita*. Imagine his arrogance. For that, because he misused his intelligence, God removed his intellect."

The coreSelf may have damaged components in the subtle body. Sometimes in the astral world, when visiting a lower astral place, someone comes to me to request being fixed in this way or that way. Thus, it is important that I not go to such places because I do not want to become responsible for interferencing with the operation of material nature where it wants someone to be insane and I feel that this person should be fixed with sanity. Recently in a conversation I explained that unless one knows the prehistory, past life of a person, one should avoid interfering with his/her destiny. The police do not like when one aids a fugitive or if a doctor secretly helps a wounded criminal.

When Jesus Christ, Lord that he is, attempted to expelled some demoniac entities from the psyche of a man, the psychotic entities questioned Christ about where they would go if he expelled them. Christ took an action and caused them to be transferred into the bodies of some pigs.

Even a person as great as Jesus Christ had to face the responsibility for interfering with the disagreeable process of nature, what to speak of me.

Celibacy Misunderstanding / Thigh Conquest

Recently I worked on breath infusing below the torso, below the trunk of the subtle body, below the base chakra, below the groin area, just the thighs and where they are hooked into the torso, and the legs and feet, as well as the knees and ankles.

By the way the ankles are a wonderful place to infuse with fresh breath. So are the knees. The initial instruction to do this was from Yogeshwarananda but he did not emphasize it. Recently, Lahiri stipulated that it must be done. Due to his stress, I shifted to comply with the instruction.

I have nothing to lose, because if I will be stuck with this subtle body hereafter, then it is best that I elevate it as much as possible before it is, at last, disconnected for the last time from the physical casing.

When materialistic persons save money for a venture, they do not play around. They will cut any throat, stab any belly and do whatever is necessary to get that money hoarded sufficiently. From them I learnt something about how to be serious and not to let anything get in the way of what one should do to secure an elevated subtle body hereafter.

It would be preferred that I would go to a divine world hereafter, but how do I know for sure if that will happen. I have an alternative plan that I should elevate the subtle body, so that if I do not find myself in a divine world, then at least I will be attracted to a high astral region.

What about my friends on earth?

I will not think of them. Their positions are dictated by fate just as mine is. If I was the master of fate, it would make sense to think about friends because then it would be a problem for me as to where I would put them but since I am not the absolute, I do not have it as a responsibility to design the future of the world.

Fate, or the real master of fate, produces the future of the world as we go along. We see it happening about us one each side. There is really very little we can do about what fate decrees. The little gaps which fate allows us to draw art or to carve reputations should be put to the best use depending on how resourceful one is.

Recently with the help of Lahiri Baba, I attacked the thigh region of the body. I did work on this before during the years when I worked strenuously to change the sexual attitude of the physical body which I derived from my parents. However, there was an area of the thighs which eluded my confrontation, which avoided being handled by me.

Fortunately, by the grace of Lahiri Baba, I got a hint that this area lurked in the background. It hid from my vigilance. This happens in yoga where the ascetic achieves certain wonderful things, and still certain areas are completely missed because those areas are protected from his interference.

Subtle material nature has plans. Surely, it does. But that does not mean that it intends to reveal all secrets. Look how many years it took for human beings to master organic chemistry.

Did nature hide that information all along?

If one associates with the advanced yogis, there is a chance that the secrets will be shown. One will realize how little control one has over the psyche.

The thighs are the enemy of student yogis who intent to master celibacy. It does not matter what one does with the genitals, if one uses them or ceases to use them or even if one amputates or surgically sews it up. None of these actions have any effect on celibacy of the subtle body. Gross actions of sexuality or the lack of such actions, does nothing to upset nature's secrets of subtle sexuality. Dormant sex desires, submerged muted sex desire is a complete sham in the matter.

So long as the thighs carry the authority to support the sexual chakra, whatever one does for celibacy which does not attack the alliance between the thigh and the sex chakra, is a sheer waste of time.

Celibacy has nothing to do with if other people keep track of one's sexual activities. Celibacy has nothing to do with if I know that you are sexually active or not.

Ultimately celibacy is an in-house action, like kriya yoga is overall, where it concerns what the psyche does by itself. It does not concern who I am with sexually or who is with me sexually or who you are with sexually. It has to do with what happens in the psyche between the components of consciousness and how these components respond to various stimuli.

More important though is the realization of the veto power of fate. Principled people need to have something in fine print, hard copied and hard wired into law, which states that there is absolute celibacy. But that is not what I describe. In the celibacy I describe, fate is taken into account as it is in everything else which I describe. Fate is that little zero which when it is put under any other number no matter how large that number it, it reduces that number to nothing.

If fate exerts against isolation, the effort at celibacy, will fail.

The influence of the thighs must be smashed if the yogi intends to reach the siddhaloka places. There is a zero possibility to go there if the thighs are no subdued. They must be totally reconfigured.

The first part of this endeavor is to realize how the thighs are configured. The natural way is for the energy of the thighs to link into the body into the pubic area, where the energy from each thigh curves in to mix and form a sex energy support system of liquid and psycholgical hormones. The yogi must stop this linkage and redesign the thighs so that the energy no longer loops inwards to the sexual area.

Any army must have a food source. If there is no eating, there is no physical power and not even psychological power. If one can remove the basic support of the sex expression feature of the groin area, naturally the power of this area will diminish.

This does not mean that nature will change. It will not. It will continue as it is. But for the accomplished yogi, he/she will have a phase of the subtle body which does not have the natural configuration. That phase can be used after final departure from the physical system to get a transit to be with the siddha perfected yogis.

In celibate practice a person may have sexual energies in his/her psyche which does not belong to the self but which are deposits which belong to others. This means that for celibacy the total sexual energies are never available for 100% control. Only the part which belongs to the individual is there for such control. The rest can be used by the other persons concerned.

This begs the questions:

Who owns the body?

Do I own the body totally?

If some person has a 15% stake in my sexual energy, can I force that person to not use that sexual energy? Is that a correct action?

In the story of King *Bharat's* birth as *Jada Bharat* (Stupid *Bharat*), he had to carry the palanquin of King *Rahugana* just as if he (*Bharata*) was a slave. Why was he compelled? He was a great yogin. In the past life he was the son of *Rishabha* (ri-shab-ha) who is rated as an incarnation of Vishnu? Why did such a person have to act as someone slave, as a servant of a person who was not spiritual advanced and who was a political idiot?

But of course, my self-righteous friends will say that this does not apply to celibacy. But I disagree. I do not see the difference. If I do not own the body in terms of service, if I can be conscripted as someone's slave, then what is the difference if I am involved sexually?

Celibacy really means how one moves away from all non-mandatory sexual activities. The problem is to come to an agreement on what is mandatory. There we are at an impasse obviously, because our opinions about what is necessary, vary.

Celibacy is Complicated

This is a practice for women who are interested in containment, conservation and upward distribution of whatever sexual energy is generated in the female psyche. Due to the different way of operation between the male situation and of the female, some procedures used by males have no application with females. Some used by females have no use in the male subtle physiology.

Personally, I have no concern with the practice for females. I have never attended a session by senior yogins where they teach females the kriyas. However, from time to time, some information about these methods is transmitted into my psyche for transmission to specific females on the physical plane.

Female sexual apparatus may be viewed as being a closed sack of energy which is tuned downwards and which has a string which ties the sack so that the substance within it cannot leak. However, once the string is slackened, naturally as with any container which is inverted, gravity will pull whatever is in the sack out of it.

In this process, effort is made to turn the sack about so that its natural configuration is that it faces upward. This means going against the grain of nature. Once the sack is turned upwards, and if the yogini can get it to remain in that format, the flow of energy downward ceases.

From within the trunk of the subtle body, the yogini may also enter that form and grab the mouth of the sack from time to time and pull it up so that the wall of the sack does not become lax, since if it does it may collapse downwards resulting in the downward flow situation all over again.

Those who want to achieve celibacy need to practically define what they should do to achieve this.

What is celibacy?

That is the big question. The definition must include the subtle body as well as the karmic impositions which may be cast by providence. I am not interested in celibacy which means not having sex desire unless there is a clear explanation if that is possible and how the person can achieve that in reality.

Always be prepared to answer a few questions. For example:

Where do the ancestors of your body fit into the celibacy definition?

What percentage of the sexual energy produce in your body is under your full autonomy?

How will you manage fated incidences which are based on confrontations with others with whom you have sexual obligations?

Sky of Consciousness Contact / Yukteswara

For the past ten days I was visited by the person who became known as the guru of Paramahansa Yogananda. This is Yukteshwara. He is interested in the kriya which has to do with retracting and dissolving the nutrition orb, which is something that drives us in the mundane evolutionary cycle on the basis of the perpetual need to acquire some type of energy to keep going.

The situation in material existence, the obvious conclusion about this, is that the big fish eat the minnows. But there is another more ghastly but hidden side which is that the smallest microbe is effectively parasitic on the biggest fish. For his part the big fish sees himself as king and rightly so, but for the truth sake, while the big one procures the smaller of its species, the microbes carefully move in.

Some microbes, the more compassionate, less greedy ones, think that it is best to sample some portions so that the host creature can live. But some other microbes do not consider that. They think that compassion is cosmetic way of dealing the final blow. One of these microbes spoke to the other like this:

"If we do not kill it, something else will. If we half-kill it, it will suffer. Let us exhibit the full mercy. Let us give it the one and final blow."

This is sponsored by the nutrition orb.

Yukteswar's subtle body looked more or less like his last physical form, which means that since then he has not taken an embryo. He is a permanent astral being. His subtle body has an energy in it, where one senses that it is exist under the shelter of Lahiri Baba. This is like when you see an infant with its mother. Wherever the mother goes, the infant follows. The child is always within reach of the mother.

Yukteshwara said that he was interested in how I used the *bhastrika pranayama* to achieve pratyahar practice which is the precursor for the *samyama* meditation procedures of Patanjali. There are two systems. One is that you sit to meditate and that is that. This is popular. The other is the more aggressive, more energy intensive process, where you do *pranayama* practice, then sit to meditate. Ancient yogis in the tradition of the kriya lineage from Babaji did *anuloma-viloma pranayama* mostly but I do *bhastrika*.

But there is no argument as to how a person can master *pratyahar* sensual energy withdrawal just before meditation *(samyama)*. We do not care to argue about that. If you have the accomplishment by some other method, say by eating ice-cream or curry, we have nothing to give you but praise. Many people say that they have such mind control that they are only required to sit and meditate. Others claim that they can visualize this or that and it causes their thoughts to stop so they can meditate. Others say that they chant a mantra and then they can meditate.

Yukteshwara made the classis statement which students make when they notice their guru gives novel instructions to a newcomer. He said,

He never showed us that. We did not do it that way. We never saw him do it that way. How is it that he instructed you to do that, if even he did not do it? Never mind, if it is successful. The mystery of why it was not taught remains. Why you? Why did he not show this to others since this is so effective with the nutrition orb. You have no idea how some yogis suffer because of not achieving the dissolution of that orb. One has to hold locks for years in the astral world in order to keep the orb from becoming active again, because once it does, one is finished and one must take another embryo with the risks which that entails.

Many students are baffled when a teacher tells a newcomer some secret kriya through which that student gets an accelerated practice and its resulting success. What to do about this?

Yukteshwara examined the *thrust-down* kriya where infused breath energy goes straight down at a slant to the pubic floor and like a powerful jet of air, blasting everything from that area. He examined the two-loop grasp which squash-in and then pull up the nutrition orb. He was satisfied that this practice is effective.

After that I did a skull blast breath which is the original process of *kapalabhati* (skull breath). This involved not using kundalini in the brain, only using breath infusion into the brain. This is for evacuating all negative energy from the brain space area.

After this when I sat to meditate, I had some luck reaching chit akash sky of consciousness. The first contact was a split-second flash of light which came in from a high angle from about 80 degrees up from the line of sight in the head of the subtle body. When that blinding flash of light comes from that high up, it is from the *paramatma* supersoul personality with his reserve of spiritual potencies in tow. The second good indication was that in the naad sound in the back of the head, the lower back part on this occasion, there was a flash and then there was a new completely different light which has a slight golden glow to it. This is the naad light. That did not flash and go away. That stayed consistently.

Then there was an ordinary third eye vision into this physical world, where I was in a hallway and then a teenaged girl who was with a woman saw me and stared. No one else there could see me but her. When this happened, I was aware of being in the hallway and being in a physical body which sat in a tight lotus posture.

The third eye may see into this physical world, into the astral levels and also into the chit akash. The student must learn to discern which is which or he/she may be misled by misjudging one type of perception for another.

However, third eye perception into the physical world is an indication of being in the proximity of the chit akash sky of consciousness even though it is not direct contact with that spiritual level. Such proximity is an achievement, a reason for a yogi to smile during meditation.

Spontaneous Naad Light

This morning many things happened during breath infusion and meditation practice. Unfortunately, I cannot put my finger on most of it. It is like when one drives though heavy fog. There is much out there but you cannot see it.

Breath infusion was done early beginning at 3.30am. It continued until 4.20am. There were many small infusion charges which fired here and there in the psyche, first mostly in the trunk of the subtle body, then in the thighs, neck and head of it.

When I sat to meditate in about 3 seconds after, there was a flash glow. I was in naad sound and naad light simultaneously. This is a major development where without effort I was in naad light. This is called *dhyana* or 7th step of yoga compared to having to make effort to achieve this which is *dharana* 6th step of yoga.

When this happened, I congratulated naad with a feeling of:
O, you are here. That is favorable. Stay with me. Stay close.
Naad!
The greatest of the sweethearts!
The best of the lovers!
The ultimate breast to suckle!
The most wrapped around arms!

Infusion Energy Ripples

This morning's breath infusion was much about infusion energy and not so much about kundalini on the spine. This was a shoot up of energy from the place where the thighs are linked to the trunk of the subtle body. From there in the center of the thighs, the energy moved upwards in waves.

How was it?

It was a twinkly tweaking energy which felt like a camphor-mint coolness sending out ripples of itself up through the trunk of the subtle body until it reached under the shoulders and vanished. This is part of freeing various parts of the psyche from being under the kundalini energy survival configuration.

When I sat to meditate, unlike yesterday when I was in naad light and sound after about three seconds, it took about eight minutes. Then I found myself in naad light.

Reason?

The mind hashed over details of this and that. Then suddenly as if someone threw a switched it stopped. I found myself to be a listener and perceiver in naad sound and naad light.

This is progress, every bit of it!

My Boyhood Criminal Acts

During meditation this afternoon, a supernatural being presented evidence of some criminal things I did while I was a juvenile. It was the incidence of breaking lizard eggs. Where I lived as a boy, there were many lizards. Some lived in the house. Some others came into the house and departed as they pleased. The buildings were not air tight.

Every so often I would find their eggs which would be in hollows in wood or in a hollow in the ground or in a crevice. Sometimes I could take an egg and let it drop to a hard surface where the shell would crack. There would be a tiny lizard in there at some stage of its embryonic development. Of course, that meant the death of the creature.

This supernatural being who came was unseen even to my subtle body but seen to subjective supernatural perception which perceives the invisible beings. In my subtle head he showed the eggs which I damaged. Even though everything in my subtle head was in darkness, I could see those eggs just as I did when I was about nine years of age and did these criminal acts. I thought to myself, "For sure some suffering will be felt because of this."

The supernatural being said this," We will excuse this, because of the age of your body at the time and because of the lack of parental guidance."

I replied, "That is all well and good, except that nature took note of it. It is sure to sever my hand or arranged some damage sooner or later in one of these lives. What have you guys got to do with it. Nature unto itself governs this. It enforces its own counterbalance. But I do appreciate the pardon, since it means that punishment will come from one agency only."

Just after this, the supernatural being left. I considered his visit to be an omen of death. Usually as one gets nearer and nearer to death, one may get such visitations. One may also vividly see things one did even in childhood, especially criminal acts even those done in so called innocence.

As I loop through these lives, certain fates are up ahead waiting for me. These are manufactured by nature with subtle energies from my former actions, some of which were meritorious and some which were criminal.

Celibacy: Idealism or Realism

In the celibacy aims, there is the idealism and there is the realism. Which do you strive for?

To be practical an ascetic should strive for the realism, because the idealism has frustration and misunderstanding as part of its process. It is better to be open-minded to providence, rather than to be preset with ideals which providence will either refuse to honor or create harsher penalties for.

It is the same question, I asked before:

- Who owns the body?

It is not a simple question.

When my children were infants, I had major proprietorship over their bodies. I engaged them in many ways. There is no point in owning something and not getting service from it.

Now that they reached adulthood, I can no longer extract such services from their limbs. Thus, the question of who owns their bodies rears its ugly head again, because for sure my ownership right in relation to them, is permanently suspended.

Because these children are intelligent and institutionally educated, there arises another question as to who owns the mind.

Really, who owns the mind in the case of someone who is employed in such a way that he/she spends eight to ten hours per day thinking on behalf of an employer?

In celibacy the question arises as to how celibate can one be.

What portion of the sexual energy can one devote to celibacy?

What are one's rights to use the total amount of sexual energy for one's ascetic aspirations?

Nutrition Orb / Naad Blend

Please see the diagram below which shows a kriya which I did for two weeks. It was based on an inspiration from Lahiri Mahasaya. This was of interest to Yukteshwara who came to see how it was done and as to its effects.

At this stage I cannot say that I have the full scoop on this. However presently this involves two aspects, one which is naad and one which is the retraction and gradual elimination of the nutrition orb. This is necessary if the yogi wants to live in a dimension where food is not required as it is in this physical world.

From all indications in the instruction given by Sri Krishna to Uddhava, a yogi must wash out sushumna nadi central spinal passage completely by using the naad vibration to shatter the sushumna's wall and remove its controlling holding on the psyche.

Naad is used according to Krishna to blend the sound from down in the cleared *sushumna* with the naad sound which is coming from outside the psyche and which penetrates into the mind of a yogi. Krishna said that there would be a blend of musical notes when this happens.

O yeah!

Until that happens in our individual experiences, we should take his word for it.

I found that when naad is pulled down into the *sushumna* into the neck and into where *sushumna* trails out in the lower brain, naad does not necessarily follow the yogi there. If it does it does not blend.

What I experienced is that you are either with naad above in the subtle head or in the outside back of it, or you are in a naad or you are in the vibration which is in the *sushumna* itself. In the beginning of the practice, the two do not mix as Krishna described.

We have to take Krishna's word for it, so if it does not mix in our case, it means that something is amiss or that we are on a plane of consciousness where the mixing will not occur no matter what anyone says.

In this diagram below naad appears to bulge from the back of the head. The coreSelf for its part finds that it cannot cause naad to surround the nutrition orb and so it is ambivalently stuck as it was, between its attention going to the nutrition orb and to the naad.

The *tongue push back* kriya which has become a legendary kriya among pseudo yogis, is a farce for most people who practise. Some cut their tongues because of what they heard this action can do. Ninety-nine percent (99%) of these persons are evolutionary misfits and have no right pursuing kriya practice but somehow, they heard of these ideas and then decided that they would make yoga a utility.

In this practice however the *tongue push pack* has nothing to do with cutting the frenum or any part under it. The student only needs to push it back and keep it pushed into the soft area which it makes contact with.

The nutrition orb which is located at that touch point will manifest only for those yogis who pulled up kundalini and have the trunk and thighs of the subtle body cleared of stale energy at least to the efficiently of about 86%. You can do this practice even if you are not sure that you achieved that but the full success depends on the achievement.

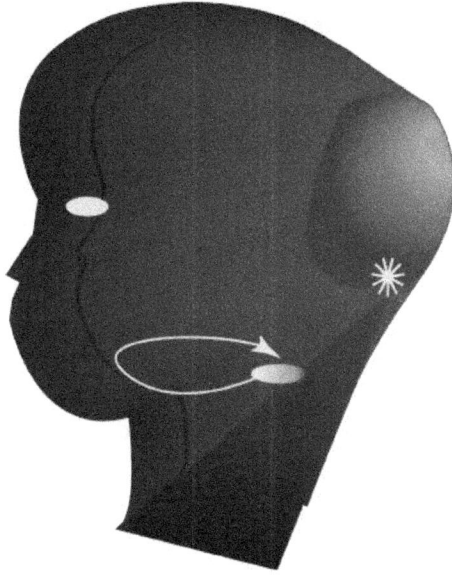

naad zone protrusion outside of subtle head

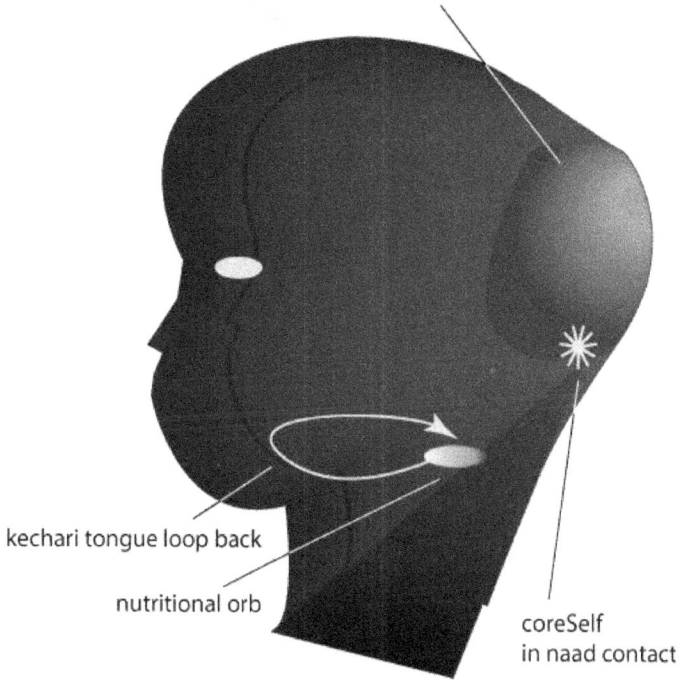

kechari tongue loop back

nutritional orb

coreSelf
in naad contact

Scattering Pleasure Bliss Charge

There is what may be called the *push in until it shatters* kriya, which is vital if the student is to get free of the addiction of relying on the kundalini lifeForce to do everything in the psyche except enjoy. Over all we were manifested in this creation with an enjoy mentality as if we are masters of a world which was created just for our consumption.

For us to transcend the situation and break out of the confinement of focalize pleasure acquirement, we need to change the configuration of the subtle body, so that it does not focalize on any one thing to derive its pleasure needs. There is no denial of these needs. There is admittance with the understanding that the kundalini's native arrangement has unfavorable aspects to it, which we just cannot afford, and are not pleased with in the least.

If a student wants to be a miserable failure, all he/she has to do is to state that there will be a wash out of the focalize sensual pleasures where that will be no more, and there will be instead, a scattering of pleasure where one part of the body is no longer specialized for hunting certain gratifications.

People will want to fight such a guru with teeth and nails and whatever else is available which can be used as a weapon. Individual body naturally means individual focus on individually preferred sources of gratification, and yet some of us sobered enough to realize that this system which was designed by the kundalini, is inefficient.

Why?

Because the coreSelf has to sell itself to get the focalized fulfillments. It has to act as a servant of the psyche instead of being the power in it. No one wants to be down under but that is the position of the coreSelf in the system designed by the kundalini lifeForce.

What to do about it?

Vigorously practice by some effective kundalini yoga method through which you can raise kundalini daily and get it to abandon its homeland which is the *muladhara* chakra. Harass it daily to get it to move from there, twice per day. Like any reptile, if you fatigue and harass it enough, it will abandon its nest and go elsewhere.

The exception is that while with a reptile, you may not care where it goes once it leaves, with the kundalini you must be concerned. You must apply the mental, emotional and physical restrictions to force kundalini to go in a particular direction.

Once you subjugate kundalini, the next step is to take advantage of the situation and dominate the entire trunk of the subtle body. Infuse energy into it directly with or without respect to kundalini. When there is a compression of the infused breath energy anywhere in the psyche, go there. Infuse more air into it. Keep doing this until that compressed energy lump shatters into a trillion pixels of energy which scatter in all directions and which gives a special pleasure-bliss charge to that part of the psyche.

Naad as the Sweetheart

As everyone knows, we are fascinated by anything which is new and desirable, like that first lover. Some of us did not have that so we do not know what that means but still even those who did not have that may remember a first something that was most desired.

My first desired object in this life was my mother's breast. For some reason, I just could not have enough of that. Maybe I was starved of milk in previous lives and then nature lumped all those frustrations together and released them in the infancy of this body.

My second most desired object was my mother herself, because as providence would have it, I was separated from my mother when I was about four years of age. After that it unfavorable because a grandmother no matter what she does is not a mother. It does not matter if she does a better job of it than the mother would have, still it appears that she is the enemy being that she is the representative of cruel fate, of the universal form of Krishna in the form of an imposed irreversible providence.

I used to cry to see my mother but she was far away. My tears displeased the other relatives who did their best for me. A few weeks ago, I got an email from a sweetheart of mine whom I used to know over some forty years ago. This happened because people can now search for their lost loved ones online. But what would happen if there was no internet? That is simple because the subtle body would find those persons anyway. After the demise of those persons, their subtle bodies would find each other in an effort to come to some resolution about long lost love.

A yogi may sometimes hide astrally by slipping into *difficult to find* dimensions. He may not be discovered by others, who will think that for sure he is either dead or liberated.

What is the situation here where repeatedly we form relationships with loved ones and then we are severed from those relationships and then again, we meet in some other life or in an astral world? These relationships are reformed and then again there is a breach and this goes on continually.

Today while meditating I was in love with naad sound. I considered this:

Now that I found my long lost dear one, the naad sound, I will stick with my sweetheart once and for all. I will never leave her company. But there may be somebody out there who after reading this, begins to think:

What is the matter with that fool? I am the one for him not a sound in the mind? Why does he hear these mental sounds?

In mediation for the first three minutes there was this quiet chatter in the mind, nothing blatant and obvious, nothing too compelling. Then I became aware of naad sound in the back and naad light but it was a dim light like when people who are in love want to be private.

I moved back into naad. When I touched naad it said.

"Where were you? Why are you three minutes late? Do not stay away from your sweetheart. Be kind to your darling, you cruel man."

Naad, a Real Love Affair

Meditation this morning was like a wedding. As a boy growing up in Georgetown, British Guiana, I marveled at the way brides behaved for their weddings. There was first the fussing and chatting, the anticipation of tremendous happiness. There would be the measuring and re-measuring of the bride's body by the dress maker, the purchase of the materials to make the dress, the lace, the sequins and so on. Then there would be the emotional confidence, the blushing of the cheeks, the over confidence, the idea that this would be the day of days.

There would be the wrapping of the hands around the breast during the try on of the dresses. Some of my female relatives were dress makers. I would see this happening. There was this fever of enjoyment and feeling of being conquistadors over the males. There was the suspicion that perhaps something may go amiss and shatter the bride's heart like a Tiffany fine art glass ornament which fell to a marble floor.

I would look on and marvel, only to get that stare returned with a silent message of,

"You will never know what this is like, what happiness this is, you little tart. Run along. You are not gifted to know this."

Then the big day would arrive. There would be the fussing as the bride got dressed. The dress was always too small. She would have to be squeezed as the zipper was drawn up. Sometimes the zipper would burst and the bride eyes would pop out of their sockets, but the older women had their needle and threads and got moving, sewing it. Then again, the squeezing especially at the waist because for some reason, who knows why, that area had to be thin no matter what. Then up to the breasts which had to bulge out, only God knows why. The bra in those days had fish bone or some metal flat bars in the fabric. These little pieces of whatever had their job to do; propping up the breasts irrespective of if they sagged naturally or stood up on their own, turning their nipple faces to the sky with youthful arrogance.

Because I was a boy, a little kid, I could be present. This was when I was about seven years of age. Sometimes suddenly a breast would jump out and the ladies would laugh. I would look at the poor thing and wonder why they were squeezing it into place but I would not say anything because I did not dare, before a heavy hand would come flying into my face or I would get a stern look of

"I will deal with you later you little oaf."

Then there would be the shoes to put in with the heels. These shoes for some reason, only God knows, would be so tight that it took two persons to get it on the bride's feet. Her flesh would bulge out of it. Then her veil, then her gloves, white gloves.

All the while my little brain, being short on emotional intelligence was hot with questions of,

Why this?

Why that?

What is the need?

Then a taxi would arrive. The bride would be shoved into the back seat, literally shoved. In that car would be two other women who accompanied her. They would speak with excitement as if they spoke another language?

The taxi went to the church. People waited to see the bride. She came out blushing and squashing, waving if she could get her wits in order. She would enter the front door of the church or walk down the aisle if the groom was already there.

He for his part, the nobody in the affair, would stand like a fish out of water, gasping for air, scared, the whim that he was, the incidental factor. His friends would look with sorry faces. Their fathers, some who thought it was important to be there, or those who had to be there as a matter of duty, would be serious also, like butchers waiting with guns to kill animals, the minister would be there with a bible in his hand.

Then the ceremony. The organist would pay the *here comes the bride* refrain. The bride would venture down the aisle. Everyone would stare. She was the Queen for the Day. The groom who was near the altar, would look down the aisle like a lost sheep shivering in its hoofs in the dead of night in the middle of the forest where the wolves howled.

Then when the organist stopped, the priest would begin the ritual. He did this before. He would do this again. Then the moment of victory, the crest of the whole thing was when the priest gave permission for the bridegroom to kiss the bride. The bride's face would turn into a bubble of joy. All other people would look to see this delightful moment of moments. As a boy with little emotional sense, a total dummy in the matter, I would be saying silently in my mind, "What is the big deal here?"

Then there would be the departure from the church. A decorated car would wait on the street. The bride and groom would enter it. The groom had to know his place, just in case he bungled because purses of the bride's relatives came flying at his face. He got the bride seated on the side which was nearest to the church door. Once she was seated, he rushed to the other side to sit beside her.

Now, as I remember this and share this experience with you, I understand what the experience was about.

That is only because I had a similar experience with naad sound this morning in meditation. The only thing I could compare that with was these experiences of marriages when I used a boy body.

When I sat to meditate, immediately without any gap I was in naad. I met naad without making an effort to do so. This is called *dhyana* (7th stage of yoga) with naad. I felt that I had just married naad. Then a moment after there was the kiss just like at the marriage when the bride would be kissed and her wildest dreams came true. I really for the best of me do not know what flashed through her mind at the time but I got the feeling that this experience was similar.

It is with naad, a real love affair, so intimate as to make me recall the tremors of the incidence of the marriages of hopeful young ladies when I was seven years of age.

Yoga Siddha Body Adaptations

In the system designed by kundalini which is for our exploitation, the thigh energy is used primarily for surcharging sex hormones with passionate energy for passionate enjoyment during sexual exchanges. Nature for its part used this energy for reproduction but it has with it sexual enjoyment which is the part we are hypnotized by.

Obviously only a fool will reduce the sense enjoyment, in this case sex enjoyment when he/she can max out on much desired pleasure. We are, after all is said and done, pleasure seekers at heart.

Some people come to yoga seeking to delete the pleasure needs of the psyche but this desire is impractical because it is not what you want but what nature is willing to share with you. Since pleasure is an enjoyable feature, the idea of eliminating it makes no sense.

Celibacy is a desire that comes about mainly by two traumatic bases which are the realization that:
- sex desire is a loan shark operation of material nature
- sex desire is a slow kill operation like the hopeless situation of a beached whale

A loan shark is a financial business which charges a high interest rate and which has criminal intentions which initially, are hidden from the borrower. Nature does not show upfront what will happen when one gets involved in sex enjoyment. There will always be a big bill later but nature does not show the charges up front. Even if it did the consumer would not understand because he/she has no means of tallying the debt.

There are cases of great yogis who got involved in sex desire and who knew what the charges would be. Still, they could not resist. I am sometimes challenged in similar incidences which prove conclusively that knowing that you will be splattered to bits for jumping out of a flying aircraft, may not stop the action from taking place.

Knowledge is not always a saving grace, especially when it is given by nature, where it knows that giving the knowledge will not equip the person with the power to stop the action which the knowledge explains.

Sex desire includes certain responsibilities but nature may not show these upfront. Therefore, one is likely to facilitate it and then later discover the liabilities.

Sex desire is like an empowerment system, like when a whale takes a ride on a large wave which heads to the beach. Sometimes whales like to have fun. Some throw caution to the wind and take chances on large waves, except that sometimes these waves head to a shallow beach which the whale fails to estimate.

The body of a whale requires a certain depth of water to function, otherwise it becomes stranded and cannot get back to sea. When a whale rides a huge wave which beaches it, the whale eventually dies from starvation and dehydration. It is a slow and awful death.

Sex desire is something like that where nature puts the psyche into a pleasure wave which rise and rises and rises. Then it crests and heads for the shallow sands. One is then dumped there and left for dead.

I berated sex desire but what does that mean in the practical sense? Poor people must take loans even though the interest rate is abusive. Whales will ride waves even though they will be beached on occasion. The information does not necessarily change anything for anybody.

The thigh energy is there to serve the sexual reproduction/enjoyment function of the psyche. I propose that this system be disrupted. Here are the diagrams.

siddha yoga
advanced human
thighs render
no service to genitals

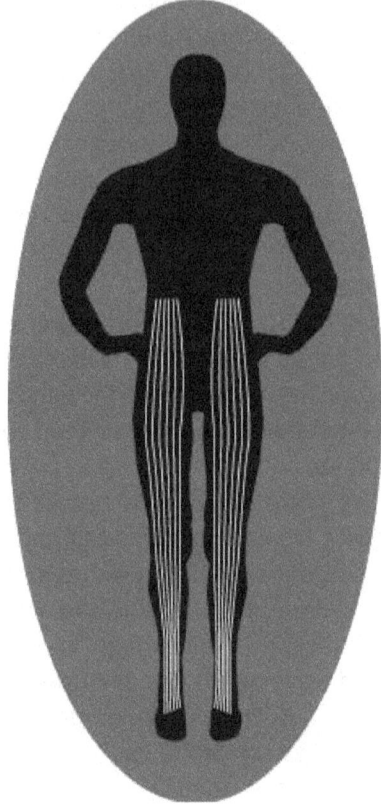

primitive man
with thighs serving genitals

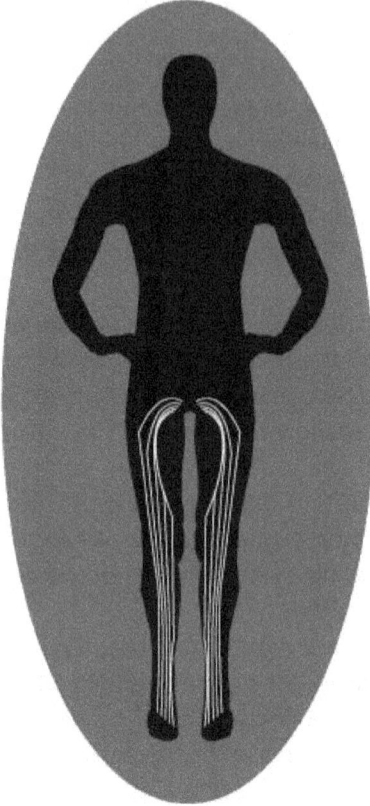

Yoga Siddha Form Creation

During afternoon breath infusion Lahiri left. He was satisfied that he assisted me. Two procedures he shared were

- nutrition orb pull up
- thigh/leg/foot clearance by pull-up anti-gravity action

In the end he said:

"I helped you sufficiently. I will go. With that you should reach where you desire."

Both methods are indirectly related to celibacy but in a sense, they are not related to it. That is the paradox. This may seem confusing but nature is an enigma which no limited being can figure.

The nutrition orb cannot be accessed until sex desire is disabled. This does not mean that the ascetic does not perform sexual acts. It means that the value system in the psyche for sex desire be underwritten with a zero so that like in mathematics, the largest number becomes nothing if it is qualified by zero.

The orthodox approach to celibacy is a farce because material nature is unwilling to support it fully. The ascetic must use another method which is to remove the value system for it. Then the sex desire even if it is a raging storm has no power under it.

Once this is achieved, the nutrition orb comes into perception and can be dealt with. A yoga guru cannot help with this. One should reach the stage where one perceives the orb then a guru will appear and give help.

The second process which has to do with the thighs, legs and feet is a *draw-up* kriya which is an *anti-gravity pull* procedure. Because of the construction of the subtle body to use the gravity of the earth for its operations, if one wants to go against gravity, one must work against the natural way. Once one gets the thighs not to serve the sexual access area, there arises suddenly this freedom to access the energy in the legs and feet. One can then pull this energy by a suction action. One can clear those parts of the psyche of used subtle energy. This is the creation of the yoga siddha form.

Glow Lights in Meditation

There are least two glow lights to observe which indicate slight contact with the chit akash sky of consciousness. Any time one finds oneself in either of these lights, one should stay put and habituate the self to remain in them like a frightened child who is placed in the arms of its mother.

If one experiences these glow lights in other tones or hues, that is acceptable. The main identity of these lights is the fact that they are just like a dim glow of light, like using a low watt bulb, to light a large room. How well do you think it will illuminate the area? Barely, it will barely do anything and still it will give some slight luminescence which can be observed.

In the case of a bulb, I can point to it and say, "There it is. That is the source of the glow."

In the case of naad meditation or intellect orb light, there is nothing to point to. It seems that there is no source of the glow. If an invisible object emits light, one may see the light but one will not see the source. If a sound emits a light, the yogi will not see the sound even though he/she may perceive the light. In this case, sound is vibration without a vibrator.

A comparison may be given as in the case of a fruit tree which is shaken by a strong human being. We can see the human. We know that the shaking is a result of his muscular action. In an earthquake however when the fruit tree shakes, we cannot pin point a source because even the ground under the tree would be moving.

Naad light is not something you can compel to appear. For instance, we heard that some people can focus between the eyebrows and compel the third eye to open. Okay, say that we accept that someone can do this.

But with naad he cannot compel the light of naad to appear. It appears while one listens to naad. Then one will see a golden glow energy which will increase the sense of security one feels when one is absorbed in naad. There will be this increase ease of feeling and a slight friendly happiness is felt. One should remain with this for as long as it remains or for as long as one's time schedule permits.

The other glow light which I will describe is the intellect orb. This glow is of the same intensity, low watt, but the color is silver-white. Will you perceive it in another tone or hue?

Who knows?

While naad sound is toward the back and not so much in the front of the subtle head, naad light is towards the front of the subtle head. You will see the glow but you will see no orb. The glow will give you an added sense of security and a quiet happiness.

Both glow lights are indications of proximity to the chit akash sky of consciousness.

Enjoy these if they ever grace your meditation.

Blindsided by Kundalini / Dangerous?

Every so often, I get an email from someone who is afraid to raise kundalini. The person may read a book of mine and then get challenged to raise kundalini but may be scared of doing so all the same.

Today I had an experience during breath infusion practice that may be regarded as supportive of those who feel that raising kundalini is dangerous and that it should not be done because it may cause irreparable harm to the body.

I had several breath infusions burst within the trunk of the subtle body. These fired one after the other. I kept infusing the air to be sure that charges were compressed. This cause the trunk of the subtle body to be filled with translucent light. Once when I stood up with locks applied, I notice that there was a shift in consciousness where my existential footing suddenly and abruptly changed

I wore a blindfold but I thought to peek to make sure that my body stood. Before doing this, I applied the locks more securely. I keep the neck and mind locks in place. Suddenly there was an urge to open the eyes. The left eye became filled with light, then the right eye too, but there was no vision.

I was blind in each eye. I could see nothing except inside the subtle eyeball which was superimposed into the physical eyes. In those eyeballs the infused energy pushed its way in and compressed itself in the eyeballs. It was pixilated, pearly and translucent. There was no vision. Each eyeball was like granite marble made of translucent solid light.

Is this dangerous?

Could I be permanently blind?

Perhaps, I should desist from this practice.

What do you think?

Astral Demands

Last night there was astral contact with the father of my body. He is now deceased. My astral body was at a religious function in Guyana. While most of the people attending were in the downstairs area where the priest did the rituals, I was upstairs hiding so that most attendees would not realize that I was present.

Suddenly, a voice began calling my name as if to say, "I have to see him. I know that he is here. It is urgent."

Then the presiding priest being disturbed by the visitor, said, "Acharya, come out. A man is here to see you."

He addressed me as Acharya, a word which means teacher in Hindi.

Just then I saw my father cross into a spell-perimeter. Usually once this spell-perimeter is made by the officiating priest, no one can cross. Somehow because he has a karmic connection to me, my father easily crossed the astral cordon but he had the sense to jump outside of it immediately after he made the request.

I came from the upstairs. I transited through the air following behind my father. He got on a three-wheel vehicle and began driving on a road. He emitted an instruction that I should follow him.

After a short distance down an astral dirt road, he arrived at a junction where the road split into two roads. In the middle of the split there was a house which had an open bottom floor which was piled with mercantile commodities. Some of these were foodstuffs.

My father walked over to a pile of beans and rice and then went to a rectangular one-foot deep trough in which there were fish and shrimp.

I followed him. He took three fishes and some shrimp. The owner of the place came suddenly. He figured the cost of the items. After that my father disappeared into the astral dimensions and I returned to the religious function.

I shared this experience to give some view about how the astral world operates and how whimsical some astral associations are, even to the extent of affecting one's astral body to do things which have very little meaning.

My Body of Innocence

This morning I had the opportunity to inspect the new mind which was acquired with this body when this body was created in the mother's psyche. The mystery of birth and death shadowed humanity for all ages. Despite our knowledge of just about everything else, we are stymied as to what exactly takes place at the birth and then the death of a specific body. This happens now. Still we are unable to make head or tail of it.

This morning, a step mother, came to visit during the meditation period. She got my vibrational address from my father, to whom she was married some years ago. She passed on from her body and so did he, but she took a new body in South America. Her subtle body assumed the stepmother pattern form.

She found me by using an identity alignment energy which was in the subtle body of my father. She said this:

"You are the son I always wanted but never got. Even though I treated you badly, still I was attached to you and wished that you were my biological production as my dear son."

After she left, there appeared a series of incidence from when I lived with my father and this person and her daughter in San Juan, Trinidad. I stayed with them there for about two months. I used to go to a ravine to look at minnows and crayfish. This place was within walking distance of their home. My father for his part showed little interest in his children in terms of teaching them anything. With him it was a puppy love affair which happened in his spare time. He was not available on a daily basis. He was a seaman.

The real value in this astral occurrence with this step mother however was the fact that her presence caused my subconscious stockpile of memories to open completely. This never happened before with such clarity in this particular way. I realize what my identity was at the time. I realized that during the formation of the present body in the mother's psyche I was awarded, so to speak, not just a new body but a new mind.

This may be termed as the body of innocence. It is a new body, rather than an innocent body except that human beings like to say that such a body is innocent because it has no culture of activities which it performed previously. It has no maturity experience to form conclusions or informed judgements.

Looking around in the psychological version of that new body, was like going into an empty room which has no furniture, no wall-hangings, no rug, nothing; just a blank place. I looked around in it. I look down at it, but there was nothing there. Even though I could feel it there was no vision of it through the subtle eyes. It was an invisible body even to itself. Imagine if you can feel your hand but when you look there is nothing there. You feel that you stand but when you look down there are no legs and feet there.

Then I saw that gradually over time, over years, things begin to appear in the room of that blank psyche. There was nothing else there, no past life, no subconscious mind, just nothing. I was totally segregated from my subconscious stock pile of memories from other lives. Then at about sixteen years of age a change occurred where some subconscious information was released. Then everything changed accordingly.

Serving Others as Equals?

The idea that no person ought to be greater than another, has value only in so far as it is a utility for paring down arrogance. The view that love simple gives is totally untrue. Love may be camouflaged under the *only gives* appearance but love in fact is the most demanding aspect in relations. It is disciplined and requires everything of a person eventually.

It is about giving, yes, but about taking too.

Jesus served his disciples by washing their feet for two reasons. One was to let them know that they needed to be concerned with caring for others, especially those whom he would put into their trust just as God had put them as his responsibility. But this is not an equal sharing, where Jesus was the equal to each disciple. It is more like the infant and the mother. The two are not equal. The infant is helpless and can neither clean or nor feed itself. In that case the mother serves the child for the very reason that the mother is superior. It is the superiority in this case which caused the mother to service the child.

Service to someone does not always mean that the servant (serving person) is the inferior. It may not mean that the serving person is the superior. It may not mean that the serving person is the equal of the other. Serving means that the service should be done irrespective of the social or existential grade of the servant and the person served.

A person may be greater and still be required to serve. That does not make that person equal to the other. The sun serves on a daily basis but we are in no way equal to it.

If God shines your shoes, that Supreme Being is still that, is still God. Nothing changed. You are neither equal to nor superior to that being.

The second reason for Jesus' foot-washing example, was to teach his disciples that there would be people who would be less-than themselves, just as they were *less than* Jesus. Still they would be required to wash the feet of those persons. It was a way of saying:

Do not feel that *greater than* always means to be on the receiving end. It also means being on the serving end with the *lesser than* as the recipients. Look at how carefully and particularly I tend you. Get some understanding of how you are to care for others.

Absolute Silence Meditation

I did an absolute silence meditation yesterday. This is when in meditation one finds oneself in an absolute silence of mind, just so without any effort on one's part, and one is afraid to do anything mentally, emotionally or psychologically to disrupt this state of consciousness.

It is then that the yogi feels like a monkey on a broken limb which hangs out in the middle of nowhere from which he can neither jump to another branch, nor to the trunk of the tree nor to any other tree, nor even to the ground.

The monkey thinks:

"My death is imminent. I cannot reach the ground without smashing my head. I cannot go up the limb because a slight jerk or movement would cause it to disconnect from the tree. I cannot swing over to another branch or to the trunk because this limb will tear if I place stress on it. This is the end. This is my death.

"I should remain here in a still posture, holding until I can no longer do so, then I will fall to my death."

When a yogi enters the thoughtless state all by the grace of providence, by some breath infusion, or by some other cause, he should remain absolutely silent and be scared of any mental or emotional action just as the monkey is scared if a branch it is on tears, and it hangs high without any way to transferring to any other support.

Just as the monkey will be scared to move, so the yogi should be afraid of doing anything which will upset that thoughtless state. This state is technically called *unmani*.

Sexual Relationship Equations

It is dangerous to want to service many sexual relationships. There is no telling how providence might tally these and how it will set these to be serviced in the future.

Many questions come to fore about the priorities of providence and as to whether these would be in one's interest.

What should I do with my girlfriends, potential girlfriends and even those from past lives whom I did not encounter in the present lifetime?

This is a misleading question. It presupposes that I can do something with my girlfriends, potential girlfriends and the ones from past lives whom I did not encounter in the present lifetime.

The truth is however that none of these relationships may be serviced if providence does not facilitate. First, I must be given access to these girlfriends. Once access is allowed, I must be allowed to service these in the conjugal way. Suppose I am given access in a non-conjugal way, then what?

Will there be frustration? Will there be a subconscious mismatch?

Will I feel undone?

Will I become grumpy under the circumstance because of suspecting intuitively that fate suspends the desired pleasure and robs me of the satisfaction I should enjoy?

In what order will providence allow me to service the relationships, and in which world system or dimension, and at which time?

I remember some persons from my youth in this body, whom I met and who used adult forms and were socially like mothers to me, but who were girlfriends from previous existences. These individuals did not objectively know of those past lives, but felt some activation of conjugal affection regardless and were downright amused and confused simultaneously when they encountered me in this life.

Why did providence do that?

How was I to shuffle through the emotional complexity?

Suppose one of these girlfriends felt that I should be her one-and-only companion and that no one else should be in the picture, how will providence accommodate that and also take care of other desires of other girlfriends?

Will I live in an era where males are allowed polygamous relationships? Or will I be restricted in a society in which only monogamous situations are permitted?

The woman Draupadi was allowed five champions for husbands. Will I be transferred into a world where one of my girlfriends is permitted that type of marital liberty?

If I was compared to a turret, spinning and clicking into positions where I would face one of my girlfriends at each position, how many positions could there be and how many dissatisfactions would occur with how many girlfriends who may feel that the allowance to my attention was not sufficient?

What would each of these girlfriends do in response?

Would each be frustrated, unhappy and sullen?

Radha and Krishna

What was the relationship between Radha and Krishna?

Radha was identified as a gopi girl who was in love with Krishna. She was one of many such gopi girls but she is accredited as the foremost of the group. Krishna did not marry Radha. She was in the vaishya farming community while Krishna was brought up under that social circumstance but was biologically of the political caste.

Krishna asserted his biological pedigree after he was invited to fight some wrestlers who were the bodyguards of King Kamsa. After Kamsa was assassinated by Krishna, Krishna's biological father, Vasudeva took steps to affirm Krishna's pedigree and had Krishna (and Balarama) trained formally in the politics of the time.

Krishna then married women who were of the political families. According to the Srimad Bhagavatam which is the primary source for information about Krishna, he did not return to the farming community where he grew up after he left to deal with Kamsa who suppressed his parents and relatives. Once, Krishna did again see Radha and his other gopi girlfriends. This was when there was a religious festival at Kurukshetra. Then the gopis (Radha included) refused to go before Krishna because he was dressed formally as a politician, as an aristocratic person of the ruling caste.

Lack of Spiritual Progress Calculated

One necessary part of spiritual progress is no progress during some phases of one's life. This is bound to happen and should be figured into the success factor. If you run a large department store then pilfering by employees needs to be calculate so that you know there will be a certain loss annually as a result.

Failure to do this will cause confusion and misinterpretation. It may cause disillusionment and discouragement.

During the past week, my meditation practice took a punch in the gut due to having to relocate and also due to various non-yogic associations. This is a part of the course of progression. In other words, stagnation, slowing down, retardation, even going backwards, losing one's footing in a certain practice, are natural parts of progression under the present circumstances.

- Do not be discouraged by it.
- Forge head in spite of it.
- Take no thought because of finding yourself in the dumps.
- Pick yourself up and move on from wherever you are even if you recognized that you passed those progression points before and are now at a lower stage.

Hearing Naad Casually

Attentive listening to naad, becoming absorbed in naad deliberately, is totally different to hearing naad casually. Some students said that they hear naad continuously. It is easy for them to hear naad. But that has little to do with attentive listening.

This morning during meditation, it took about thirteen minutes before I was attentively listening to naad. Even then the absorption was not as rich as needs be. There is the circumstance where I lost my love affair with naad. This is like when I had a rift with a girlfriend, with the foremost one. Being with her did not produce the highlighted much desired enjoyment and pleasure. We quarreled. Something happened to influence the relationship for the worse. We lived at the same residence but we were like strangers who were huddled together by circumstance but who had no affinity for each other.

After I made the contact with naad, I realized that things changed for the worse. The sweet relationship I had before was no longer there. I thought to myself:

This is depressing. My girlfriend changed. She is not agreeable.

What should I do?

How can I live with her hostility?

After those thoughts I considered that I should put myself in the back of the head near the neck where the neck joins into the base of the skull. I felt that if I stayed there things would soon normalize. I would be my *jolly go lucky* self again. My girlfriend would return. I would be happy again.

I waited and waited. Nothing happened. The relationship did not change.

I was down and out, in the dumps because of this.

I had an idea. I linked with the nutritional orb. I pulled it up and to see if naad would help me in that endeavor like it did before. However, it did nothing to assist.

I was left with the nutrition orb being pulled up to the throat to where the tongue touches the soft palate at the back of the mouth but the lovey dovey feeling was gone. How drab!

I was like a man with a lover who did not love him.

Like a lonely sailor adrift on a makeshift raft in an ocean, no one to talk to, no smile to see on a pretty face, nothing, just salt water and bare sky in all directions.

My Non-Romantic Girlfriend

Meditation this afternoon was an improvement over meditation this morning when naad was like a stranger who turned her face away from me while we rode the bus to work in the morning. The woman must have had a flare-up with her husband or some tragedy in her home before she left for work. When she got on the bus, she was unwilling to speak to anyone. Not even, good morning, did she say; not a glance, not a smile, not even a neutral glance, nothing.

In the beginning, naad was like a friend this afternoon but not like a girlfriend, just as a friend. By the end of the session, this plain friendly sound was like a non-romantic girlfriend.

What is that like?

It reminds me of a girlfriend I used to have when my body was nine years of age. She was a pretty girl as far as I was concerned. I was attracted to her for sure. But there was no sexual flavor to it, just a gender-difference attraction. It was with a bit of neutral love with friendship and desire to be near each other but that was it.

It was a relationship that was devoid of sexual interest. It was as close as nature permits in such situations where there is no possibility of sexual expression. In this session of meditation naad began with just friendship. Then by the end of it, I could embrace naad like seeing a girlfriend when I was identified as a nine-year-old body.

One interesting thing that happened which I did not notice, or compare before, was naad light variation. Before in this life my introduction to naad light only happened after my love affair with naad began. During the friendship stage before, there was to my perception no naad light, even though there was vibration manifestation and vibration light production which was a dark blue, dark grey, dark brown energy.

Now in the naad non-romantic girlfriend stage, naad emitted a light which was brighter than in the romantic girlfriend state. This light in the non-romantic girlfriend stage is brighter like say a 25-watt bulb, while the romantic girlfriend state it is more like a 5-watt bulb which gives a cozy feeling to support a romantic encounter.

Meditation may go downhill but it can climb and ascend again. The student should be willing to make that rise to where he/she was before.

Under House-Arrest by Naad

Meditation this morning was a progression from the digression the practice suffered recently. At least for the first fifteen minutes, there seems to be no connection to naad, no idea of it. Then I realized that I was in touch with naad except that it acted as a silent sentry guarding me as if I were a prisoner under house arrest.

When authorities hold an important political prisoner, they do so with care to be sure not to hurt the captive. They make him feel as if he is not under arrest. I realized during the meditation that I was in touch with naad but naad was silent as if it did not desire to disturbed me.

Imagine a sound vibration which becomes totally silent, where it is present and is in control and still it is not felt in any way.

Cosmic Sense of Identity Light

During meditation a special thing happened which was the contact with the *chit akash* through streaks of cosmic sense of identity light which came into my psyche horizontally. Usually contact with the cosmic sense of identity come in from high up. It strikes the individual sense of identity as a bright ray-flash of stunning light.

In this experience it was different where the light came in from the horizontal in line with the center of my temple and on the left side only. It was streaks of white and colored translucent light, instead of one flash ray of blinking luminescence.

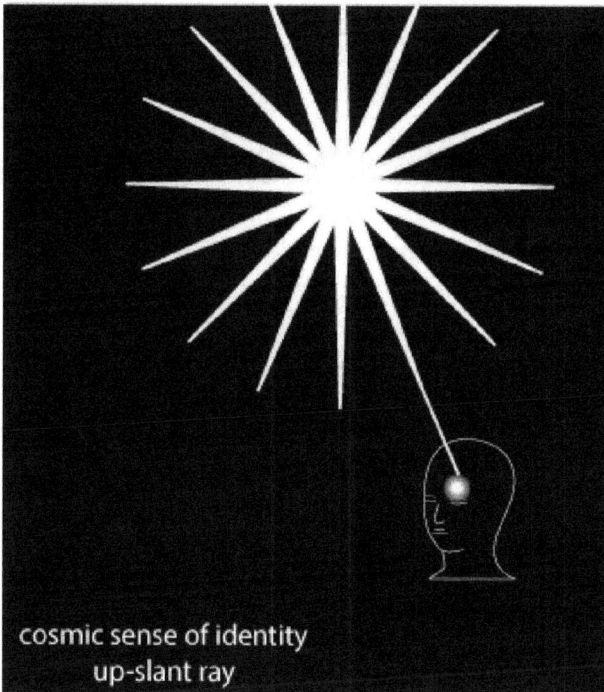

cosmic sense of identity
up-slant ray

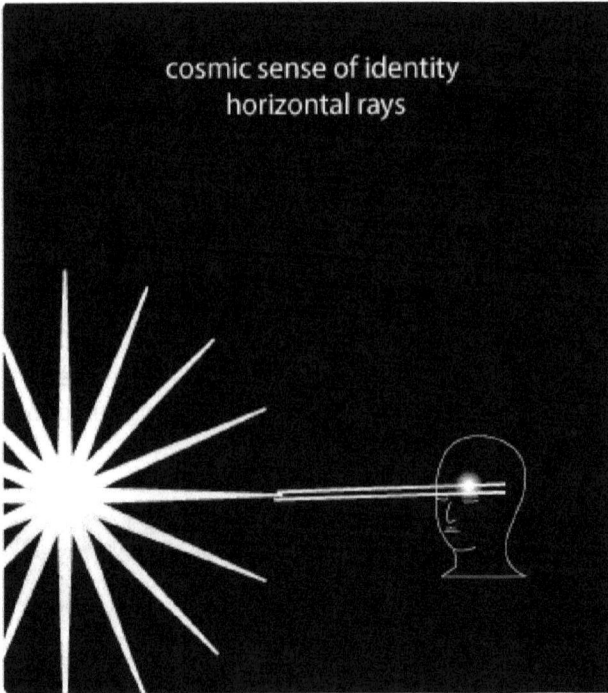

cosmic sense of identity
horizontal rays

The inability to raise kundalini is always due to fault in the technique. Even though one thinks one follows the instruction to the letter, still one may not be. One may omit or include something which causes the failure. The main cause for students who were trained, is the inability to make the breath energy become concentrated and to be pushed down through the navel area into the pubic zone and then to the base chakra. Any inefficiency in these actions may result in kundalini not rising.

Can a student make kundalini rise in the conventional way, if he/she was provided with a much-desired sex partner?

To make a point, I will put my reputation on the line and say this:

If kundalini does not rise during practice, it may if one is sexually engaged, rise through the genitals?

If kundalini will rise for sexual pleasure but it will not for breath infusion, we can conclude that it is prejudiced against breath infusion and is disinclined to rising up through the spine but it is very eager to discharge its energy through the genitals.

This is similar to what happens in the operation of digestion and excretion. In some of us, there is no problem digesting. In fact, we become obese as a result of a very efficient digestion, but when it comes to excretion we are stymied. But the same kundalini which causes efficient digestion is reluctant to sponsor prompt excretion.

There is a way to check to see if one had an impact on kundalini by doing the infusion. That method is to observe the quality of the meditation session. If the session was on a high plane, it means that kundalini did rise even though it did not do so in a sensational way.

To support this statement, consider that sooner or later, according to the intensity of the practice, one will reach a stage where *sushumna nadi* central passage will remain clear and open continuously. Then kundalini will have no built-up charge of energy to discharge in a rush of pleasure. Kundalini will come into the brain on a fulltime basis. The yogi will not have those moments of intense pleasure from it as before. But then there will be infused energy compaction, and its resulting bliss experiences.

Are we expectant of and addictive towards a rush pleasure climax?

Sure, we are.

That is the condition which we have from nature.

However, the spiritual situation is different because it is not focalized on the genitals. It is evenly distributed in every part of the psyche.

Naad in the Teacher-Student Relationship

I meditated with naad after doing breath infusion. I was with naad as if naad was another person beside me. I did breath infusion. It was a good session but it was a teaching session not just my individual practice. In teaching sessions other things happen. The teacher is not himself or herself, and does not practice with specific focus on his/her individual needs.

I was with naad, as I said above. Then I realized that I was like a student. Naad was the teacher. There was relationship but it was not the boyfriend-girlfriend feeling. I just could not in any way feel romantic.

Naad was the adult teacher. I was five years old student.

The relationship with naad during meditation was just like the relationship that there was between me and a kindergarten teacher. I was the willing-to-learn student, the boy who was attentive. Naad was the teacher who expertly taught and was serious about making sure that I learned what she taught.

Naad took me in hand. It trained me on how to be transcendental, how to be supernatural, how to be distant from the considerations of the physical world.

After fifteen minutes, the relationship changed. Naad was like a friend I had when studying Algebra. We studied and shared ideas of formulas. During the discussions there was no interest in girlfriends, none whatsoever. We forgot that we had interest in girls our age.

Yogi in Love

In meditation this morning, naad was indifferent to me, like being with a stranger, like when a man is spurned by a lover and is left to pine away.

What should a yogi do under the circumstance?

What else, besides meditate on naad but in a mood of not disturbing naad, not being grumpy about it, being patient, staying close to naad without a sour attitude.

I came out of the meditation for a short while, just to make a notation about this, so as to alert students who fantasize or who received hype about meditation on naad as if it is always a friendly much desired state.

Even though the meditation began on this down note, it developed into a positive and romantic relationship, where near the end, I found myself to be very endearing to naad.

Then it flashed that this final state during the session was like when a man walks with a woman on a lonesome beach, with their hands together in the fantasy of love, where they feel that they are the only two people in the world and that the entire universe was designed just for their pleasure. These are two conceited people but it is a sweet form of conceit.

Of course, they are not the only two people in the world. And of course, the world was not designed around them. And of course, the world will see to it that in the future they come to their senses to know that they have absolutely no significance. Still, for the time being, they are in love. Everything supports their feelings.

The whole thing, billions of stars shining in the blue night, was manufactured just for that moment when they met and their hands were clasped together with the spasms of romance. This was how they felt at that moment.

About three days ago, I got a flash message from Lahiri Baba which stated that the non-romantic relationship with naad arose from a lack of chitakash energy in the psyche of a yogi, especially resulting from a lack of clearance of the energies from the thigh downward.

Yogis usually focus on the spinal column and the head of the subtle body. This is a good practice and is required at a certain state. However, if one advances and does not become stagnant or dogmatic, one will develop focus on the entire subtle body, the whole psyche. Then the relevance of cleaning every part of it will be evident.

There is a magic bullet for students who began yoga after fifty years of age, and who want to sit in easy pose without the leg or thigh falling sleep. It is this:

Tolerate it. Train your mind to accept it, so that during meditation when it happens your mind regards it as normal and regular and continues with the meditative focus being used at that time.

The mind gets jumpy about certain things. For some of these, it can be retrained where it handles the incidences in a passive non-alarming mood but some other things the mind will never get used to, and will continue reacting violently and surprisingly.

You should know for sure, that even advance yogis suffer from cramps and circulation shut down when sitting in easy pose and especially when sitting in tight lotus *(padmasana)*.

Some years ago, I sat in a tight lotus to meditate I used to sit in an even tighter one. Due to the aging of the body and its decreased capacity for youthful vigor, I was forced to sit in a not-so-tight lotus despite my burning desire to do so. This is like when an old man finally meets the love of his life, but fate set it up to happen when he is between sixty and seventy years of age.

At the time even though he has desire and even though the desire is strong and he can appreciate it, still he is not productive on the active sexual end of the bargain. It is full of disappointment, embarrassment and heartache. I had a friend who suffered from this for many years. Hearing his descriptions of the disappointment was heart rendering.

If yoga is your sweetheart and if you found your true love in yoga after sixty years of age, it will be somewhat disappointing if you do not achieve certain aspects in a perfect and exemplary way. Better to find love at seventy than to go through the entire life and not find it and to be on the last breath, thinking,

When will the love of my life appear?

How can I die and not ever see love personified?

But here is something which I know for sure. In the beginning when I got a yoga teacher (Arthur Beverford), I did lotus posture with difficulty in extreme pain. That was in 1970. I sat in it, which is foolish to do if the lotus posture is not easy for you. I would suffer through the pain and with brute mental force made myself internalize or focus on the center of the eyebrows. But that causes an inefficient meditation because one has to maintain tolerance towards the aches, pains and cramps and that portion of your attention does not go into the meditation.

However later on, I could sit in lotus and not have to worry about pains for about fifteen minutes. After those fifteen minutes, I had to ease out of the posture because there were severe pains which the mind could not tolerate.

Now after years of practice, I can sit in lotus posture for thirty minutes or even for an hour. At about forty-five minutes for the most, the cramps and circulation effects will set it. Then if I already shifted over to a higher state of consciousness or into another dimension, I do not feel the condition of the physical body until I resume ordinary perception. Thus, the cramps have no relevance while one is transited over into another plane of consciousness but as soon as one shifts back, one feels them and is force to uncoil the legs.

There are other similar things which may happen. For instance, sometimes when I return to physical consciousness, I become aware that the head is slumped over and the neck has a pulled or strained muscle. Sometimes the tongue is pushed stiffly into the lower teeth and is pinched between two tightly spaced teeth. One discovers this when one returns.

Subterranean Descent / Devil's Millhopper

Due to the presence of Bernard Adjodha in Gainesville, Florida as well as of Vishak, a caste brahmin from India, I got the opportunity to visit a place known as the Devil's Millhopper. This is located near Gainesville.

It is a depression in the earth due to the caving in of ground material into a large cavern within the earth. Going down was easy. It felt that one should look forward to it. There were people helping others to get down.

This is similar to have a vice like smoking, drinking alcohol, taking narcotics, and indulging in sexual excess. One is encouraged to do it, where it does not require any special endeavor.

When we got to the bottom, there was not much to see. I felt like the invisible people who encouraged us to go down, were suddenly absent. There was a faint smell of dampness, sulphur and sour water, like when the earth is waterlogged with sewage. The vegetation grew. There was crystal clear water running and blackish-brownish stagnant water.

On the way when we were up on the ground level, just before descending, we passed a man who seemed like something had hit him in the face. His body lost color. His eyes blared. He looked like he has seen hell and managed to escape but that he was prohibited from sharing the experience. It was bright daylight and without looking at any of us, he walked on like a ghost with a sunrise deadline for slipping through the night.

After five minutes at the bottom, I began to feel that something had gone terribly wrong. Visions of the subterranean astral regions of the earth, began to arise in my mind but I could see that other persons were also uncertain but just could not put their fingers down on anything. For one thing, no one would admit that this was a terrible mistake. You do not descend into hell with a *merry go lucky* attitude, at least not if you are sober.

After about ten minutes down there, I began to muster the courage to leave the place, but there was a spell on everyone. A lady and her child who were there when we arrived, silently left without staring at any of us. It was as if she spoke to some unseen person and the conversation just happen to be over. She had to leave us there.

I then realized that the only people who were normal at that place, the only people who greeted each other cordially were those who had not descended down into the Devil's Millhopper.

Then after about fifteen minutes average, one of our party said something about going up. We all turned and followed as he ascended to the ground level. Of the total of five persons, two of them took off up the stairs like bats never looking back as they flew out of hell. The rest of us slowly made our way up the winding stairs. It felt like we are going against gravity. My feet were heavy. My heart was fatigued. My lungs wondered what gas I inhaled. My muscles strained against a slowing force which wanted me to go to the bottom of the Millhopper.

As soon as I stepped back to the top, to the ground level, there was a whiff of fresh air, something which was absent at the bottom of that place. I then recalled that there are subterranean astral places which were just like this in terms of causing the astral body to become extra heavy and stagnant.

Neanderthal Student Yogis

In the astral world last night, I had a conversation with some human-looking Neanderthal hominids. They complained of how the humans treat them and about the lack of opportunity in the human society for their kind.

Sometimes I wonder why certain people adopt yoga practice? If you were time-jumped into the modern age and your real time-life was during the Neanderthal period of hominids, then being in the modern situation is a sure challenge and being in the digital age is somewhat amusing and very confusing.

Why not become a student yogi?

Is yoga not for rapid evolutionary advancement?

The answer is simple:

No, it is not!

Evolutionary advancement is strictly in the hands of nature. It has nothing to do with yoga. You cannot evolve merely by doing yoga, even by doing kriya yoga. To evolve you have to be subjected to the rigors of nature. That is what produces the evolutionary strides.

If your species ceased by nature, scraped as it was, suspended forever, and if somehow you grafted to the modern humans, it does not mean that you are as evolved as the modern human species.

How do you deal with this insecurity?

Yoga will not provide a solution for you. It cannot replace nature.

Does that mean that you should do no yoga?

It does not mean that but it means that you should not think that yoga can do what it has no authority to adjust.

How will you evolve?

The answer is simple:

You will not evolve until nature provides an environment in which you could prosper. In the meantime, you should lay low in the society of the modern humans, watching them and waiting for nature to flip them out of the scene and reintroduce your species.

We know that yoga assists you if we see that you are humble to nature which is your total evolutionary access, the key to success, the way for you to grow the human profile from the inside out

Sudden Kundalini Rise

Usually the first dramatic experience one gets with kundalini is sexual climax experience, but one may not realize that this energy is kundalini. When kundalini rises through the spine into the brain, is it considered to be kundalini. However, this is misinformation, because kundalini is involved in everything the body does and everything which happens within the body itself.

With sex experience one is not trained to observe kundalini astutely. Nature pushes us in the direction of observing it as enjoyers only. Suppose I go to a Broadway play. The only thing that is required of me is to buy a ticket, enter the premises and take a seat. I am an enjoyer of it. I am not required to endeavor in any way. This is like how we regard sex experience.

Yet there is another way to relate to a Broadway play. That is to enter by the back entrance, take a part in the play, learn the lines to be recited, practice acting and then be on the stage at the time when the play is to begin. In that case one is not the enjoying observer. One is the working performer.

Doing kundalini yoga is like being the working performer, where one must remember what to recite, and how to act it out. One should do it for the enjoyment of the audience. One should laugh when one should, even though for one it is not funny. One must be angry during some stages and pretend to kill another performer even though one is non-violent. One cannot eat popcorn. One cannot recline in a seat drinking a beverage. During recess one must hurry and change the outfit to assume another part when the curtains open again.

Since we were trained to be observing spectators for whom the play is a source of enjoyment, when we first train in kundalini yoga, it seems very awkward.

A recurring question is:

During sexual climax experience does one scientifically observe the experience, how the energy flows, where the energy is derived, how the energy reaches climax?

Sex experience is private and confidential. Nobody stops to do anything besides enjoy. Nature does most of it with a little help and then one is subjected to the intense pleasure.

In kundalini yoga however one must be attentive to note any rise in the energy no matter how small, to compress it in and in, to channel it, to squeeze it back and confine it to certain areas, to keep the locks rigid. Thus, a new training is required.

Vigilance is required when doing kundalini yoga. Student should watch inside the psyche to see what the energy does, as to where it goes, as to how it moves, as to how it is compressed by the locks, as to its intensity and coloring if there is any type of visual or touch perception.

Small rises of kundalini? These should be observed. In fact, these are more important then the large and very obvious rises. These tell the student that there is a high degree of sensitivity and psychic perception, which is a plus in this practice.

There is a rule where in the lineages the yogis do not discuss their experiences except with their teachers and with other advanced students. This is an old principle.

Apart from this the big secret about the failure to report what happens in *samadhi* trance states, is that the yogi may have no memory equipment while in those states. Instead of admitting this many teachers, even very advanced ones, say that the experience was so fantastic that it could not be described and that words could do no justice to it and that one must experience it oneself.

I have never had an experience which I could not describe but what happened when I failed to explain it, was that I did not have the vocabulary or I could not pin down something similar in the ordinary experience which I could refer to as being similar to the experience.

Some experiences are vague initially but if they recurr, clarity dawns. This was never due to the fantastic-ness of the experience. It was due to the fact that I did not have the supernatural sense perception to integrate the experience. If you are blind, then if you are struck by a bright light, how will you explain it. Of course, you may report truthfully that it was fantastic and beyond description.

If there is a vague experience, usually within three days I would develop the proper supernatural perception to see it clearly. In rare cases, it may take three weeks or three months even but usually it is within three days, and then the supernatural perception is available.

There is called shaktipat bestowal of supernatural perception. That is different because that is where there is a deliberate transmission from a yoga guru and then the student sees supernaturally as a result.

A student may tune into the nature of a yoga teacher, and from that connect develop supernatural perception even with no obvious bestowal from the teacher.

Since in some trance states there is no memory formation, or stated precisely, memory formation is just not possible, then the only way to remember what takes place is to emerge from a trance state and record what happened in brief notes. Then re-enter those trance states.

But for a beginner this is risky because if he/she leaves a trance state then he/she may be unable to resume it.

I do so because of years of practice and because of having an innate sensitivity. Once I know that I am in a no-memory-possibility state, I leave that state, make notes and return into that state.

Later when I see those notes after leaving the trance state, I can describe what happened.

The question is:

Why is there no memory capacity in some trance states?

The answer is that in some states there is no memory capacity because there just is not any.

It is not a problem of not having memory capacity there. The issue is recognizing that the state is such. One has no way to send information to the edge of that state.

Index

About the Author

Michael Beloved (Yogi *Madhvāchārya*) took his current body in 1951 in Guyana. In 1965, while living in Trinidad, he instinctively began doing yoga postures and tried to make sense of the supernatural side of life.

Later in 1970, in the Philippines, he approached a Martial Arts Master named Arthur Beverford. He explained to the teacher that he was seeking a yoga instructor. Mr. Beverford identified himself as an advanced disciple of *Śrī* Rishi Singh Gherwal, an Ashtanga Yoga master.

Beverford taught the traditional Ashtanga Yoga with stress on postures, attentive breathing and brow chakra centering meditation. In 1972, Michael entered the Denver, Colorado Ashram of *kundalini* yoga Master *Śrī* Harbhajan Singh. There he took instruction in *bhastrika* pranayama and its application to yoga postures. He was supervised mostly by Yogi Bhajan's disciple named Prem Kaur.

In 1979 Michael formally entered the disciplic succession of the Brahmā - Madhava-Gaudiya Sampradaya through *Swāmī* Kirtanananda, who was a prominent sannyasi disciple of the Great Vaishnava Authority *Śrī Swāmī* Bhaktivedanta Prabhupada, the exponent of devotion to Sri Krishna.

However, yoga has a mystic side to it, thus Michael took training and teaching empowerment from several spiritual masters of different aspects of spiritual development. This is consistent with *Śrī* Krishna's advice to Arjuna in the *Bhagavad Gītā*:

Most of the instructions Michael received were given in the astral world. On that side of existence, his most prominent teachers were *Śrī Swāmī* Shivananda of Rishikesh, Yogiraj *Swāmī* Vishnudevananda, *Śrī Bābāji Mahasaya* - the master of the masters of *Kriyā* Yoga, *Śrīla* Yogeshwarananda of Gangotri - the master of the masters of *Rāj* Yoga (spiritual clarity), and Siddha *Swāmī* Nityananda the Brahmā Yoga authority.

The course for kundalini yoga using pranayama breath-infusion was detailed by Michael in the book *Kundalini Hatha Yoga Pradipika*. This current book was composed from meditation and breath-infusion notes which were originally shared in staple bound booklets as Yoga Journals.

Michael's preliminary books relating to this topic are *Meditation Pictorial*, *Meditation Expertise*, and *Meditation ~ Sense Faculty* (co-author). Every technique (kriya) mentioned was tested by him during pranayama breath-infusion and *samyama* deep meditation practice.

This is a result of over forty years of meditation practice with astute subtle observations intending to share the methods and experiences. The information is published freely with no intention of forming an institution or hogtying anyone as a disciple.

Publications

English Series

Bhagavad Gita English

Anu Gita English

Markandeya Samasya English

Yoga Sutras English

Hatha Yoga Pradipika English

Uddhava Gita English

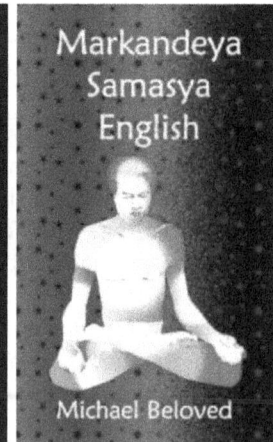

Yoga Sūtras English

Michael Beloved

Haṭha Yoga Pradīpikā English

Michael Beloved

Uddhava Gītā English

Michael Beloved / Madhvāchārya dās

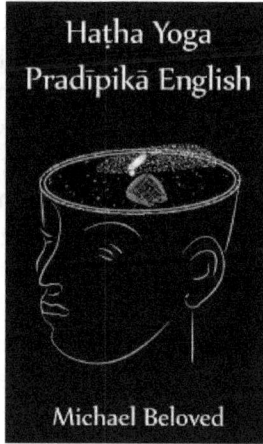

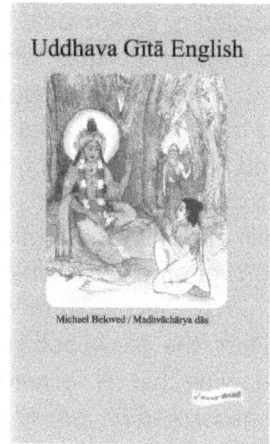

These are in 21st Century English, very precise and exacting. Many Sanskrit words which were considered untranslatable into a Western language are rendered in precise, expressive and modern English.

Three of these books are instructions from Krishna. **In *Bhagavad Gita* English** and **Anu Gita English**, the instructions were for Arjuna. In the **Uddhava Gita English,** it was for Uddhava. *Bhagavad Gita* and Anu Gita are extracted from the Mahabharata. Uddhava Gita was extracted from the 11th Canto of the Srimad Bhagavatam (Bhagavata Purana). One of these books, the **Markandeya Samasya English** is about Krishna, as described by Yogi Markandeya, who survived the cosmic collapse and reached a divine child in whose transcendental body, the collapsed world was existing.

Two of this series are the syllabus about yoga practice. The *Yoga Sutras* of Patañjali is elaboration about ashtanga yoga. Hatha Yoga Pradipika English, is the detailed information about asana postures, pranayama breath-infusion, energy compression, naad sound resonance and advanced meditation. The Sanskrit author is Swatmarama Mahayogin.

My suggestion is that you read *Bhagavad Gita* **English**, the **Anu Gita English, the Markandeya Samasya English,** the *Yoga Sutras* **English,** the **Hatha Yoga Pradipika** and lastly the **Uddhava Gita English**, which is complicated and detailed.

For each of these books we have at least one commentary, which is published separately. Thus one's particular interest can be researched further in the commentaries.

The smallest of these commentaries and perhaps the simplest is the one for the Anu Gita. We published its commentary as the Anu Gita Explained. The *Bhagavad Gita* explanations were published in three distinct targeted commentaries. The first is *Bhagavad Gita* Explained, which sheds lights on how people in the time of Krishna and Arjuna regarded the information and applied it. *Bhagavad Gita* is an exposition of the application of yoga practice to cultural activities, which is known in the Sanskrit language as karma yoga.

Interestingly, *Bhagavad Gita* was spoken on a battlefield just before one of the greatest battles in the ancient world. A warrior, Arjuna, lost his wits and had no idea that he could apply his training in yoga to political dealings. Krishna, his charioteer, lectured on the spur of the moment to give Arjuna the skill of using yoga proficiency in cultural dealings including how to deal with corrupt officials on a battlefield.

The second Gita commentary is the Kriya Yoga *Bhagavad Gita*. This clears the air about Krishna's information on the science of kriya yoga, showing that its techniques are clearly described for anyone who takes the time to read *Bhagavad Gita*. Kriya yoga concerns the battlefield which is the psyche of the living being. The internal war and the mental and emotional forces which are hostile to self-realization are dealt with in the kriya yoga practice.

The third commentary is the Brahma Yoga *Bhagavad Gita*. This shows what Krishna had to say outright and what he hinted about which concerns the brahma yoga practice, a mystic process for those who mastered kriya yoga.

There is one commentary for the **Markandeya Samasya English**. The title of that publication is Krishna Cosmic Body.

There are two commentaries to the *Yoga Sutras*. One is the *Yoga Sutras of Patañjali* and the other is the Meditation Expertise. These give detailed explanations of ashtanga Yoga.

The commentary of Hatha Yoga Pradipika is titled Kundalini Hatha Yoga Pradipika.

For the Uddhava Gita, we published the Uddhava Gita Explained. This is a large book and requires concentration and study for integration of the information. Of the books which deal with transcendental topics, my opinion is that the discourse between Krishna and Uddhava has the complete information about the realities in existence. This book is the one which removes massive existential ignorance.

Meditation Series

Meditation Pictorial

Meditation Expertise

CoreSelf Discovery

Meditation Sense Faculty

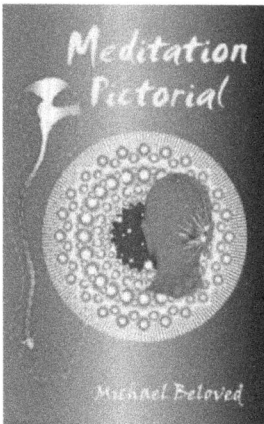

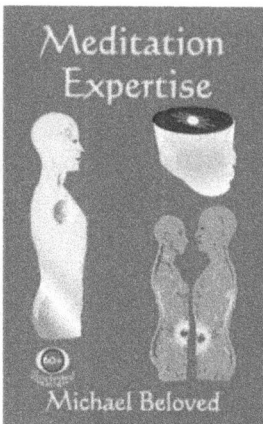

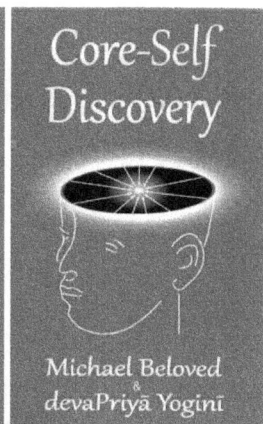

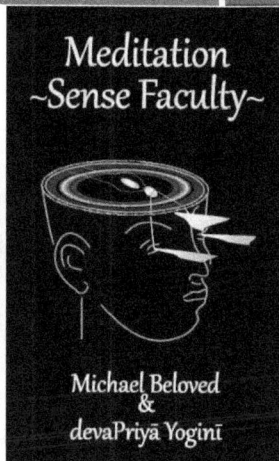

The specialty of these books is the mind diagrams which profusely illustrate what is written. This shows exactly what one has to do mentally to develop and then sustain a meditation practice.

In the **Meditation Pictorial,** one is shown how to develop psychic insight, a feature without which meditation is imagination and visualization, without any mystic experience per se.

In the **Meditation Expertise,** one is shown how to corral one's practice to bring it in line with the classic syllabus of yoga which Patañjali lays out as the ashtanga yoga eight-staged practice.

In **CoreSelf Discovery,** (co-authored with *devaPriya Yogini*) one is taken though the course of *pratyahar* sensual energy withdrawal which is the 5th stage of yoga in the Patañjali ashtanga eight-process complete system of yoga practice. These events lead to the discovery of a coreSelf which is surrounded by psychic organs in the head of the subtle body. This product has a DVD component.

Meditation ~ Sense Faculty (co-authored with *devaPriya Yogini*) is a detailed tutorial with profuse diagrams showing what actions to take in the subtle body to investigate the senses faculties. The meditator must first establish the location and function of the observing self. That self must be screened from the thoughts and ideas which usually hypnotize it.

These books are profusely illustrated with mind diagrams showing the components of psychic consciousness and the inner design of the subtle body.

Explained Series

Bhagavad Gita Explained

Uddhava Gita Explained

Anu Gita Explained

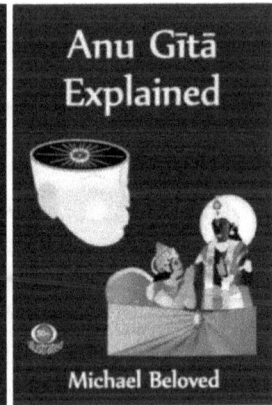

The specialty of these books is that they are free of missionary intentions, cult tactics and philosophical distortion. Instead of using these books to add credence to a philosophy, meditation process, belief or plea for followers, I spread the information out so that a reader can look through this literature and freely take or leave anything as desired.

When Krishna stressed himself as God, I stated that. When Krishna laid no claims for supremacy, I showed that. The reader is left to form an independent opinion about the validity of the information and the credibility of Krishna.

There is a difference in the discourse with Arjuna in the *Bhagavad Gita* and the one with Uddhava in the Uddhava Gita. In fact, these two books may appear to contradict each other. In the *Bhagavad Gita*, Krishna pressured Arjuna to complete social duties. In the Uddhava Gita, Krishna insisted that Uddhava should abandon the same.

The Anu Gita is not as popular as the *Bhagavad Gita* but it is the conclusion of that text. Anu means what is to follow, what proceeds. In this discourse, an anxious Arjuna request that Krishna should repeat the *Bhagavad Gita* and again show His supernatural and divine forms.

However, Krishna refuses to do so and chastises Arjuna for being a disappointment in forgetting what was revealed. Krishna then cited a celestial yogi, a near-perfected being, who explained the process of transmigration in vivid detail.

Commentaries

Yoga Sutras of Patañjali

Meditation Expertise

Krishna Cosmic Body

Anu Gita Explained

Bhagavad Gita Explained

Kriya Yoga Bhagavad Gita

Brahma Yoga Bhagavad Gita

Uddhava Gita Explained

Kundalini Hatha Yoga Pradipika

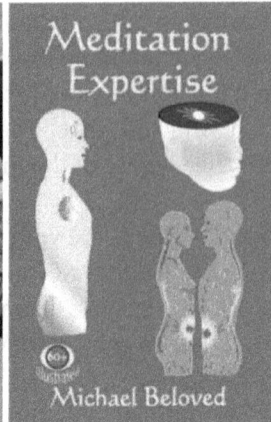

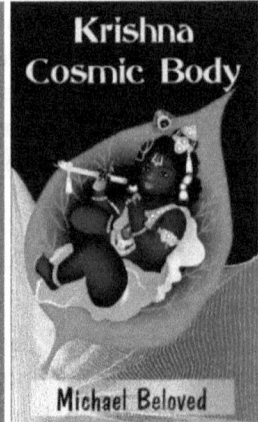

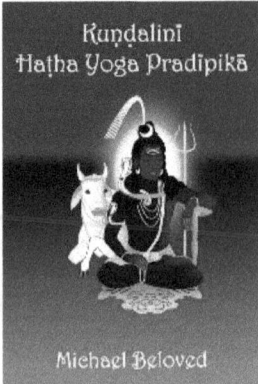

Yoga Sutras of Patañjali **is** the globally acclaimed text book of yoga. This has detailed expositions of yoga techniques. Many kriya techniques are vividly described in the commentary.

Meditation Expertise is an analysis and application of the *Yoga Sutras*. This book is loaded with illustrations and has detailed explanations of secretive advanced meditation techniques which are called kriyas in the Sanskrit language.

Krishna Cosmic Body is a narrative commentary on the Markandeya Samasya portion of the Aranyaka Parva of the Mahabharata. This is the detailed description of the dissolution of the world, as experienced by the great yogin Markandeya who transcended the cosmic deity, Brahma, and reached Brahma's source who is the divine infant, Krishna.

Anu Gita Explained is a detailed explanation of how we endure many material bodies in the course of transmigrating through various life-forms. This is a discourse between Krishna and Arjuna. Arjuna requested of Krishna a display of the Universal Form and a repeat narration of the *Bhagavad Gita* but Krishna declined and explained what a siddha perfected being told the Yadu family about the sequence of existences one endures and the systematic flow of those lives at the convenience of material nature.

Bhagavad Gita **Explained** shows what was said in the Gita without religious overtones and sectarian biases.

Kriya Yoga *Bhagavad Gita* shows the instructions for those who are doing kriya yoga.

Brahma Yoga *Bhagavad Gita* shows the instructions for those who are doing brahma yoga.

Uddhava Gita Explained shows the instructions to Uddhava which are more advanced than the ones given to Arjuna.

Bhagavad Gita is an instruction for applying the expertise of yoga in the cultural field. This is why the process taught to Arjuna is called karma yoga which means karma + yoga or cultural activities done with yogic insight.

Uddhava Gita is an instruction for apply the expertise of yoga to attaining spiritual status. This is why it explains jnana yoga and bhakti yoga in detail. Jnana yoga is using mystic skill for knowing the spiritual part of existence. Bhakti yoga is for developing affectionate relationships with divine beings.

Karma yoga is for negotiating the social concerns in the material world. It is inferior to bhakti yoga which concerns negotiating the social concerns in the spiritual world.

This world has a social environment. The spiritual world has one too.

Currently, Uddhava Gita is the most advanced and informative spiritual book on the planet. There is nothing anywhere which is superior to it or which goes into so much detail as it. It verified that historically Krishna is the most advanced human being to ever have left literary instructions on this planet. Even Patañjali *Yoga Sutras* which I translated and gave an application for in my book, **Meditation Expertise**, does not go as far as the Uddhava Gita.

Some of the information of these two books is identical but while the *Yoga Sutras* are concerned with the personal spiritual emancipation (kaivalyam) of the individual spirits, the Uddhava Gita explains that and also explains the situations in the spiritual universes.

Bhagavad Gita is from the *Mahabharata* which is the history of the Pandavas. Arjuna, the student of the Gita, is one of the Pandavas brothers. He was in a social hassle and did not know how to apply yoga expertise to solve it. On the battlefield, Krishna gave him a crash-course on yogic social interactions.

Uddhava Gita is from the *Srimad Bhagavatam (Bhagavata Purana),* which is a history of the incarnations of Krishna. Uddhava was a relative of Krishna. He was concerned about the situation of the deaths of many of his relatives but Krishna diverted Uddhava's attention to the practice of yoga for the purpose of successfully migrating to the spiritual environment.

Kundalini Hatha Yoga Pradipika is the commentary for the Hatha Yoga Pradipika of Swatmarama Mahayogin. This is the detailed process about asana posture, pranayama breath-infusion, complex compressions of energy, naad sound resonance intonement and advanced meditation practice.

This is the singular book with all the techniques of how to reform and redesign the subtle body so that it does not have the tendency for physical life forms and for it to attain the status of a siddha.

These books are based on the author's experiences in meditation, yoga practice and participation in spiritual groups:

Specialty

Spiritual Master

sex you!

Sleep Paralysis

Astral Projection

Masturbation Psychic Details

Spiritual Master
Michael Beloved

sex you!
michael beloved

Sleep Paralysis
Michael Beloved

Astral Projection
Michael Beloved

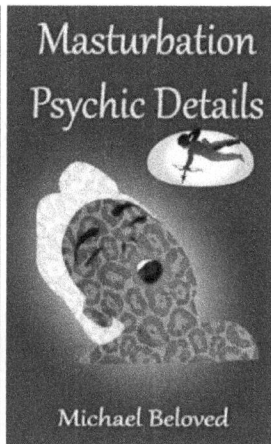

Masturbation Psychic Details
Michael Beloved

In **Spiritual Master**, Michael draws from experience with gurus or with their senior students. His contact with astral gurus is rated. He walks you through the avenue of gurus showing what you should do and what you should not do, so as to gain proficiency in whatever area of spirituality the guru has proficiency.

sex you! is a masterpiece about the adventures of an individual spirit's passage through the parents' psyches. The conversion of a departed soul into a sexual urge is described. The transit from the afterlife to residency in the emotions of the parents is detailed. This is about sex and you. Learn about how much of you comprises the romantic energy of one's would-be parents!

Sleep Paralysis clears misconceptions so that one can see what sleep paralysis is and what frightening astral experience occurs while the paralysis is being experienced. This disempowerment has great value in giving you confidence that you can and do exist even if one is unable to operate the physical body. The implication is that one can exist apart from and will survive the loss of the material form.

Astral Projection details experiences Michael had even in childhood, where he assumed incorrectly that everyone was astrally conversant. He discusses the lifeForce psychic mechanism which operates the sleep-wake cycle of the physical form, and which budgets energy into the separated astral form which determines if the individual will have dream recall or no objective awareness during the projections. Astral travel happens on every occasion when the physical body sleeps. What is missing in awareness is the observer status while the astral body is separated.

Masturbation Psychic Details is a surprise presentation which relates what happens on the psychic plane during a masturbation event. This does not tackle moral issues or even addictions but shows the involvement of memory and the sure but hidden subconscious mind which operates many features of the psyche irrespective of the desire or approval of the self-conscious personality.

inVision Series

Yoga inVision 1

Yoga inVision 2

Yoga inVision 3

Yoga inVision 4

Yoga inVision 5

Yoga inVision 6

Yoga inVision 7

Yoga inVision 8

Yoga inVision 9

Yoga inVision 10

Yoga inVision 11

Yoga inVision 12

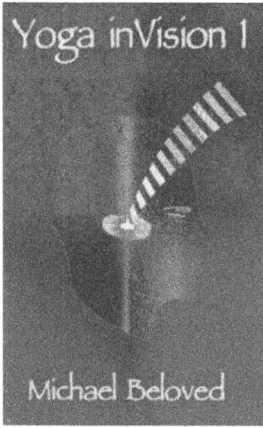

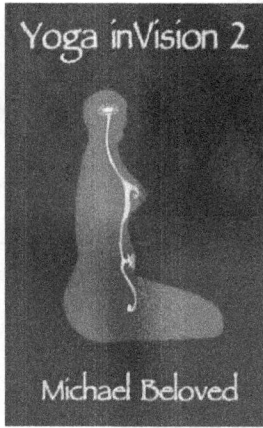

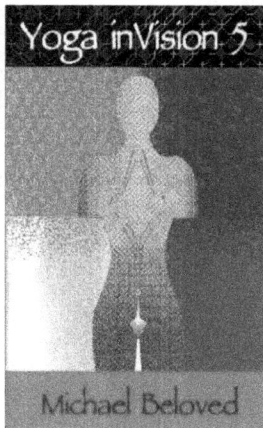

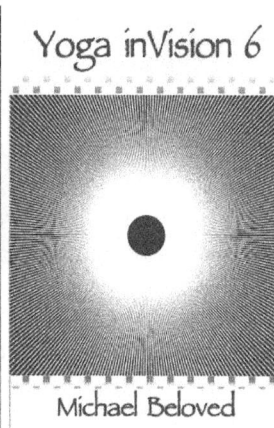

Yoga inVision 1 — Michael Beloved

Yoga inVision 2 — Michael Beloved

Yoga inVision 3 — Michael Beloved

Yoga inVision 4 — Michael Beloved

Yoga inVision 5 — Michael Beloved

Yoga inVision 6 — Michael Beloved

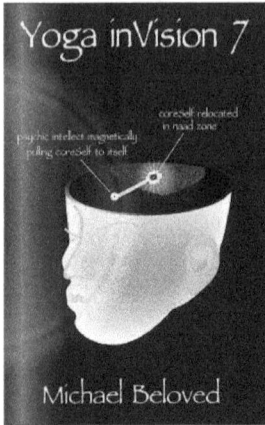

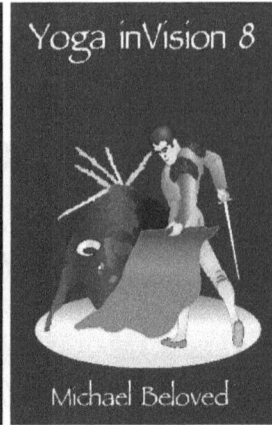

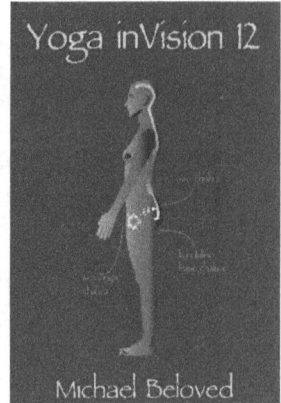

Yoga inVision 1, the first in this series, describes the breath-infusion and meditation practices during the years of 1998 and 1999. There are unique, once in a lifetime as well as recurring insights which are elaborated. inFocus during breath-infusion and the meditation which follows is an adventure for any yogi. This gives what happened to this particular ascetic.

Yoga inVision 2 reports on the author's experiences from 1999 to 2001. Each day the experience is unique, illustrating the vibrancy of practice. Many rare once-in-a-lifetime perceptions are described.

Yoga inVision 3 reports on the author's experiences from 2001 to 2003.

Yoga inVision 4 reports on the author's experiences from 2006 to 2009.

Yoga inVision 5 reports on the author's experiences from 2006 to 2008.

Yoga inVision 6 reports on the author's experiences in 2010.

Yoga inVision 7 reports on the author's experiences in 2011.

Yoga inVision 8 reports on the author's experiences in 2011.

Yoga inVision 9 reports on the author's experiences in 2012.

Yoga inVision 10 reports on the author's experiences in 2012.

Yoga inVision 11 reports on the author's experiences in 2012.
Yoga inVision 12 reports on the author's experiences in 2012-2013.

Online Resources

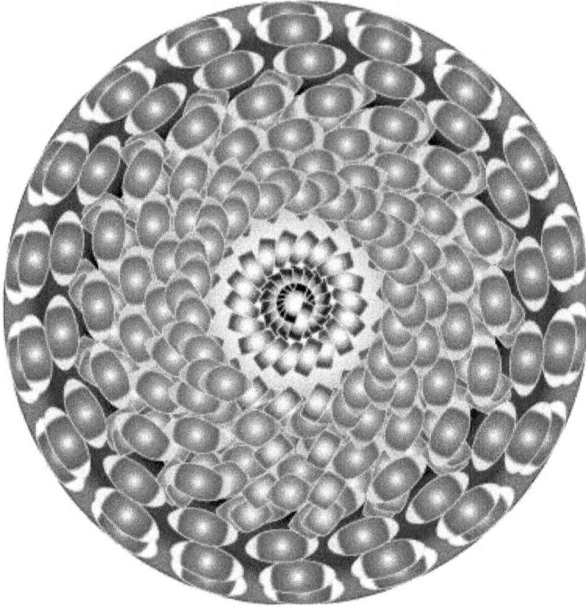

Email: michaelbelovedbooks@gmail.com
                 axisnexus@gmail.com

Website: michaelbeloved.com

Forum: inselfyoga.com

Posters: zazzle.com/inself

www.ingramcontent.com/pod-product-compliance
Lightning Source LLC
Chambersburg PA
CBHW070039110426

42741CB00036B/2851